Challenges to Democracy: The Next Ten Years

Challenges to Democracy: The Next Ten Years

Edited by **EDWARD REED**

With an Introduction by
Robert M. Hutchins

Published for the
CENTER FOR THE STUDY OF DEMOCRATIC INSTITUTIONS
by
FREDERICK A. PRAEGER, *Publisher*
New York • London

FREDERICK A. PRAEGER, *Publisher*
64 University Place, New York 3, N.Y., U.S.A.
77-79 Charlotte Street, London W.1, England

Published in the United States of America in 1963
by Frederick A. Praeger, Inc., Publisher

All rights reserved

Library of Congress Catalog Card Number: 64-12516

Printed in the United States of America

CONTENTS

Challenges to Democracy: The Next Ten Years

ROBERT M. HUTCHINS

President, The Fund for the Republic

ROBERT OPPENHEIMER has said, "One thing that is new is the prevalence of newness—the change in scale and scope of change itself—so that the world alters as we walk in it; so that the years of man's life measure not some small growth or rearrangement or moderation of what he learned in childhood, but a great upheaval." Stanley Morison, when he was editor of the *Times Literary Supplement,* said that the possession of the eleventh edition of the *Encyclopaedia Britannica,* published about fifty years ago, was really a wonderful thing, because it reflects a world that has totally disappeared.

The world is new, we think, and we think it is going to get newer. There are some signs that this development may not be altogether attractive. It may be, in fact, that our situation is changing too fast for our ideas. The ideas upon which this country was founded are the finest flower of the eighteenth century. They were the flower of the dialogue of that day, and they were meant to continue it, not to end it. Today, in a totally new situation, unless these ideas are re-examined and revitalized, they are likely to degenerate into slogans. A slogan is a form of words that can be indefinitely repeated without putting any strain on the mind. The task of reinterpretation and re-evaluation is the task of the Center for the Study of Democratic Institutions. If we can compare small things with great, we might think about what Lincoln did with the phrase "all men are created equal." This phrase did not originally include black men. Speaking of the Founding Fathers, Lincoln said that they meant to set up a standard maxim for a free society that would be familiar to all and revered by all; constantly looked to, constantly labored for, and, even though never perfectly attained, constantly approximated, and therefore constantly spreading and deepening its influence and augmenting the happiness and value of life to all people of all colors everywhere.

The Constitution of the United States does not mention such democratic institutions as corporations, labor unions, administrative agencies, cities, or schools and colleges; and its references to the common defense, the press, the church and state were made in a totally different context. On the other hand, the problems with which the Constitution *was* concerned are now presented in an entirely new shape. The Constitution was concerned very largely with the problem of federalism in the relations between the states and the federal government. This was based on geography; today the geography no longer exists. The city of Chicago is now in four states. As late as 1909, the leading sociologist in the country, Charles Cooley, said that the United States had no capital city. This was a routine remark for a sociologist to make in those days, but today even a sociologist knows that there is a capital city in the United States. Another subject with which the Constitution is tremendously concerned is the subject of checks and balances. It may be that checks and balances favor the maintenance of the status quo. It has been prophesied that the United States will never have another depression "because we know all the buttons to push." But the question is, under a system of checks and balances, whether one can get to the buttons.

The best summary of all this is perhaps provided by thinking about what Jefferson thought the basis of democracy was going to be. To Jefferson, democracy in the United States was going to succeed, although he thought it had failed everywhere else. It was going to succeed in the United States because we were all going to be self-employed, we were all going to live on farms, we were all going to be so well educated that we could face any new problems that arose, and we were all going to be educated in civic virtue through local government. Now, about 79 per cent of us are employed by others; almost none of us lives on a farm—the number of farms has declined by 31 per cent in the last ten years; I cannot recommend American education as a basis for the elevation of the democratic spirit; and anybody who expected to learn civic virtue through participation in local government would be sent to a psychiatrist.

Under these circumstances, it is not surprising that democracy is having a hard time all over the world and that even in the United States there are grave doubts about its effectiveness and survival. The Center for the Study of Democratic Institutions believes that it can be made to work. This is one reason why, in celebration of the tenth anniversary of The Fund for the Republic, it assembled in a two-day Convocation in New York City the distinguished group of individuals who make up the contributors to this volume. The problems and procedures of this Convocation, as they are presented in the following papers, are the problems and procedures of the Center for the Study of Democratic Institutions. These problems are not those customarily listed in university catalogues. Nor do they ordinarily appear in the programs of political parties or in messages on the State of the Union. On the one hand, the Center is not engaged in academic research or instruction. On the other, it is not a party, a lobby, or a propaganda agency. It tries to provoke and promote thought by the method employed at this Convocation, by discussion. Its effort is to symbolize and advance the civilization we are seeking, the civilization of the dialogue.

This Convocation, and the work of the Center, have been based on the proposition that the unexamined life is no life for man. The society that is unaware of itself can survive in a world like this only through the special providence that is said to look after fools and drunkards, and it can achieve the common good only by accident. In a world like this a nation without centers of independent thought and criticism, without an organized way of continuously re-examining its aims, re-appraising its policies, and bringing the changing facts of life home to its people may find itself lurching along the road to nowhere as it drives its ancient political carthorse beneath supersonic jets into mushroom clouds.

We are all children of the Enlightenment and, like the Enlightenment, we believed that all we needed was more knowledge. One of the Enlightenment's chief representatives, the historian Gibbon, in his celebrated chapter summarizing the reasons for the fall of the Holy Roman Empire, relieved the fears of Europe by saying that there would never be another barbarian conqueror. The reason was simple. War, said Gibbon, now requires a knowledge of a large number of arts and sciences; hence, to excel in war the barbarian must cease to be barbarous. Since man first discovered how to master the forces of nature, all history has been tending toward this goal. Gibbon's final remark is this: "We may, therefore, acquiesce in the pleasing conclusion that every age of the world has increased and still increases the real wealth, the happiness, the knowledge, and perhaps the virtue of the human race."

The conclusion is pleasing but false. If we look at the whole human race, we see that the rich have got richer and the poor are poorer. Although knowledge has grown, happiness and virtue have not. And we have learned that a barbarian conqueror equipped with knowledge is *more* barbarous as well as more dangerous than any of his unlettered predecessors. We have to continue to search for knowledge, but we see now that knowledge without wisdom has brought us to the edge of destruction and may at any time push us over the brink. The road to wisdom is candid and intrepid thinking about fundamental issues with a view to action in the here and now. This is the object of the Center for the Study of Democratic Institutions. This is the kind of thinking that I believe appears in the series of papers presented at the Convocation and reproduced in this book.

We have to recapture, revitalize, and reinterpret the great ideas and ideals that animated those who laid the foundations of our democratic institutions. In this way, we Americans may become competent to rise to the height of our times. In this way, we may hope to form a more perfect union, to establish justice, to insure tranquility, to promote the general welfare, and to secure the blessings of liberty, not only to ourselves and our posterity, but to all men everywhere.

1.

*The Role
of Government
in the Economy*

GUNNAR MYRDAL*

Economist and Author

THE role of government in the economic life of the United
States is bound to be an increasing one. The primary role of
government in the economy I conceive to be the one of creating conditions for business that result in rapid and steady
economic growth. There are several reasons why the present
relative stagnation in the American economy is dangerous
for the successful pursuance of America's foreign policy. In-
ternally, it is apt to create rigid class chasms and, in particular, to cause the growth of an underprivileged class not
sharing in the nation's opportunities, which would be a development contrary to American ideals. To get America out of
the rut of relative stagnation with mild recessions, weak and
hesitant recoveries, and a rising trend of unemployment will
require very much more of long-range planning and of government intervention.

As a matter of fact, the trend toward "big government" has
prevailed for a long time. America, like all the other rich
countries, has moved far on the road toward the organizational welfare state—though as yet not as far as some of the
most advanced of them—with an immense amount of public
intervention and a widely dispersed system of economic planning of a pragmatic and, as yet, largely uncoordinated type.
What is now becoming an urgent necessity in America is, in
the first place, a much better coordination of already exist-

*Editor's note: This is an abridgment of the paper delivered by Dr. Myrdal at
the Convocation. The original was, at a later date, greatly expanded into a
book, *Challenge to Affluence*, published by Pantheon Books in 1963.

ing government controls—that is, their integration into a more perfect, deliberate, and rational long-range planning. As a result of this planning and coordination, it would certainly be possible to scrap a lot of specific controls, which have spuriously grown up ad hoc. They would be replaced by more general controls. Indeed, successful planning should free the citizen from a lot of nuisance public intervention, of which there is astonishingly much in America. But there will have to be a very considerable widening of the public sector, by which I mean that the government will have to increase its responsibilities for a larger part of consumption and, consequently, of employment and production.

These conclusions do not make me happy, but rather fill me with foreboding that the American people may have to go through severe crises before they really come to grips with the task of improving and enlarging their government. For one thing, studies and experience have made me realize what an exceedingly difficult task government planning is in any country, even where the preconditions for social engineering are very much favorable than they are—at least at the present time—in the United States. For this reason, I would never suggest government intervention except when necessary for the pursuance of really important interests and ideals. I would always feel deeply satisfied if things were to take care of themselves. In choosing means for government control of the economy, I would always prefer the most general, the least specific means, implying a minimum of discretionary power for courts and, particularly, for administrators. Whenever I could work the controls simply by an adjustment of prices, I would find this highly advantageous. I would, for reasons of both efficiency and democracy, prefer such decentralizing arrangements as would push the actual business of regulatory intervention down to state, district, and local authorities, effectively controlled, so far as possible, by elected assemblies, and to the organizations in the institutional infrastructure within the framework of the government apparatus, provided they are reasonably well balanced, so that together they can function as agencies for public policy.

It is a very long time since I looked with any exhilaration toward the prospect that technological development and other fundamental changes in our national communities and in the world would force us to plan and control ever more intensely our economic life. In America, which has no parliamentary cabinet government assuring an automatic synchronization of the political will of the Executive and the Congress, legislation is usually not prepared with the care desirable for planning and coordination of government activities. Draft bills also run bigger risks of either not being enacted at all or being enacted in an ill-considered and distorted form. Administration on all levels in America is still far from having the security and the efficiency that is required for the same purpose.

There is, moreover, in America a greater lack of democratic balance in the institutional infrastructure below the level of the national government than in those countries which are most similar to America in basic valuations and ambitions—for example, the other Anglo-Saxon countries and Scandinavia. Thus, the majority of workers are unorganized in America, and the people as a whole are not organized to press their interests as consumers. At least for the time being, a much more than desirable share of responsibility for not only the direction but even the execution of public policy has to be carried by the national and state governments, which themselves have not the structure that would make them ideally fitted for this task. The United States Government is under the compulsion to deviate further from laissez-faire in order to substitute legislation and administration for the largely non-existing workers' and consumers' organizations, as to a considerable extent it has already done to defend the interests of the shareholders who are equally dispersed and powerless vis-à-vis corporation management.

A basic cause of all this is that the citizen's participation in public life, taken in its broadest sense, is lower in America than it generally is in similar countries. Under these circumstances and in this institutional setting, the citizens in all social strata, as the opinion polls glaringly demonstrate, also show a distressing lack of intellectual understanding of the issues at stake and demonstrate attitudes that lag far behind the rapid changes of social reality. Much that can be safely delegated to local self-government in other advanced countries and to the cooperation and bargaining among organizations in a well-balanced institutional infrastructure will have to be done in America through direct controls by the government and its agencies. Meanwhile, whatever the government can do to strengthen the people's participation and organizational activity on those levels below the central government should certainly be done.

The record of economic development in the United States during the last decade is unsatisfactory. When it is all added up, the average annual growth rate comes out as considerably less than 3 per cent. The American economy seems to have settled down to a sequence of recessions, short-lived and inadequate upturns, and periods of stagnation in between. If there is any consistent pattern, it looks as if the recoveries after the recessions tend to become ever more hesitant and to result in an ever more incomplete re-employment of the unemployed in proportion to the rise in output. I have seen no evidence to make it probable that the American economy by itself—that is, as a result of the forces now at work in that economy, including present governmental policies—will get out of this rut.

The famous built-in stabilizers have, until now, prevented the recessions from developing into serious depressions. But such an eventuality cannot be excluded. That a depression would not be permitted to develop into anything like the Great Depression of the 1930's but would call forth vigorous government action is a statement that does not satisfy me. The policies should have been applied in time to prevent such a depression. Or rather, because the established pattern of development is unsatisfactory, government policies should be planned and executed in order to set the economy into an entirely new pattern of rapid, steady growth.

In the foreign relations of the United States, a difference in growth rate can immediately be translated into a difference in power to press forward solutions of international problems that satisfy its interests and ideals. The importance of keeping up America's economic strength in its relations with the Soviet world and with the underdeveloped countries is obvious and does not need any further comments. There has been little open discussion about America's need to be economically strong in its relations with its friends, particularly in Western Europe.

America's relations with Western Europe are now on an entirely different basis from what they were in the days of the Marshall Plan. America is well entitled to feel satisfied that its rescue action at that time was so successful that most Western European countries now enjoy a rapid and steady economic growth. Remarkably enough, this holds particularly true in regard to what had been the weakest and most troubled countries on the European continent—that is, *"das neue Europa"* of Hitler's dream world, Germany, Italy, and those countries which had been overrun by the Nazis and were liberated by the great alliance of the U.S., the U.S.S.R., and Great Britain. They are still weak in many respects; they have serious unsettled psychological and moral problems to cope with; democracy is not as firmly established there as in the Anglo-Saxon and Scandinavian countries. But economically they are striding ahead rapidly, though from comparatively low levels, and were doing so long before they consolidated themselves in a protective common market.

The snag is that meanwhile America itself has lapsed into relative stagnation. At present, America has good reasons to urge fundamental changes in the policies of its European allies in many and diverse fields. But it no longer has the economic strength to press for them effectively. America even has to suppress some of its demands or present them sotto voce. The situation is almost the reverse of the one ten or fifteen years ago. I believe that America is in danger of losing out as the uncontested leader within the Western world, and this is bound to become even more pronounced if the differences in economic growth rate remain.

Even America's *low* rate of economic growth is dependent upon very heavy armament expenditures, which swallow up half the federal expenditure budget. This is not a healthy situation for a nation that is honestly intent upon trying to reach a disarmament agreement. On an abstract level, the economists can argue that a major decrease in these expenditures can easily be compensated for. But we should be aware of the real difficulties if there is not a radical change in the way the American people and Congress look upon the role of government in the economy. The difficulties of an adjustment of the American economy to lower levels of armament expenditures are bigger because the growth rate is so low: In a rapidly growing economy, a decrease in the armament expenditures could be taken more in stride. In addition, we should not hide from ourselves the fact that the vested interests, working against an international agreement to decrease armaments substantially, must be much more forceful in an economy with an under-utilized capacity.

The low average level of economic growth during the last ten years coincides with a particularly rapid, and increasingly rapid, technological development, which enhances labor productivity. The result is a high and gradually rising level of unemployment. Full-time unemployment now fluctuates around a level of 6 per cent. This figure must be increased by perhaps half again in order to account for the partial unemployment of those workers who are put on short-time employment or who do not bother actively to seek work because jobs are not available. In neither case is the idleness voluntary.

This situation—to which correspond idle plants and machines—is serious as it stands. Add to this several changes under way that, if economic growth is not speeded up, are bound to cause a tendency toward an even greater increase in unemployment. With the coming to age of the big batches of children born as a reflection of the full employment during and after World War II, the labor force will be growing much more rapidly in the decade ahead than in the last one. Technological progress, the revolutionary character of which is stressed by the common use of the term "automation," is accelerating and is now more and more directed toward displacing labor. So far as material products are concerned, a bigger output can be produced with an ever smaller work force. The increased use of computing machines also will be releasing white-collar workers on the lower managerial levels.

Somewhat less often observed and commented upon is the tendency of the changes now under way to increase the class chasms in the American society and to stiffen the class structure. Technological progress does not release labor in a uniform way but directs labor demand more and more toward the skilled and educated and still more toward the highly skilled and highly educated. The incidence of unemployment tends increasingly to fall most heavily upon those who, for social and economic reasons, have less skill and education.

The population development under way gives its peculiar twist to this unfortunate situation. The increase in the rise of the labor force in the present decade consists almost entirely of the entry upon the labor market of a rapidly increasing number of young workers. Back in 1950, about 2 million American youths reached 18 years of age; now the figure is 3 million, and in 1965 it will be 4 million. In the next decade, the age group between 25 and 45 will, on the contrary, increase very little; that between 25 and 30 will actually decrease. It is clear that with prevailing and widespread unemployment a disproportionate part of these young newcomers in the labor market will be among the permanently unemployed or live under a permanent risk of becoming unemployed unless very much larger facilities for education and training are speedily provided and, at the same time, the American economy develops so rapidly that it can absorb much more labor than it does now.

In a situation with such big risks of unemployment as the present one, even the trade unions are unwillingly becoming instrumental in increasing that substratum of American workers who are unemployed or have only more or less casual jobs. The process of automation is particularly speedy in sectors of the American economy where there are effective trade unions. These unions are thus forced to press for job security for their own members even when this creates incentives for the employers not to engage new workers. In a situation of growing unemployment, the unions often feel their bargaining strength weakened and find it more difficult to take a consistent and strong stand for what, from the point of view of all American workers and the nation as a whole, is the main interest—full employment. They are in danger of being reduced to protective organizations for a number of separate groups of job-holders who, even if they are all taken together, represent only a minority, perhaps one quarter, of the workers. To an outside observer, it seems, when everything is taken into account, almost a miracle that large units of the American trade union movement have seen it possible to take such a broad-minded and progressive position on national policies as they actually have done.

Much of the rising unemployment also falls upon minority groups and implies a serious setback in the progress of national integration. The largest minority group still at the greatest disadvantage is that of the Negroes. From about the beginning of the last war, there has been a definite trend toward improved race relations in America, a development that is the more remarkable since, for the sixty years preceding, there had been no great change in the status of the Negro in America. One important cause of this encouraging trend was undoubtedly the high level of labor demand that was sustained, on the whole, until about ten years ago. An increasing number of Negroes were allowed to acquire skills, join trade unions, and get seniority and job protection in new fields that were opening for Negroes.

But Negroes are still the "last to be hired and the first to be fired." Apart from a tiny upper and middle class of professional and business people, mostly thriving behind the remaining walls of prejudice, and a now considerably larger group of skilled and union-protected workers, the majority of Negroes are much poorer and have less training and education than the average white American. They are, consequently, more vulnerable, particularly in the present situation. To this large number of Negro workers and workers in other minority groups must be added the poor white people everywhere in America, who will also be pressed down in this substratum which is excluded from the prosperity of the nation at large and the progress of the American way of life.

I have assumed that the primary role of government in the economy is to keep the economy expanding and to maintain high employment. This is recognized in American legislation, as it is in that of all other rich countries. I have tried to demonstrate that during the last decade the United States Government has not been able to fill this role satisfactorily. The first and obvious policy conclusion, therefore, is that the government should take measures that can result in economic expansion. This means, generally speaking, that it should cause an increase in aggregate demand. This can be induced by a great variety of possible measures. There is an element of sense in the argument that, since the main thing is to get the economy going at full speed, it is not of great importance what particular ones are chosen.

Some of them—for instance, the lowering of tax rates— would not imply that the government would become more involved in the economy than before. But the interest in assuring not only a start but a steady continuation of more rapid growth makes it necessary to be discriminating in the choice of policy measures, at least after having provided the first spurt to the economy. What matters is not only the rate of investment, new employment and growth, but their patterns. This raises a need for careful long-range planning. It also tends generally to push the government into taking a much greater responsibility for the use of the national resources.

My first observation refers to the relative exaggeration in the popular view of the great abundance and affluence of American society. This is undoubtedly partly responsible for much undue complacency about American economic growth and even for a widespread feeling that the limit for the expansion of production is near. The fact is, of course, that there is a very large number of crying needs in America that, if they were translated into effective demand, could sustain rapid economic growth for a long time to come. This cannot be done except by government intervention on a large scale.

The existence of these unmet needs will, for a considerable time, not make it either necessary or desirable to share unemployment by shortening the working week still further.

It has decreased in this century from sixty to forty hours, which is one of the great gains the American people have reaped from economic progress. But neither in America, nor in other Western countries, has the level of culture yet reached so high that more than a minority is able to make decent use of still more time between work and sleep—and that highly educated minority is usually working much longer hours.

One category of such needs is, of course, based on the low levels of living of the fifth of the American people who are officially recognized as falling below the poverty line. Another fifth or more of the population does not share to any substantial extent in the abundance commonly assumed to characterize American society. The affluent society is largely a myth, except for a privileged upper stratum.

There is, however, so much solid truth in the appreciation of the technological revolution under way and of the capacity of the American economy to expand production rapidly in almost every field, if a higher growth rate were permitted, that a rise in the living levels of the underprivileged social strata becomes not only a desideratum from a social point of view, but almost a condition for long-term economic advance. Never in the history of America has there been a greater and more complete agreement between the ideals of economic progress and of social justice. The former goal is not attainable if large-scale policy measures are not taken to reach the latter goal.

For the purpose of giving more purchasing power to the poorer sections in American society, there are a number of redistributional policy means available. The one that implies least government intervention is, of course, a radical reduction of the tax burden in the lower income brackets. Other means are assistance to organized labor in the weaker sections of the labor market or increases in the minimum wage level. The high concentration of poverty among certain categories, such as the elderly, the invalided and the sick, single mothers, and families with many children, is a strong reason to expand the system of social security, a field where America is still far behind the countries that are most similar to it in basic values.

In some respects, however, the government will have to become more directly involved in providing services that are now not available, or not available on a large enough scale. As I have tried to show, unemployment in America is increasingly becoming a structural and not a cyclical matter. Merely raising aggregate demand will not lift the growth rate to the height that is possible. It will soon create a scarcity of skilled and educated workers, while leaving a residual unemployment among the others. The training and education of young people must expand very much more than proportionately to mere population growth. The need for much greater efforts in the educational field is, moreover, further increased by another cumulative factor: The expanded demand for teachers who must have their schooling and training. Particularly in the field of vocational training, America needs very much greater efforts. It also needs a new philosophy. Such training, as is the case with education in general, should not be left to lead to dead ends, but should be instrumental in making it possible for young people to move sidewise to other occupations and upwards to higher responsibilities. In the dynamic phase that America has now entered, this is necessary in order that training shall not be wasted.

At the same time there is an urgent need also for a retraining of older workers in order to prevent the emergence of a group of second-class workers who are permanently unemployed or only casually employed. It should be added that only in an expanding economy is there a real chance of successful efforts at rehabilitating laid-off labor or labor in the danger zone. In a situation of widespread unemployment, the

retrained will have difficulties in finding jobs and will slump
back to their previous status.

In filling these needs, it will be necessary to invest much
larger resources in schools and hospitals. But there are many
other public investments that are now unreasonably neglected. There is, of course, no excuse for a rich country to
tolerate huge slums in the big cities and lesser ones in the
smaller cities at the same time that it allows a large part of its
manpower and other productive resources to go to waste.

It is fairly generally recognized by those who have studied
the problem that there is a serious and irrational bias against
public consumption and investment in America. It is a result
of the combination of high-pressure salesmanship for private
consumption and traditional suspicion against increasing
public budgets. It cannot correspond to what people would
really prefer if they could as readily follow their impulses to
buy the means of collective consumption as they can to buy
private consumers' goods, and if the former were equally well
advertised. In the cities, where so much long-term investment
is needed if they are to become really effective as containers
of human life and efficient work, this becomes the more
serious since almost the whole population increase now goes
to swell the number of city dwellers, particularly in the big
metropolitan districts.

Since the primary means for increasing aggregate demand
must be decreased taxation and increased public expenditures, the public budget will not be "balanced" in the
American sense of this term. At least, at the start of an expansionist policy this is clear. Whether it holds good also in
later years, when a higher rate of growth and fuller employment have been reached and thus the basis of taxation broadened, is more uncertain. It will depend partly upon the speed
by which the government succeeds in increasing public expenditure in the directions indicated above. The tax rates

may then have to be raised. But whether increased tax returns and increased expenditures should need to counterbalance each other exactly is not in any sense obvious.

The question, in any case, is not very interesting. The concept of a "balanced budget" in which taxation pays for all public expenditures independently of the character and incidence of taxation and expenditures is an entirely irrational construct, which is nowadays given significance only in American popular and political discussions. What really matters is a "balanced economy," which in different settings—dependent among other things on the size and type of public expenditures and of taxes—may require an "over-balanced," "balanced," or "under-balanced" budget. It is encouraging that rational ideas of functional finance are increasingly accepted by the business community in America. But the fact that such a large number of American voters and responsible politicians still think in terms of "balancing" the budget is in itself important. It decidedly increases the difficulties of rational economic planning and of getting the American people and the Congress to accept the policy measures that are needed to get the American economy into a pattern of rapid and steady growth.

A real risk is that a higher growth rate will overstimulate investments, generally or in certain fields, so that after a short time the result will be an inflationary development, which, under certain conditions, may come so fast that sooner or later it will have to be broken by causing a recession. This is contrary to the goal of public policy, which must be that economic growth is not only rapid but also steady. To accomplish this objective will require careful planning and the availability of flexible means for controlling the volume of investment. Even if monetary controls of a general type are clumsy and largely ineffective, and even if, in particular, the long-term rate of interest in a rapidly expanding economy should be kept low and steady, this should not exclude the possibility that discriminatory controls applied to credits for home construction or for installment buying may not be useful. But, in the main, I would be looking for policies in the fiscal sphere, such as taxes adjustable on short notice on energy, on investments in particular fields, and on consumption. Allowances for capital depreciation, as well as for the costs of advertising, should also be adjustable. Varying the level of public expenditure, particularly of the investment type, also belongs in these categories. Even if, ideally, such adjustments should be made automatic, reacting to changes in certain indices, their ability to stabilize economic growth would, of course, require very much improved long-range planning.

About the risks for inflation, I would like to make two general points. First, we now know from recent experiences in many countries that there is no close relation between the rate of economic growth and the rate of inflation. Much depends upon the balance in which the growth process proceeds. Prices may rise while the economy is lagging, and they may keep steady though it is pushing ahead. Second, in the present stage of American economic development the social effects of a low rate of progress are so grave, particularly in the lower strata, that I should frankly confess that I am prepared to take a moderate rising price level if that should be a condition for economic growth.

However, I believe that the higher utilization of capacity following more rapid growth will tend to lower costs so substantially that inflation will not be a condition for economic progress, particularly if the government is prepared to extend its controls over investments and, perhaps, over prices and labor costs. In regard to price control, I sometimes ask myself whether the United States Government, which for decades has fought monopoly with such courage and even vehemence by means of legislation and court action, and yet failed to prevent a continuous concentration of market power, would not be prepared to tone down its rather fruitless fight against monopoly and ask instead for a share in controlling administered prices, which are so decisive for the general trend of prices.

There has been more interest in demanding greater government control of wages, though the principle that wage levels, as well as other conditions for employment, should be left to the collective bargaining in the labor market is so powerful that, as yet, government intervention has not become a general practice (except the legislation on minimum wages in the large unorganized sections of the labor market). At the same time, the American economy is from time to time disturbed by very serious labor conflicts.

As a Swede, I know from experience about the conditions for gradually reaching a situation in the labor market where the bargaining process proceeds effectively to solutions satisfactory to the public interest, preventing both excessive rises of wages in certain sections, too low wages in others, and not giving rise to open labor conflicts of any importance. Almost all workers should be organized, not by compulsion but because it has become a matter of course. Unions should be open and democratically governed, and the members should have a fairly high rate of active participation in running them. Unions should be industrial and not split in craft unions. Considerable power should be vested in a central organization of all unions, which articulates the common interest. The employers should, on their side, be organized in a parallel way. All legal conflicts concerning the interpretation of contracts should be brought under the courts. Collective bargaining in economic matters between the parties should develop over the years into a very serious, but basically friendly, exercise. The two sets of organizations should gradually mature to the degree that together they can serve as de facto agencies for public policy.

Such an order in the labor market of America is only a distant possibility, and many believe that it will never be reached. Under present conditions, I can see reasons not only for legislation about minimum wages in the large unorganized sections of the economy and about the constitution and functioning of the unions in the other sections, but also for some form of government participation in the collective bargaining process itself to prevent too big wage increases in the few strategic industries in America that greatly influence general price development and also have strong unions. But in democratic America, I cannot see such wage controls applied without also being supplemented by controls upon prices and profits. This would lead to increasing the role of government a great deal. It is an illustration of the thought I have already expressed, that in order to reach a similar level of order in line with public policy, the United States is under the compulsion to deviate further from laissez-faire to substitute for deficiencies in its institutional infrastructure.

In regard to the exchange difficulties, it is clear that the fear of losing gold has been a powerful reason for the unwillingness of the United States Government to venture on an expansionist policy aimed at getting the American economy going at full speed. On this question, I have to declare myself as a heretic to widely prevalent views. If the American economy were set on the road to rapid and steady growth, this would by itself change anticipations, make Americans less interested in seeking investment outlets abroad, and, at the same time, induce foreigners to invest more in American securities in order to share in American economic progress. American policy has run into a vicious circle, for its anxiety about gold losses induces it to be satisfied with the relative economic stagnation that itself is a main reason for the lack of confidence in the dollar.

It seems to me that America has an entirely irrational fixation on the importance of preserving a big gold reserve and of not using it as a reserve that should be expandable. If legal and other restrictions were lifted and gold then started to move abroad even faster than it has until now, what would it matter? America's strength is what is, and can be, produced in this country, not the gold in Fort Knox. Enough of the gold would probably soon come back if the American economy were expanding and the cost and price situation not getting out of hand.

The more basic problem is, of course, to achieve a more perfect organization of the international money market. When the two countries that provide the world with international currency, the United States and Great Britain, have been pressed into deflationary policies at home, which are now endangering the stability of economic growth everywhere—and not least in the underdeveloped countries—we are facing basically the same problem that Gustav Cassel, my late teacher, friend, and predecessor at Stockholm University, wrestled with after World War I. Politically, he was anything but a radical, and I feel comforted in recalling that my views are not more radical than his forty years ago.

Like him, I am aware that this problem can be solved in many ways. And, like him, I would give preference to a simple solution, calling for a minimum of institutional changes, since it is always difficult to reach international agreement on beautifully perfected but complicated schemes for international cooperation. That any move toward international monetary stability increases the role of the government in the economy does not need to be stressed. Meanwhile, we should be aware that America's national policies are of crucial importance, even for the international organization of the money market. America should lead the world in more generous international liquidity arrangements, just as it should in growth rates.

I have stated the need for careful and intensive long-range planning in economic development. It is needed not only for framing government policy but also for providing a basis for planning in private business, which otherwise has to operate with a complex of important parameters given only in the form of the crudest guesses. However, among the things that have apparently not changed in America, and specifically in Washington, is the nearsightedness of politicians and experts.

There is an astonishing number of competent people who can, off-hand, give a detailed and comprehensive analysis of how all important economic indices have recently been moving and how they are likely to move in the months ahead. Everybody is excited about what is going to happen next, who is in and who is out, who is behind whom, and who thinks what. In regard to economic development, an altogether undue interest is attached to when the next recession or the next upturn is going to occur, a matter of very little significance to America or to the world. I will confess that not even as a shareholder do I take much interest in this sort of pastime, since I do not afford myself the time to be a speculator.

With regard to the long-range developments, there is a contrasting lack of interest. What is produced is mostly in very general and philosophical terms. Not only the President and the Congress, but also leaders in business, are left without that image of the future which is needed for rational action, particularly when it implies long-term investment or other decisions that have consequences far ahead—as, indeed, most legislation about taxes, tariffs, and everything else does.

What is needed are forecasts of what will happen to the American economy in five, ten, and twenty years. The fact that there are interrelations among the various factors—as there are in a population forecast among deaths, births, age structures, and population increases—is the reason why such prognoses make real contributions to knowledge. The economic forecasts should be worked out for alternative rates of growth and for different directions and patterns of policy.

They will spell out what is possible, what is alternatively necessary to do in order to reach and maintain a postulated growth rate, and what it will imply in terms of employment and the movement of people, educational efforts, investment, and so on. The high level of econometric expertness in America and the perfection of the computing machines make it feasible to work out such models with much more specificity and exactitude than was the case only a few years ago.

Therefore, unless the United States Government takes on greatly increased responsibilities, there is little hope of getting America to become again a country with a progressive economy, of saving America from serious damage both to its power in foreign relations and to the internal unity of the nation. To attempt to give the government a greater role in the economy without utilizing the superb intellectual resources that America possesses and now disperses on tasks of much less importance would be part of the waste in this country of abundance.

The work on long-term forecasts and programs would also have a wider educational function in America, besides giving the needed basis for rational policy formation in government and business. Only by painting on the wall in definite and concrete figures the opportunities that could be realized by a change in policies can America be made to wake up to its old ambitions and the new necessities. I am afraid that the resistance of prejudice and vested interests, mostly misunderstood, will postpone this awakening and that the development in the years to come will be a checkered one. The more important is it, then, not to leave unutilized this powerful means of educating the general public. Trust in education has through generations been part of the American creed, and I am glad to end on that note.

2.

Technology and Democracy

LEWIS MUMFORD

Author; President, American Academy of Arts and Letters

I SHOULD like to begin by redefining, very tentatively of course, the central concept of democracy—a term now confused and sophisticated by indiscriminate use, and often treated with patronizing contempt. Can we agree, no matter how far we might diverge at a later point, that the spinal principle of democracy is to place what is common to all men above that which any organization, institution, or group may claim for itself? This is not to deny the claims of superior natural endowment, specialized knowledge, technical skill, or institutional organization; all these may, by democratic permission, play a useful role in the human economy. But democracy consists in giving final authority to the whole, rather than the part; and only living human beings, as such, are an authentic expression of the whole, whether acting alone or with the help of others.

Around this central principle clusters a group of related ideas and practices with a long foreground in history, though they are not always present, or present in equal amounts, in all societies. Among these items are communal self-government, free communication as between equals, unimpeded access to the common store of knowledge, protection against arbitrary external controls, and a sense of individual moral responsibility for behavior that affects the whole community. All living organisms are in some degree autonomous, for they follow life-patterns of their own; but in man this autonomy is an essential condition for his further development. We surrender some of our autonomy when ill or crippled, but to surrender it every day on every occasion would be to turn life itself into a chronic illness. The best life possible—and here I am consciously treading on contested ground—is one that calls for an ever greater degree of self-direction, self-expression, and self-realization. In this sense, personality, once the exclusive attribute of kings, belongs in democratic theory to every man. Life itself in its fullness and wholeness cannot be delegated.

In framing this provisional definition, I trust that I have not, for the sake of agreement, left out anything important. Democracy, in the primal sense I shall use the term, is necessarily most visible in relatively small communities and groups, whose members meet frequently face to face, interact freely, and are known to each other as persons. As soon as large numbers are involved, democratic association must be supplemented by a more abstract, depersonalized form. Historic experience shows that it is much easier to wipe out democracy by an institutional arrangement that gives authority only to those at the apex of the social hierarchy than it is to incorporate democratic practices into a well-organized system under centralized direction, which achieves the highest degree of mechanical efficiency when those who work it have no mind or purpose of their own.

The tension between small-scale association and large-scale organization, between personal autonomy and institutional regulation, between remote control and diffused local intervention, has now created the critical situation that has brought us together here. If our eyes had been open, we might long ago have discovered this conflict deeply embedded in technology itself.

I wish it were possible to characterize technics with as much hope of getting assent—with whatever quizzical reserves one may still have—as in this description of democracy. But the very subject of this paper is, I confess, a controversial one; and I cannot go far in my analysis without drawing on interpretations that have not yet been adequately published, still less widely discussed or rigorously criticized and evaluated. My thesis, to put it bluntly, is that from late neolithic times in the Near East, right down to our own day, two technologies have recurrently existed side by side—one authoritarian, the other democratic; the first system-centered, immensely powerful, but inherently unstable, the other man-centered, relatively weak, but resourceful and durable. If I am right, we are now rapidly approaching a point at which, unless we radically alter our present course, our surviving democratic technics will be completely suppressed or supplanted, so that every residual autonomy will be wiped out, or will be permitted only as a playful device of government, like national balloting for already chosen leaders in totalitarian countries.

The data on which this thesis is based are familar to most of us, but their significance has, I believe, been overlooked. What I would call democratic technics is the small-scale method of production, resting mainly on human skill and animal energy, but always, even when employing machines, remaining under the active direction of the craftsman or the farmer, each group developing its own gifts, through appropriate arts and social ceremonies, as well as making discreet use of the gifts of nature. This technology had limited horizons of achievement, but, just because of its wide diffusion and its modest demands, it had great powers of adaptation and recuperation. Until now, this democratic technics has underpinned and firmly supported every historic culture until our own day, and redeemed the constant tendency of authoritarian technics to misapply its powers. Even when men paid tribute to the most oppressive authoritarian regimes, there yet remained within the workshop or the farmyard some degree of autonomy, selectivity, creativity. No royal mace, no slave-driver's whip, no bureaucratic directive left its imprint on the textiles of Damascus or the pottery of fifth-century Athens.

If this democratic technics goes back to the earliest use of tools, authoritarian technics is a much more recent achievement. It begins around the fourth millennium B.C. in a new configuration of technical invention, scientific observation, and centralized political control that gave rise to the peculiar mode of life we may now identify, without eulogy, as civilization. Under the new institution of kingship, activities that had been scattered, diversified, cut to the human measure were united on a monumental scale into an entirely new kind of theological-technological mass organization. In the person of an absolute ruler, whose word was law, cosmic powers came down to earth, mobilizing and unifying the efforts of thousands of men, hitherto all too autonomous and too decentralized to act voluntarily in unison for purposes that lay beyond the village horizon.

The new authoritarian technology was not limited by village custom or human sentiment. Its herculean feats of mechanical organization rested on ruthless physical coercion, forced labor and slavery, which brought into existence machines that were capable of exerting thousands of horsepower centuries before horses were harnessed or wheels invented. This centralized technics drew on inventions and scientific discoveries of a high order—the written record, mathematics and astronomy, irrigation and canalization; above all, it created complex human machines composed of specialized, standardized, replaceable, interdependent parts—the work army, the military army, the bureaucracy. These work armies and military armies raised the ceiling of human achievement, the first in mass construction, the second in mass destruction, and both on a scale hitherto inconceivable. Despite its constant drive to destruction, this totalitarian technics was tolerated, perhaps even welcomed, in home territory, for it created the first economy of controlled abundance—notably, immense food crops that not merely supported a big urban population but released a large trained minority for purely religious, scientific, bureaucratic, or military activity. But the efficiency of the system was impaired by weaknesses that were never overcome until our own day.

To begin with, the democratic economy of the agricultural village resisted incorporation into the new authoritarian system. So even the Roman Empire found it expedient, once resistance was broken and taxes were collected, to consent to a large degree of local autonomy in religion and government. Moreover, as long as agriculture absorbed the labor of some 90 per cent of the population, mass technics were confined largely to the populous urban centers. Since authoritarian technics first took form in an age when metals were scarce and human raw material, captured in war, was easily convertible into machines, its directors never bothered to invent inorganic mechanical substitutes. But there were even greater weaknesses: The system had no inner coherence—a break in communication, a missing link in the chain of command, and the great human machines fell apart. Finally, the myths upon which the whole system was based—particularly the essential myth of kingship—were irrational, with their paranoid suspicions and animosities and their paranoid claims to unconditional obedience and absolute power. For all its redoubtable constructive achievements, authoritarian technics expressed a deep hostility to life.

By now the point of this brief historic excursus may be evident: That authoritarian technics has come back today in an immensely magnified and adroitly perfected form. Up to now, following the optimistic premises of nineteenth-century thinkers like Auguste Comte and Herbert Spencer, we have regarded the spread of experimental science and mechanical invention as the soundest guarantee of a peaceful, productive —and, above all, democratic—industrial society. Many have even comfortably supposed that the revolt against arbitrary political power in the seventeenth century was causally connected with the industrial revolution that accompanied it. But what we have interpreted as the new freedom now turns out to be a much more sophisticated version of the old slavery, for the rise of political democracy during the last few centuries has been increasingly nullified by the successful resurrection of a centralized authoritarian technics—a technics that had in fact long lapsed in many parts of the world.

Let us fool ourselves no longer. At the very moment Western nations threw off the ancient regime of absolute government, operating under a once divine king, they were restoring this same system in a far more effective form in their technology, reintroducing coercions of a military character no less strict in the organization of a factory than in that of the new drilled, uniformed, and regimented army. During the transitional stages of the last two centuries, the ultimate tendency of this system might be in doubt, for in many areas there were strong democratic reactions; but with the knitting together of a scientific ideology, itself liberated from theological restrictions or humanistic purposes, authoritarian technics found an instrument at hand that has now given it absolute command of physical energies of cosmic dimensions. The inventors of nuclear bombs, space rockets, and computers are the pyramid builders of our own age; psychologically inflated by a similar myth of unqualified power, they boast through their science of their increasing omnipotence, if not omniscience, and they are moved by obsessions and compulsions no less irrational than those of earlier absolute systems—*particularly the notion that the system itself must be expanded, at whatever eventual cost to life.*

Through mechanization, automation, cybernetic direction, this authoritarian technics has at last successfully overcome its most serious weakness: Its original dependence upon resistant, sometime actively disobedient servo-mechanisms, still human enough to harbor purposes that do not always coincide with those of the system.

Like the earliest form of authoritarian technics, this new technology is marvelously dynamic and productive. Its power in every form tends to increase without limits, in quantities that defy assimilation and defeat control, whether we are thinking of the output of scientific knowledge or of industrial assembly lines. To maximize energy, speed, or automation, without reference to the complex conditions that sustain organic life, has become an end in itself. As with the earliest forms of authoritarian technics, the weight of effort, if one is to judge by national budgets, is toward absolute instruments of destruction, designed for absolutely irrational purposes, whose chief by-product would be the mutilation or extermination of the human race. Even Ashurbanipal and Genghis Khan performed their gory operations under normal human limits.

But observe that the center of authority in this new system is no longer a visible personality, an all-powerful king; even in totalitarian dictatorships, the center now lies in the system itself, invisible but omnipresent. All its human components, even the technical and managerial elite, even the sacred priesthood of science, who alone have access to the secret knowledge by means of which total control is now swiftly being effected, are themselves trapped by the very perfection of the organization they have invented. Like the pharaohs of the Pyramid Age, these servants of the system identify its goods with their own kind of well-being; as with the divine king, their praise of the system is an act of self-worship; and again like the king, they are in the grip of an irrational compulsion to extend their means of control and expand the scope of their authority. In this new systems-centered collective, this Pentagon of power, there is no visible presence who issues commands; unlike Job's God, the new deities cannot be confronted, still less defied. Under the pretext of saving labor, the ultimate end of this technics is to displace life, or rather to transfer the attributes of life to the machine and the mechanical collective, allowing only so much of the organism to remain as may be controlled and manipulated.

Do not misunderstand this analysis. The danger to democracy does not spring from any specific scientific discoveries or electronic inventions. The human compulsions that dominate the authoritarian technics of our own day date back to a period before even the wheel had been invented. The danger springs from the fact that, since Francis Bacon and Galileo defined the new methods and objectives of technics, our great physical transformations have been effected by a system that deliberately eliminates the whole human personality, ignores the historic process, overplays the role of the abstract intelligence, and makes control over physical nature, ultimately control over man himself, the chief purpose of existence. This system has made its way so insidiously into Western society that my analysis of its derivation and its intentions may well seem more questionable—indeed more shocking—than the facts themselves.

Why has our age surrendered so easily to the controllers, the manipulators, the conditioners of an authoritarian technics? The answer to this question is both paradoxical and ironic. Present-day technics differs from that of the overtly brutal, half-baked authoritarian systems of the past in one highly favorable particular: It has accepted the basic principle of democracy, that every member of society should have a share in its goods. By progressively fulfilling this part of the democratic promises, our system has achieved a hold over the whole community that threatens to wipe out every other vestige of democracy.

The bargain we are being asked to ratify takes the form of

a magnificent bribe. Under the democratic-authoritarian social contract, each member of the community may claim every material advantage, every intellectual and emotional stimulus he may desire, in quantities hardly available hitherto even for a restricted minority—food, housing, swift transportation, instantaneous communication, medical care, entertainment, education—but on the one condition that one must not merely ask for nothing that the system does not provide, but likewise agree to take everything offered, duly processed and fabricated, homogenized and equalized, in the precise quantities that the system, rather than the person, requires. Once one opts for the system no further choice remains. In a word, if one surrenders one's life at source, authoritarian technics will give back as much of it as can be mechanically graded, quantitatively multiplied, collectively manipulated and magnified.

"Is this not a fair bargain?" those who speak for the system will ask. Are not the goods authoritarian technics promises real goods? Is this not the horn of plenty that mankind has long dreamed of and that every ruling class has tried to secure, at whatever cost of brutality and injustice, for itself? I would not belittle, still less deny, the many admirable products this technology has brought forth, products that a self-regulating economy would make good use of. I would only suggest that it is time to reckon up the human disadvantages and costs, to say nothing of the dangers, of our unqualified acceptance of the system itself. Even the immediate price is heavy; for the system is so far from being under effective human direction that it may poison us wholesale in order to provide us with food or exterminate us in order to provide national security, before we can enjoy its promised goods. Is it really humanly profitable to give up the possibility of living a few years at Walden Pond, so to say, for the privilege of spending a lifetime in Skinner's Walden Two?

Once our authoritarian technics consolidates its powers,

with the aid of its new forms of mass control, its panoply of tranquilizers, sedatives, and aphrodisiacs, could democracy in any form survive? That question is absurd; life itself will not survive, except what is funneled through the mechanical collective. The spread of a sterilized scientific intelligence over the planet would not, as Teilhard de Chardin so innocently imagined, be the happy consummation of divine purpose; it would rather ensure the final arrest of any further human development.

Again, do not mistake my meaning. This is not a prediction of what *will* happen, but a warning against what *may* happen. In characterizing the authoritarian technics that has begun to dominate us, I have not forgotten the great lesson of history: Prepare for the unexpected! Nor do I overlook the immense reserves of vitality and creativity that a more humane democratic tradition still offers us. What I wish to do is to persuade those who are concerned with maintaining democratic institutions to see that their constructive efforts must include technology itself. There, too, we must return to the human center. We must challenge this authoritarian system that has given to an underdimensioned ideology and technology the authority that belongs to the human personality. I repeat: Life cannot be delegated.

Curiously, the first words in support of this thesis came forth, with exquisite symbolic aptness, from a willing agent— but very nearly a classic victim!—of the new authoritarian technics. They came from the astronaut John Glenn, whose life was endangered by the malfunctioning of his automatic controls, operated from a remote center. After he had barely saved his life by personal intervention, he emerged from his space capsule with these ringing words: "Now let man take over!"

That command is easier to utter than obey. But if we are not to be driven to even more drastic measures than Samuel Butler suggested in *Erewhon,* we had better map out a more positive course—namely, the reconstitution of both our science and our technics in such a fashion as to insert the rejected parts of the human personality at every stage in the process. This means gladly sacrificing mere quantity in order to restore qualitative choice, shifting the seat of authority from the mechanical collective to the human personality and the autonomous group, favoring variety and ecological complexity, instead of stressing undue uniformity and standardization, and, above all, reducing the insensate drive to extend the system itself, instead of containing it within definite human limits and thus releasing man himself for other purposes. We must ask, not what is good for science or technology, still less what is good for General Motors or Union Carbide or IBM or the Pentagon, but what is good for man—not machine-conditioned, system-regulated mass-man, but man in person, moving freely over every area of life.

There are large areas of technology that can be redeemed by the democratic process once we have overcome the infantile compulsions and automatisms that now threaten to cancel out our real gains. The very leisure that the machine now gives in advanced countries can be profitably used, not for further commitment to still other kinds of machines furnishing automatic recreation, but by doing significant forms of work unprofitable or technically impossible under mass production, work dependent upon special skill, knowledge, and the esthetic sense. The do-it-yourself movement prematurely got bogged down in an attempt to sell still more machines; but its slogan pointed in the right direction—provided we still have a self to do it with. The glut of motor cars that is now destroying our cities can be coped with only if we redesign our cities to make fuller use of a more efficient human agent, the walker. Even in childbirth, the emphasis is already happily shifting from an officious, often lethal, authoritarian procedure, centered in hospital routine, to a more human mode, which restores initiative to the mother and to the body's natural rhythms.

The rebuilding of a democratic technics is plainly too big a subject to be handled in a final sentence or two; but I trust I have made it clear that the genuine advantages our scientifically based technics has brought can be preserved only if we cut the whole system back to a point at which it will permit human alternatives, human interventions, and human destinations for entirely different purposes from those of the system itself. At the present juncture, if democracy did not exist, we would have to invent it, in order to restore, fortify, and replenish the spirit of man.

GERARD PIEL

Publisher, "Scientific American"

Just a generation ago, the title "Technology and Democracy" would have stood for a roundabout way of saying Progress. In the present American climate, it evokes the problems that are gathered under the dispirited heading of Change. The word Change is a gingerly locution for Revolution—not Revolution in the grand old sense of American Revolution, but Revolution as it is beheld from the uncomfortable vantage of a seat in the tumbril.

The alienation of the worker diagnosed by Karl Marx a century ago has given way to the middle-class malaise of *anomie,* alienation not only from society but from self. Affluence is the terminus of the American Dream, affluence from which, in Edward Albee's transcription of the voice of the people, "You get no satisfaction!" The skyscraping cities of the land have become ghettoes, as Morton Grodzins and his colleagues have shown, transformed by a menacing new pattern of metropolitan segregation. "The destructive blight of ugliness," says Mason W. Gross, spreads out upon the landscape in "the creeping, crawling hideousness" of the suburbs. With "an educational system that does not educate, a system of mass communications that does not communicate," in the words of Robert Hutchins, we have become incapable of "the discussion by which political issues are determined." The margin by which we elect a national administration precisely measures the breadth of political discourse. What could come of such an election in these times but an administration impotent in policy and struck with the power of decision by cybernation?

Americans find themselves looking abroad with unaccustomed envy to the future-dwelling peoples of the newly buoyant economies of Western Europe, with anxiety to the harshly forward-driving Socialist systems, with dismay to the new nations of the world's poor, so eager to embrace any system that will bring them to our dubious estate. At home, Americans are looking backward. Some to the 1930's, which is what they mean by "Let's get America going again!" Some to the bustling laissez-faire normalcy of the 1920's. Many more to the 1860's, in the atavistic celebration of the War Between the States that, on January 1 of 1963, overlooked the centenary of the Emancipation Proclamation.

The Center for the Study of Democratic Institutions asks us to look back to 1776 and to answer this question: Can democratic institutions framed in the landscape of a rural republic secure liberty, equality, and the pursuit of happiness in a modern industrial society? That is, whether the individual, whose perfection was to be the goal of our society, is fated now to be the well-fed creature of a technological order that has endowed him with power to no purpose, with techniques for programming and no capacity to plan, with means that compromise all ends.

For a first approximation of an answer, we ought to seek a longer perspective than that provided by our brief, parochial history. Recent discoveries by physical anthropologists make it possible to place the modern condition of man in the perspective of two million years, or more, of history. The taxonomical status symbol that distinguishes the genus *Homo* from other primates is the making of tools—that is, technology. This transaction with the environment is of a different order from the unlearned behavior that facilitates survival; some reflexes cross at the spinal synapses. Tool-making is a function of the cerebral cortex; it involves integration of the memory, perception, and motor centers in purposeful activity. Now, the first primate in whose cortex the necessary feedback circuits closed did not much resemble *Homo sapiens*. The discovery of a few bones of his hands in association with the pebble-tools they made has reversed the traditional notion that man made the first tools; it appears rather that tools made man.

At the very least, tool-making must be reckoned as a major selective pressure in the evolutionary process that generated "the great ravell'd knot" of the human cerebrum. The record as to skulls and hand bones is scanty and incomplete, but the story can still be read in the enduring fossils of behavior— the stone tools that are counted among the most numerous of all fossils of the Pleistocene. They show that, early in the history of our genus, evolution became cultural as well as biological—Lamarckian as well as Mendelian in the sense that acquired behavioral characteristics were consciously se- lected, improved, and enlarged upon, and transmitted by teaching and learning from generation to generation. The increasing diversity of stone tools implies a corresponding elaboration of technology employing less enduring materials. The mastery of new environments commanded thereby dis- closed new possibilities and new ways of life to emergent man —one might go so far as to say new values and goals.

As long as 40,000 years ago, it appears, the diverse tech- nologies of hunting and food-gathering enabled *Homo sapi- ens* to make himself at home in every environment on earth, from the Arctic shores of the continents to remote islands in the open Pacific. These life-ways brought out the best in man. The society was the extended family, and, since few en- vironments provided an assured sustenance, members were bound by close ties of mutual interest and cooperation. None- theless, even in the struggle for daily survival, life was enriched by the articulation of the esthetic impulses in the graphic arts, music, and spoken literature; in these realms, we have learned recently to use the word "primitive" with respect. In particular, students agree, there is no such thing as a language that is primitive in the sense of rudimentary. According to Benjamin Whorf, the typical primitive language, which draws no rhetorical distinction between a thing and the state it is in, would serve more effectively than any Indo-European language to describe the world as it is known to quantum physics. Typically, also, the primitive language draws no distinction between an action and its purpose; the two are merged in the unity of experience that makes life whole.

The hunting and food-gathering way of life did not, however, evoke the full capacity of man. It was a long time, for example, before the further elaboration of technology made it possible for human society to sponsor a moral philosopher in the leisured contemplation necessary to his calling. We owe this advance in culture, no doubt, to the second great revolution in technology—the agricultural revolution on which the first city states were founded.

Imperceptibly, as the hunters and food-gatherers came into possession of more intimate understanding of their environments, they had been turning into herdsmen and cultivators. There could be no doubt about the progressive nature of this development. Whereas it required square miles of open country to support a hunter and his family, a few acres of land sufficed to sustain the farmer. Hunting was a daily gamble; farming was a gamble too, but food could be stored in the granary and on the hoof. The struggle for daily survival accordingly gave way to the economy of scarcity at some point within the last year 10,000 years in Asia Minor, perhaps independently at about the same time in China, and, in entire independence, perhaps 3,000 years ago in pre-Columbian America. There was scarcity because the increase of population always overtook increases in production. Over long periods of time compared to the span of a human life, the yet slow and halting progress of technology afforded a fixed ratio of tools and techniques to land and labor. Production increased, therefore, principally as population increased, maintaining at best an equilibrium with want.

By means of economy enforced by coercion, however, the agricultural civilizations managed to gather from the labor of four families on the land a surplus sufficient to feed one family in the city. All ancient cities show the same essential plan: within the walls, the temple, the palace, and the garrison; outside, the traces in the soil of the hovels of the slaves. The history of the next 5,000 or 6,000 years, which now began to be recorded, has little to say about these arrangements. For that matter, since history is primarily a first-person account written by the beneficiaries, it has little to say about the 80 per cent of the population that at all times was excluded from participation in history.

The inequity that sustained the economics of scarcity is an inexplicit premise of the first great discourse on democratic institutions; Plato's *Republic* makes passing reference to the *andropoda,* the "human-footed animals" who held no citizenship. Jewish law, of all the ancient codes, called for a certain minimum humanity in the treatment of slaves, but raised no question about the institution of slavery itself. Later moral philosophers could show that the rights of tenure and fief were founded on natural law. But for the most part, authority asked only the legitimacy conferred by the passage of time.

Thus securely rooted in the inequitable distribution of scarcity, agricultural civilization has persisted even into modern times. Indeed, two-thirds of mankind still lives on its meager terms and is only now awakening to the demonstrated fact that another way of life is possible. For, as their more fortunate contemporaries have reason to know, men continued to devise new tools. Around 1600, in Europe, there came a quickening in this process, which Thorstein Veblen called the life process of mankind. The quickening is easily explained: The rate of discovery and invention accelerates because the accumulating stock of technology widens the scope of human activity and so the opportunity and the occasion for new discovery and invention. By 1600, the exponential curve of invention was rising perceptibly from the historical baseline. At first in Europe and then elsewhere, history took the same abrupt turn. The surplus gathered in by the economic institutions of scarcity found a new function: The wealth of the nations became capital. With the third great revolution in technology, this parable of man, the tool-maker, brings us back to contemporary American civilization and the questions now at issue.

It is in America, of course, that the industrial revolution has reached its present culmination. Our well-known standard of living serves as the usual index of our revolutionary leadership. Americans consume three times as much in the way of goods and services, per capita, as their fellow-inhabitants of industrial civilization and more than twenty times as much—if the comparison can be made at all—as the denizens of contemporary agricultural civilization. Such figures barely suggest, however, the deeper change that industrial technology is working in the condition of man. The increasing well-being of Americans requires less from them by way of work each year. They work fewer hours of the day, fewer days of the year, and fewer years of their lives, most of them at work that few of their fellow-men would recognize as work. The census of 1960 showed that less than half of the American labor force is now engaged in productive functions.

Strangely, perhaps, it is the agriculture of industrial civilization that most clearly exposes the nature of the change technology has brought and portends in man's way of life. In contrast with agricultural civilization, where 80 per cent of the people continue to be employed or underemployed on the land, less than 10 per cent of the American labor force works on the farm. Working fewer acres each year, they produce still bigger yields—presently, enough to feed 12,000 calories to each American every day, enough to feed a billion people an adequate daily ration. The American economy upgrades these calories, via animals, to give a high fat and protein content to our daily ration of 2,500–3,000 calories. It also wastes a good deal of the food and gives a good deal of it away, and still it has a surplus to keep compulsively in storage.

In the American agricultural surplus, we behold a very different kind of surplus from that which was first gathered by the lash in Mesopotamia 6,000 years ago. It is a true, granary-bursting physical surplus; it may be taken as symbolic of the surpluses generated elsewhere and everywhere in our industrial system. The technological surplus is the opposite of the scarcity surplus: It is abundance.

The advent of abundance is not yet comprehended in the theory and practice of our economy. In truth, one must confess the opposite; our abundance is dodged, minimized, and concealed, as well as squandered, burned, and dumped. Yet we are already in transition from the economy of scarcity to the economy of abundance. Our society has absorbed the shock and responded with considerable resilience. We nonetheless resolutely pretend that we can go on managing the production and distribution of abundance through agencies created for the management of scarcity. To the degree that we have failed to come to terms with our historic achievement, we have botched and corrupted it. The inability to comprehend this failure has sadly misled the critics of our mores, who have blamed the machine for our poor management of it; more important, this compound failure has diverted public discussion from what ought to be the issues of our time and has reduced our politics to trivia.

Consider the affluence that yields no satisfaction, the convergence on mediocrity and indistinguishability that characterizes so many of the common articles of commerce—white bread, light beer, and guaranteed-odorless vodka, to mention a few among many tasteless products. This looks so much like the universal process of entropy that it is taken without question to be a bane of technology. The real truth is that technology frees the task of design and production from technical limitations. By doing so, it permits other considerations to hold sway. It is these other considerations, I submit, that bring the second law of thermodynamics into action.

The American cigarette, for example, is the product not so much of technology but of the new economics of monopolistic competition, or oligopoly. In this kind of competition, the competitors all get the same answers out of their market surveys and public opinion polls; they look over one another's shoulders in computing the same maximization of results, and so they make their products more and more alike. It can be argued that they make their products this way to take advantage of the economies of mass production; what they save on production, however, they squander on sales cost. In the language of game theory, the cigarette is the solution to a zero-sum contest with perfect information; in other words, it occupies the saddle point. The soundness of this analysis is reinforced by the recent scrambling and unscrambling of cigarette brands, occasioned by the finding that heavy cigarette smoking causes lung cancer; to this destabilizing crisis, the competitors all responded with the same new models, again principally distinguishable by packaging.

The money and the social cost of this way of managing abundance is plainly demonstrated in the American automobile. Here is, above all, a social not a technological artifact, and one symbolic of the schizophrenia to which I am urging your attention. Technological considerations of function, efficiency, and utilization of resources might dictate one or more designs for the automobile. None of the American automobiles is any one of these. The virtues of abundance are bodied forth in the form of waste—of materials, space, and fuel, to name the principal categories. And here also we see the relentless convergence on the same design, the pursuit of identical oscillations in design change, and the packaging that is supposed to make all the difference in the world. Against the argument that mass production makes the autos all alike, it can be shown again that the virtuosity of technology, integrated in the sales function, is employed to squander the economies of mass production on junk. As a supposedly durable good, what is more, the automobile is a disgrace to American technology. According to the standard practice of our durable goods industries—always with the aim of perpetuating scarcity in the face of abundance—the automobile is designed for 1,000 hours of service, to be traded in at 40,000 miles or less.

Now, it is plain that all of this had to do with the maintenance of a lively economy, with the creation of jobs, with the struggle for profit margins and other vital economic aims. But all of these compulsions, it is equally clear, arise from the economics of scarcity. They are not determinants of technology. In the place of abundance, proffered by technology, we get affluence.

The Bell Telephone Company, responding to different economic compulsions, builds to far higher standards of service. The telephone handset, the cheapest thing of its kind in the world, is built for amortization over twenty years. During that time, of course, the telephone company sees to it that you put the instrument to a great many more than 1,000 hours of service.

Turning to somewhat larger issues, let me relate how the late Erwin Wolfson, the author of the Pan American Building in New York, responded to the question "Who is responsible for ugliness?" The question was put to Mr. Wolfson and others at the First Conference on Aesthetic Responsibility, held in New York in 1962. In the course of his reply, Mr. Wolfson recalled that "the architects came up with a scheme which developed about 1.5 million square feet on a plot of 151,000 square feet, with a valuation of $20 million." To this, he added, "It just wouldn't work." I am sure he was right, for what the architects had to come up with, finally, was a scheme that developed 2.4 million square feet and a valuation, I am told, of $75 million on that same 151,000-square-foot plot. Mr. Wolfson was able to show, furthermore, that as the result of the sympathetic collaboration of the builder and the architect the Pan Am building is not as ugly as it might have been. As it stands, the building is the resultant of a multi-variable equation involving a host of economic compulsions and some aesthetic considerations, to the solution of which technology lent high flexibility and freedom.

The one element lacking any weight in those equations was the public interest. But you can look in vain, both north and south on Park Avenue from the Pan Am building, for evidence that the public interest is represented by an institutional advocate in the evolution of our most successful but increasingly less livable city. There is lacking here the countervailing forces on which our economists have urged us to rely. The abundance of choices placed at our disposal by technology is harshly narrowed to the solutions of scarcity economics. Technologically speaking, we could build our town the way we like it. Economically speaking—that is from the obsolete premises of scarcity—it gets built in a way that no one likes.

So people flee to the suburbs. The escape is made possible by our rubber-tired transportation industry, and thus by the choice-expanding power of technology. But the whole scheme is as unfair as it can be. It is designed for the benefit of the better-off at the expense of the worse-off. Reaching out in all directions from every central city in our country is a radial gradient of ascending incomes. Except for Manhattan and San Francisco and a few enclaves like Louisburg Square in Boston, the central cities are becoming racially segregated slums—that is, ghettos in the strict sense of the term. The nearer suburbs are blighted by the triumphs of highway engineering that bring traffic in speedily from the unspoiled, more distant suburbs.

When we look for the representation of the public interest in the economics of suburbanization, we make a surprising discovery. The public is represented there with the biggest expenditures in the public sector after armaments and education. This is the outlay for highways, running at the rate of $10 billion a year—not far, in fact, behind education. What is more, in the economics of suburbanization one must reckon a large portion of the education outlay: The current expenditure per child (for teaching and the like) is down from 1939 (in real dollars), but the investment in the building of schools is up. In other words, the American public has been heavily engaged in financing this transformation of its lifeways. It is a transformation that, by any reckoning, tends to cheat the worse-off, and therefore the larger numbers of people, for the benefit of the better-off. In this case, substantial public expenditure has generated no countervailing force in favor of what would seem to be the interests of the larger numbers, if not of the public as a whole. On the contrary, these taxpayers would seem to have financed their own traduction.

One might wonder how it is that the treasuries of federal, state, and local governments disburse funds so generously for highways. It is not enough to observe that rubber-tired transportation, adding up to a total expense of about $80 billion per year (including the $10 billion for highways), has an economic interest in promoting this capital subsidy and so maintains well-financed lobbies at each node in the governmental network. For the country also has a substantial rail-transportation industry, and this industry has only recently begun to make half-hearted overtures to the taxpayer. What is more, it is apparent that well-equipped, electric-powered commuter services could make the shuttle from city to suburb a much less exacting human task, would reduce air pollution, and wonderfully relieve congestion in town. But one gathers, from the Pan Am building and the impending demolition of Penn Station, that the railroads are less interested in their public franchises than in the real estate they acquired therewith. The airlines, constituting a much smaller element in the transportation sector, already draw much bigger subsidies, for operations as well as for design of their aircraft and for the building of their airports. If there is anything to the interplay of countervailing forces as a scheme for rational management of society, it is high time our citizenry generated more of them.

The need for ventilation of our political life is becoming increasingly urgent for another reason not often mentioned in public because it leads discussion into such dangerous and trackless territory. Let me go a little way into the thickets. The dark truth is that our system is sick. There is even some unanimity about the diagnosis, for economists agree that the economy is suffering from a widening gap between its capacity to produce abundance and its ability to generate effective demand in the market-place. The principal symptom is the ominously steady increase in unemployment.

No one should be surprised by this state of affairs. A technological order that employs fewer and fewer productive workers is obviously qualifying fewer and fewer consumers with the purchasing power to buy the goods it makes. Nor could we want it otherwise; it is, after all, the function of technology to ease man's labors and to multiply his product. It is up to the economic system to make the new arrangements necessary to realize the bounty of technology. In fact, our economic system has managed to do so with reasonable success until recently, though at high cost to other values, including those of our democratic institutions. Its success is the more remarkable in view of the fact that the latest revolution in technology has been subverting the underlying premise of scarcity.

Since 1900, the portion of the labor force engaged in productive functions—and these include transportation and construction as well as manufacturing, mining, and farming—has declined from 75 to 45 per cent. The decline has come farthest and fastest in farming, of course, and in unskilled labor. At the outset, these declines were offset principally in other lines of production—in the expanding manufacturing sector and its need for skilled labor. Now these demands have leveled and begun to shrink; in another generation, factory workers will be as scarce as farmers. Meanwhile, our economy has created whole new categories of employment—white-collar jobs in trade and distribution and in the services. I have already remarked on the waste involved in these activities; I must here remark that they serve the vital economic function of qualifying consumers with paychecks and so supplying effective demand for the goods produced by the declining number of productive workers.

The record shows, however, that the system could not absorb the impact of technology without external assistance. Between 1900 and 1929, the percentage of the gross national product that cycled through the public sector—that is, through the payrolls of federal, state, and local governments—increased from 3 to 10 per cent. Again, whatever other functions these jobs filled, they helped to supply effective demand. In those days, it should be added, 60 per cent of the public jobs were in state and local governments and were occasioned principally by the rising demand for the welfare and resource services of government. In the 1930's, when the mounting abundance of technology first confronted us with the paradox of poverty in the midst of plenty, national policy took explicit notice of the economic stimulus generated by public expenditures. Overnight, with popular approval, the public sector doubled its claim on the gross national product, rising from 10 to 20 per cent. The ratio of state and local to federal budgets also at that time reversed itself, and the federal government began disbursing 60 per cent of the public funds.

Today, more than 25 per cent of the gross national product cycles through the public budget. But now there is a difference. Fully 10 of the 25 per cent goes to the maintenance and supply of the military establishment. Again one must observe that whatever other function these expenditures serve— whatever their military justification—they play a vital role in the mounting economic crisis. They not only provide jobs for consumers but also for corporations. In other words, they not only increase effective demand, they also help directly to maintain the system of private enterprise by keeping corporations employed. Above and beyond the call of duty, the war economy has given us affluence.

In helping to solve our fiscal problems, however, the war economy has exacted a measurable social cost. Half of the 10 per cent that it turns over has come from an increase in the size of the public sector; the other half has come from the curtailment of the welfare and resource services of the government. Those services, as a percentage of the gross national product, have been cut by one third.

The reasons why the military are accorded free access to the public treasury while the claims of our human and natural resources evoke mighty opposition ought to be more closely explored by the students of scarcity economics. Such study is needed because it is apparent that military expenditures must play a declining role in fiscal policy from now on. Progress in military technology in recent years has drastically reduced the cost of devastation per square mile. The solid-fuel push-button Minuteman and Polaris missiles have made the more labor-intensive B-70 and Skybolt obsolete. Of the ultimate ultimate weapons, as President Kennedy has observed, we can equip ourselves with no more than a finite number. This is a serious situation because the war economy qualifies some seven million consumers with effective demand. These seven million plus the four or five million unemployed—some 20 per cent of our labor force—represent the gap between effective demand and our capacity to produce abundance.

The classical Keynesian-deficit stimulus is a forlorn hope, especially if the deficit is to be achieved by a cut in taxes instead of an increase in federal expenditure. During the past decade, we have run up a cumulative public deficit of $80 billion, and still the economy has stagnated. In the present climate, there is serious danger that any tax windfall to the consumer and to business enterprises will go into savings and surplus accounts and not into consumption and investment. In any case, equivalent public funds laid out for welfare- and resource-service functions would more surely multiply effective demand, as well as increase the abundance of our domestic life.

The most urgent need is for an increase in the budget for education. Surely an educational system that educates is essential to the restoration and enhancement of our democratic institutions. With an electorate awakened to the new possibilities—not to mention goals and purposes—that technology has opened up to human life, we can expect to see a wiser deployment of our capacity to generate abundance—a deployment of that capacity to the creation of more spacious cities, to the cherishing of natural resources, and to the attainment of a happier ecological adjustment of Americans to their bountiful environment.

These objectives can no longer be regarded as "residual," to use Charles Frankel's terms; they must come to the center of the stage as the primary "institutional" questions of politics and public policy. The public interest cannot, as W. H. Ferry has said, be left to find its way through the interstices of private interests.

Technology is concerned not alone with the means but also with the ends of life. The tool-making activity of man from his beginnings has expanded the possibilities of his existence, generated the aspirations, and previsioned the goals that lie beyond. It is only in the milieu of industrial society that we can speak of equality without the silent discount of eight out of ten of our brothers. It is by tool-making that men have at least freed themselves from physical bondage to toil and to one another. One of the aspirations that now becomes feasible, therefore, is self-government. With the open acknowledgment that our tool-making has brought a revolutionary change in man's relationship to nature, we can proceed to the necessary revisions in our relationship with one another.

COMMENTS

HYMAN G. RICKOVER

Vice-Admiral, United States Navy; U.S. Atomic Energy Commission

WE MUST clearly distinguish two basic facts about technology. The first is that although technology enables us to increase our power of mind and body, it does not dictate how we use this power. In this sense, technology is neutral. We remain the controller of our actions and we are responsible for their consequences. I am unconvinced when people tell me that rapid scientific progress, which changes fundamentally the ways we provide for our *material* wants, thereby obsoletes the fundamental ethical and moral concepts Western man has painfully evolved over the centuries. Why ever should machine-produced affluence invalidate the Ten Commandments or the Sermon on the Mount? What has improved health to do with that great Western concept of the supreme moral worth of the individual that flows from belief in the fatherhood of God and the brotherhood of man—the concept that is the foundation of our own and every other democracy in the world?

As machines relieve us of the brutal, tiring, and time-consuming labor that had been the lot of the majority of men from time immemorial, as they enable us to universalize affluence and leisure, we face a choice: We may take these benefits and live the life of the idle rich of old, pursuing a good time and not bothering about the *quality* of our own life or the life of the nation. Or, we may decide to emulate those—and there were many—who in the past considered wealth and leisure a trust, to be used for self-improvement and for improvement of their particular societies. The choice is for each individual to make. Moreover, each individual, under our form of government, has a right to speak out publicly in favor of making better use of science and technology than is possible under present conditions.

I presume that all of us accept the proposition that technology makes sense only when it produces human happiness in a free society; for Americans, at least, the two go together. Were we to prefer an affluent and carefree life for the freedom and responsibilities possessed by democratic citizens, we should be sacrificing our heritage for a mess of pottage—an inexcusable folly, no matter how good the pottage might be. Perhaps we might, for greater clarity, restate the topic to read: *How can we find ways to obtain the benefits of technology without destroying or weakening our democratic institutions?*

So much for the first basic fact of technology: It does not dictate *how* we use the increased power it gives our minds and bodies.

Now to the second fact. In using science, which is what technology means, we must heed what I like to call the categorical imperatives of science. We must respect nature, over which science gives us control, for if we don't, nature will strike back. I can best illustrate this with an example.

Today we are able to destroy insect pests and weeds with new chemicals that science has developed. The use of these scientific inventions is profitable for those who manufacture the chemicals; it is helpful to farmers who are able to get better crops, reduce human labor, and thus produce at greater profit; it benefits consumers who are offered a wider variety of food at less cost. Here is a classic case of what technology can do for us. Unfortunately, we have left out of consideration the balance of nature. If used improperly, these pesticides and weed-killers may poison soil, crops, animals, and eventually man. Rachel Carson warns us eloquently against committing this ecological sin in her book *Silent Spring*.

In my own field of work, I am constantly aware of the harm that nuclear reactors, improperly designed or operated, could do. Radiation is one of the hazards that must be constantly kept in mind. The same is true to a much larger extent of nuclear bombs. We are here getting involved in extremely tricky manipulation of powerful natural forces.

Because the general public does not fully understand the categorical imperatives of science, it cannot itself exert control in this field. Recently, the United States Court of Appeals in Washington, D. C., ruled against the city of New Britain, Connecticut, which tried to prevent a private firm from receiving and storing radioactive wastes in the city for disposal elsewhere. The court rejected the case of the people of New Britain on the grounds that "the handling of radioactive wastes there does not involve any credible possibility of contamination of the ground, air, or water."

I do not question the accuracy of this statement by the court. I wish merely to bring out that, in making the statement, the court of necessity did not base its decision on its own ascertainment of the facts, but said, in effect, that the Atomic Energy Commission knows the facts and it knows that they will not harm the city. What else could the court have done? It must rely on expert opinion. The Congress has set up the Atomic Energy Commission to provide the American people with expert opinion, and the Commission does this expertly and most conscientiously. It relies on the best scientific and engineering advice it can obtain.

But in a subtle way democracy is undermined when an important aspect of the life of individuals and communities can no longer be judged by the voter, but must be entrusted to experts who work in areas of science that the general public does not comprehend. As presently constituted, our democratic institutions—through which the will of the people normally expresses itself and which under our Constitution are required to heed that will—these institutions are themselves not well equipped to control the proper use of technology. In nuclear power, I feel we have developed the best attainable safeguards; in other technologies, we have been less successful.

I suggest we explore as a second aspect of the topic the question: How can democratic institutions best control the use of technology so that neither the individual nor the nation will be harmed?

Mr. Mumford warns that sheer size, the superhuman scale of many of our organizations, damages human values that are part of our democratic way of life. They dwarf man; they diminish his autonomy and thus his ability to function effectively as a citizen exercising the power of self-government. They become bureaucracies in which masses of people work under direction, and little room is left for individual initiative. It seems that large-scale enterprise tends irresistibly to bureaucracy, whether it be private or public. Bigness thus enters our topic of discussion. Not all of the bigness is a direct consequence of the use or misuse of technology. We are an enormously populous nation. Even if times were normal, we should need big government to keep us from harming one another.

We are only beginning to realize that for generations we have had a population explosion the like of which the world has never seen. From 1800–50, we quintupled; from 1850–1900, we trebled; from 1900–50, we doubled in numbers, and we are likely to double again by the year 2000. When we celebrate the bicentennial of the adoption of the Constitution, we will be so numerous that each of us will be left with no more than about 1 per cent of the voting power possessed by Americans in our first national election. This cannot but diminish the citizen's sense of importance and lead to political apathy, itself the greatest threat to democracy.

Technology has had little to do with this growth. Other industrial nations long ago cut down to from half to one third our growth rate. They recognized their limitations of space; we have trouble realizing that we ceased long ago to be a country in which people were scarce. When this was an underpopulated country, every man's worth was automatically enhanced because he was sorely needed. But now we have endemic unemployment, which I, for one, believe cannot be overcome merely by producing more and more consumer goods. Nine out of ten Americans now work for others, many for giant organizations. Galbraith, I believe, once pointed out that the average American family—heavily indebted by installment buying—is but three weeks removed from bankruptcy. Moreover, 70 per cent of us now live in the crowded urban conglomerations we call megalopolis.

We have managed the democratic process remarkably well, though *we are now bereft of every single special advantage the Founding Fathers considered essential to the success of democracy:* few people, much land, independent small-scale enterprise, and, finally, that greatest of all advantages, geographic isolation, which allowed us to go about our peaceful pursuits without fear of foreign invasion. As we climb relentlessly toward the billion mark in population, we shall have to give thought to strengthening local and state government, for it is in these smaller units that most people are most effective as citizens. Here we might do well to investigate what successful European democracies have done. We shall find that everywhere municipal government and state or provincial government have been deliberately strengthened, but ways have also been found to achieve national unity wherever it is needed.

Half a century ago, Woodrow Wilson remarked, somewhat wistfully, it seems to me, that "the stage of America grows crowded like the stage of Europe. The life of the New World grows as complex as the life of the Old." We still have important advantages—much more land per capita, greater natural wealth (though it is rapidly being used up), and a strong tradition of individual initiative. Nevertheless, we are neither the only, nor even in every respect the most successful, democracy, politically speaking. There *are* things we can learn from abroad, notably the way standards in such fields as general education, the training of skilled workers and technicians, and the licensing of professional people are set nationally and enforced locally. Usually such standards are established by calling on the country's best minds to cooperate with central and local authorities. Once set, most of the responsibility for putting the standards into effect falls to the local authorities.

We are a big country living in a dangerous world. Much as we deplore it, the federal government must spend vast sums on weapons technology and build up the military-industrial complex whose power President Eisenhower found so disturbing and against which he warned us in his farewell address. As part of this complex, I try to keep my own group from deteriorating into a bureaucracy. I spend most of my time selecting and training the scientists and engineers in my organization. As soon as they are ready, I give them responsibilities and then leave them alone. As long as they do it well, I do not care how they organize their work. I am myself acutely conscious of the need for allowing individual initiative the widest possible leeway in any organization, large or small. How best to do this is one of the really big problems we must solve.

Private independence and initiative are not preserved by having a plurality of huge organizations, though it is of course much better than having one huge national political-industrial organization like the Soviets. It is important for us to see clearly that what diminishes the individual is bureaucracy turned rigid. Size tends to make organizations inflexible. For those who work in them, it makes little difference whether such an organization is private or public. In our country, adverse effects on the individual may be fewer in a public than in a private bureaucracy, because the individual as a citizen is able to exert some control over the conduct of public officials and is, moreover, protected by the Bill of Rights. Those who work for a gigantic private bureaucracy face corporate officials backed by the massive economic power of the organization they control. Here Americans confront one another under conditions of extreme inequality and with the weaker guaranteed no "inalienable rights."

If we may believe the many books that have recently come out dealing with life in the giant corporation, a man looking for a job or for advancement would appear to have to submit to a degree of invasion of privacy that strikes me as intolerable, besides being quite unnecessary. No "fifth amendment" protects certain categories of job-seekers against being subjected to personality tests of dubious scientific value, which probe their soul and inquire into their family life, churchgoing habits, and whether or not they have an interest in cultural matters. Several *Fortune* articles describe the most extraordinary corporate "sumptuary rules," reminiscent of the Middle Ages, which prescribe the type of house, car, club, *even wife,* that an ambitious "organization" man is well advised to acquire. Occasionally, he may even find it advisable to reshape his personality to conform to the "image" the corporation has of its management, the image being usually that of incumbent top personnel. When one takes into consideration that in today's corporation ownership and management are almost wholly divorced, managers therefore being no less employees of the company than the lowliest scrub woman, one cannot but marvel at the growth of such authoritarian organisms in the midst of democratic America.

Of course, every corporation is free to manage its affairs as it wishes and to hire the people it wants, but there is this point to consider: Corporations have long striven to obtain full citizenship rights as "persons" in the sight of the law. They have largely attained that objective. The courts for all practical purposes treat them as state or federal citizens. Does the achievement of citizenship status then not entail on the part of corporations the obligations to assume as well the civic duties of natural citizens? In law, "right and obligation are correlative."

It seems to me a clear obligation for all bureaucratic organizations—private as well as public—to do nothing that will diminish individual autonomy. Public bureaucracies need constant watching, but they *can* be restrained. With private bureaucracies, the obligation cannot be imposed or enforced. But it can be publicly discussed, and public disapproval can be visited on those who violate the obligation.

Wittfogel's *Oriental Despotism* makes a persuasive case for the easy transition from authoritarian technology to totalitarian state. Wittfogel deals with pre-industrial totalitarianisms, all characterized by being dependent for their food supply on gigantic irrigation or other water works. These required the massing of vast armies of workers who labored under the direction of technical "experts." Wittfogel shows that the docility bred into men whose work gave no release to individual initiative facilitated the transformation of these so-called "hydraulic" societies into totalitarian governments. There are enough analogies to give us pause.

How can we guard against similar consequences as our lives are more and more dominated by gigantic enterprises? I have no answer except to urge that this is a problem that will not solve itself; it must be faced and tackled. And here I would suggest we recognize that what we have, in essence, is a *crisis of intelligence*. The wise use of technology calls for a higher order of thinking than we have so far accorded it. We have largely left it to the management of practical men. I submit that we now have scientific knowledge of such immensely dangerous potential that we ought to bring a broader range of intellectual power to bear upon its use.

I think one can make a general statement that the *practical* approach to a new scientific discovery is short-range and private, concerned with ways to put the discovery to use in the most economical and efficient manner, little thought being given to side effects and future consequences. The *scholarly* approach, if I may use this term, is long-range and public; it looks to the effects that the use of a new discovery may have on people in general, on the nation, perhaps on the world, present and future. Of course, there are men who combine the two approaches, and we find them among people whose primary interest is practical, no less than among those whose primary interest is scholarly. What is important is to recognize that each approach is necessary to illuminate the problem and help solve it. To exclude the one or the other prevents finding a way to reconcile technology and democracy.

Many activities that in the past could safely be left to private decision now involve such complex relationships and such potentially dangerous consequences that they need all the intelligence we can muster merely to be fully understood, not to mention the need to solve them in ways that will preserve our democratic way of life. This way of life is infinitely precious and worth preserving at all cost. It is also capable of giving our society great flexibility and immense strength. Therefore, the most practical person will surely have no difficulty recognizing that by giving our democratic institutions primacy over habitual ways of using technology, we preserve for ourselves and our children the greatest single advantage our way of life gives us. It is not affluence of consumer goods but freedom that will let us prevail in the grim struggle for survival that has been forced upon us.

HARRISON BROWN

Professor of Geochemistry, California Institute of Technology

THIS IS not the first revolution of truly momentous consequences that man has gone through. For example, about 7,000 years ago a tremendous technological invention appeared upon the earth's scene. For a million or two years before that time, men lived pretty much as the other animals around them. But then an invention appeared, known as "agriculture," which completely transformed the human way of life.

Let us suppose what we might have said at that time. We might have said: No longer is man free to roam over the land, seeking the food he needs, free to hunt and fish, and to enjoy the natural beauties of forest and grassland. Now he is chained to a small plot of land that he must cultivate. He uses unnatural positions during his working hours, such as stooping in the rice fields all day. Where once he ate a variety of foods, he is now confined to a cereal or two and an occasional piece of meat, tasteless indeed when compared with our traditional lizards and snakes. Worst of all, he is crowded. In the countryside, a thousand men now occupy land formerly occupied by only one. A new unnatural horror has appeared—the city—in which people live under even more crowded conditions. They stink and they are disease-ridden. Fully 10 per cent of our people live in these monstrosities, not contributing anything to man's most honorable task, that of securing food. Man has ceased to be an individual.

And what is happening to our democratic institutions? The tribal councils in which each individual could make his voice heard have all but disappeared. We are governed by a system of technology, and the technologists themselves do not know that they are governing us. Let us return to the human values of our forefathers.

We might have said that, but in actual fact we could not have said it. For there is one major, overwhelming difference between the transition we are going through today and the transition man went through 7,000 years ago. This difference is one of *rate*. Today, our society is changing with extraordinary rapidity. Seven thousand years ago, the agricultural revolution went along at a snail's pace. Seven thousand years ago, a man would live very much as his mother and father and grandparents before him had lived, and he would know quite confidently that his children would live pretty much as he had lived.

Compare that with what exists today. Most of us know the sequence that runs as follows: My grandmother would ride in a horse-drawn carriage, but was afraid to ride in an automobile; my mother would ride in an automobile, but was afraid to ride in an airplane; I will ride in an airplane, but I am afraid to ride in a jet; and my daughter will ride in a jet, but is afraid to ride in a horse and carriage.

It is this fantastic rate of change which is having profound impact upon the nature of our democratic institutions; for although we seem to be willing to tolerate it with regard to technology, we are not willing to bring about the social and political changes that will enable the technological changes to be properly absorbed.

The nature of the revolution we are going through today is one of the mobilization of science and technology, for purposes of research, and this has given rise to two big long-range dangers that I would like to accentuate briefly.

First, science and technology have placed in our hands tools of persuasion and coercion of unprecedented power, and their power is increasing. As Aldous Huxley pointed out a number of years ago, the revolt with the stick, the stone, and the musket is no longer possible in nations where these tools of persuasion and coercion are available and used. This means that the road toward totalitarianism is a one-way street in the absence of influences from the outside.

The second danger is that people place too much trust in the capabilities of science and technology to protect them and to come to their rescue. There is almost an implicit faith that we do not have to worry about the future because our science and technology will advance to the point where it will meet man's new needs. Many people believe this in connection with the arms race, which has locked us in vicious competition with the Soviet Union, action leading to reaction, then to fresh action, and the consequent compounding of the size and the effectiveness of weapons systems. We see the same attitude toward our population problem and the long-range dangers created by uncontrolled breeding. People say, "Well, at some point, science and technology will come to our rescue. They will produce enough food, and if we get to the point where we run out of space, then they will be able to shoot us to the moon and to the planets and we can make new lives there."

When we put these dangers together, I have the very strong feeling, which I share with Mr. Mumford, that we are indeed headed for very difficult and perilous times. I can only say, with the Mr. Mumford of my story, "Let us return to the human values of our forefathers."

SOL M. LINOWITZ

Chairman of the Board and General Counsel, Xerox Corporation

I START by accepting the fact that in and of itself technology is amoral; it becomes "good" or "bad" depending on what you do with it. Illustration: An automobile can transport you or kill you. So can an airplane. Atomic energy can blow us all up—or it can give us unlimited energy to reach unlimited horizons. Television can bring us Leonard Bernstein or Elvis Presley, Laurence Olivier or Paladin.

It comes down to whether we can produce the "know-what" and the "know-why" to go along with the "know-how." I refuse to be depressed by the threat of what technology will do to our democracy—precisely because I believe in democracy. I refuse to assume that we are going to use all this technology we have been developing in order to destroy our democratic institutions. I do not believe that just because we have an unbreakable toy, we are necessarily going to break all our other toys with it. In short, the challenge of modern technology is not whether to use it, but how to use it to accomplish what we want. It means little to have achieved revolutionary new advances in communications if people will not communicate; to have perfected new ways to make freedom richer if people remain enslaved; to have brought out of the laboratory new ways to sustain life if our greater concern is with how to spread death.

Our responsibility is to step back and put things into focus, decide what we want our priorities to be and which are to be put into first place. In the jargon of our times, it is as true about technology as cigarettes: "It's what's up front that counts."

If we do step back and look at the problem through the long glass of history, it is unmistakable and undeniable that technological changes have brought immense benefits to human society. Advances in technology have meant the reduction of hunger and disease, abolition of slavery, relief of bondage, extension of human life. They have led to improvements in human welfare and the alleviation of human and social needs. Nor has such technological and scientific progress left the main track. As Dr. Grayson Kirk recently pointed out, 90 per cent of the medical prescriptions being written today could not have been filled twenty years ago because the ingredients were then unknown.

True enough, as our technology has grown, the shape of our institutions and our way of life have changed. But, by and large, these changes have also been for the better. We have larger cities, larger corporations, larger labor unions, but also larger and better community institutions for social and human good, such as public health and fire and police protection. With growth, too, have come the cultural hallmarks of a technologically developed democracy today, such as art galleries, concert halls, museums, and an ever increasing number of colleges and universities.

To recognize these things is not to blink away the fact that there are and will continue to be unfortunate and undesirable consequences of advances in technology. People have been and will continue to be thrown out of work. But the great overriding reality is that technology is a substitute not for men but for the "machine work" that so often dehumanizes their labor and makes their lives drudgery.

Can we put our technology to right use so that our democratic institutions will be strengthened? We now have ways to communicate faster, to spread truth more quickly, to bring aid more effectively, to advance progress and civilization more efficiently. In our data storage and processing systems today, for example, we have ways of using machines to store data and make it available throughout the world on demand to help meet human needs, to develop undeveloped areas, to inform the uninformed. If Communism does indeed thrive on ignorance and misery, then this technology properly harnessed can become a massive bulwark against its spread.

Even more significant is what the new technology will mean to our program of education. For if one thing is certain, it is that the advanced technology depends on the educated man to create it, to make it work, to keep it running, to improve it. The narrow craftsman trained in his "splinter specialty" will no longer be able to manage things in a technological society. Progress in this kind of society and economy will depend more on education than on all the other traditional criteria of an authoritarian society, such as family, social position, inheritance, and the like. For only the properly educated will be qualified to understand and to take the responsibility for decisions.

One magnificent by-product of the new technology should, therefore, be to impel us toward a far better educated—and, therefore, a stronger—democratic society than ever before. Such a citizenry can begin to fulfill the true potential of a democracy. It will demand governmental representatives able to deal widely with the complex problems of the new age in such areas as space, atomic energy, defense, regulation of industry, commerce, labor, and the whole world around us. It will be less apt to be intimidated by the name-caller, the tub-thumper, the breast-beater, the rumor-monger, and it will understand far better why democratic institutions must be cherished and strengthened.

But how about those who become disemployed, who are, in fact, not able to meet the educational requirements of the new technology? Perhaps Toynbee's concept of challenge and response may take on new meaning here. Perhaps, as machines take over "machine work," people will be released to take over "people work," in a world where millions of people desperately need the help of millions of other people in developing even fundamental technical skills. In that sense, technology could become not a force riding man but a force liberating man, freeing him to reach out a helping hand to those who need what he can give.

Perhaps the greatest impact of technology on our democratic society will be to stimulate government, industry, and labor to join together in the creation of a great "People's Corps," for which the world has long been waiting as our strongest and most effective program of person-to-person international aid and cooperation.

3.

The Elite
and the Electorate:
Is Government by
the People Possible?

J. WILLIAM FULBRIGHT

United States Senator from Arkansas

THE question before us can be answered simply: Government by the people is possible but highly improbable. The difficulties of self-government are manifest throughout the world.

The history of political thought in the last century and a half is largely one of qualification, modification, and outright repudiation of the heady democratic optimism of the eighteenth century. "The play is still on," writes Carl Becker, "and we are still betting on freedom of the mind, but the outcome seems now somewhat more dubious than it did in Jefferson's time, because a century and a half of experience makes it clear that men do not in fact always use their freedom of speech and of the press in quite the rational and disinterested way they are supposed to."

The major preoccupation of democratic thought in our time has been its continuing and troubled effort to reconcile the irrefutable evidences of human weakness and irrationality, which modern history has so abundantly provided, with a political philosophy whose very foundation is the assumption of human goodness and reason. The dilemma has troubled all the free societies of the West, none more so than the United States, whose national experience until a generation ago seemed to represent the realization of classical democratic theory.

In addition to defects of concept and content, classic

democratic thought is marked by a strikingly unhistoric spirit. It grandly and inexplicably conceived of democratic society as an organ created by a single act of human will and reason, ignoring the empirical lessons of the centuries of English history through which representative government had been tortuously evolving in the face of numberless obstacles and diversions. If Englishmen could fall prey to such delusions, it was far easier for Americans, whose revolution lent some credence to the abstractions of rationalist philosophy.

The revolutionaries of 1776 inherited a society that was already the freest in the world. Its freedom was built on solid foundations of English traditions and constitutional principles, which formed the bedrock of future stability. The revolution was not directed against a feudal *ancien régime* but against the most liberal and progressive monarchy of Europe, whose "oppression" of the colonists had consisted in recent and limited infringements on *long-established* rights. The great advantage of America, said Alexis de Tocqueville in a profound insight, lay in not having had "to endure a democratic revolution."

The American experience has thus had the appearance but not the reality of a society built by fiat to the specifications of rationalist philosophy. We have been permitted the romance of imagining ourselves revolutionaries when in fact our democracy is the product of long tradition and evolution. The mischief of our rationalist illusion is that it leads to erroneous inferences about our own free society and about the prospects of government by the people elsewhere in the world. Most notably, it blinds us to the powerful limitations on human action imposed by history, to the incalculable difficulties of building a free society, and to the basic incapacity of man to create viable institutions out of the abstractions of pure reason. Society, said Edmund Burke, is indeed a contract, but "as the ends of such a partnership cannot be obtained in many generations, it becomes a partnership not only between those who are living, but between those who are living, those who are dead, and those who are to be born."

The descent from democratic optimism in Western political thought has been more than borne out by events. As a result of the great conflicts of the twentieth century, the world-wide dominance of the Western democracies has been lost. These conflicts and upheavals have thrown the democracies on the defensive and generated powerful strains within the free Western societies themselves. There has developed, writes Walter Lippmann, "a functional derangement of the relationship between the mass of the people and the government." "The people," he writes, "have acquired power which they are incapable of exercising, and the governments they elect have lost powers which they must recover if they are to govern."

The impact of mass opinion on vital issues of war and peace, in Lippmann's analysis, is to impose a "massive negative" at critical junctures when new courses of policy are needed. Lagging disastrously behind the movement of events, Lippmann contends, public opinion forced a vindictive peace in 1919, then refused to act against a resurgent Germany in the inter-war years, and finally was aroused to paroxysms of hatred and unattainable hopes in a second world war that need never have occurred. The impact of public opinion, says Lippmann, has been nothing less than a "compulsion to make mistakes."

For a politician who serves at the pleasure of his constituency, the course of prudence is to adhere to prevailing views. To be prematurely right is to court what, to the politician at least, is a premature retirement. We come at last to the ironic inversion of the classic democratic faith in the will of the people: Not only does public opinion fail to hold the politician to the course of wisdom and responsibility but, on the contrary, to take the right course requires a singular act of courage on the part of the politician. A few might share the Wilsonian view that "there is nothing more honorable than to be driven from power because one was right." Far more prevalent is the outlook of Lloyd George, who on more than one occasion quite candidly rejected proposals whose merit he conceded on the grounds that he did not wish to be "crucified" at home. In the Lloyd George view, which is a prototype—and not without some merit in my opinion—there is little glory and still less constructive purpose in being defeated for failing to do the impossible.

Can we reconstruct the excessively optimistic democratic thought of the eighteenth century into a chastened but more realistic philosophy of government by the people? I believe we can, and this belief, I think, is prevalent among the wisest of statesmen and scholars.

The philosophers of the Age of Reason emphasized the hopes and possibilities of a free society, but the strength and viability of democracy rest not only on its aspirations but also on its accommodations to the limitations of human wisdom, to man's inability to perceive the infinite. Democracy, Winston Churchill once said, is the worst form of government men have ever devised—except for every other form. Or in Jefferson's words: "Sometimes it is said that man cannot be trusted with the government of himself. Can he, then, be trusted with the government of others? Or have we found angels in the form of kings to govern him?"

If men are often irrational in their political behavior, it does not follow that they are *always* irrational and, what is more important, it does not follow that they are *incapable* of reason. Whether in fact a people's capacity for self-government can be realized depends on the character and quality of education. It seems to me an astonishing distortion of priorities that the American people and their government gladly spend billions of dollars for space exploration while denying desperately needed funds to their public schools. I do not believe that a society that has shamefully starved and neglected its public education can claim to have exploited its fullest possibilities and found them wanting.

The case for government by elites is irrefutable insofar as it rests on the need for expert and specialized knowledge. The average citizen is no more qualified for the detailed administration of government than the average politician is qualified to practice medicine or to split an atom. But in the choice of basic goals, the fundamental moral judgments that shape the life of a society, the judgment of trained elites is no more valid than the judgment of an educated people. The knowledge of the navigator is essential to the conduct of a voyage, but his special skills have no relevance to the choice of whether to take the voyage and where we wish to go.

The distinction, of course, is between means and ends. The experience of modern times shows us that when the passengers take over the navigation of the ship, it is likely to go on the rocks. This does not mean that their chosen destination is the wrong one or that an expert would have made a better choice, but only that they are unlikely to get there without the navigator's guidance.

The demonstrated superiority of democracy over dictatorship derives precisely from its refusal to let ruling elites make the basic moral decisions and value judgments of society. The core of classical democratic thought is the concept of free individuality as the ultimate moral value of human society. Stripped of its excessive optimism about human nature, the core of classic liberalism remains valid and intact. The value and strength of this concept are its promise of fulfillment for man's basic aspirations. The philosopher and the psychoanalyst agree that, whether it issues from reason or instinct, man's basic aspiration is for fulfillment as a free individual.

A reconstructed philosophy of self-government, accepting

the weaknesses as well as the strengths of human nature, must place heavy emphasis on the development of the human *capacity* for rational moral choice. The challenge to public education is nothing less than to prepare the individual for self-government, to cultivate his capacity for free inquiry and his more humane instincts, to teach him *how* rather than *what* to think—in short, to sustain democracy by what Ralph Barton Perry has called "an express insistence upon quality and distinction."

A reconstructed philosophy of self-government must replace an ingenuous faith in human *nature* with a realistic faith in human *capacity,* recognizing that self-government, though the best form of political organization that men have devised, is also the most difficult. Democracy, in short, must come to terms with man's weaknesses and irrationalities while reaching out for the best that is in him.

Such a revised approach to democracy has certain implications for the way in which we organize our government and conduct its affairs. As Americans with our deeply rooted and fundamentally healthy distrust of government power, we might start by at least re-examining certain long-held convictions based on this distrust of power. We might at least consider the proposition, as expressed by Lord Radcliffe, that "liberty looked upon as the right to find and to try to realize the best that is in oneself is not something to which power is necessarily hostile," that, indeed, "such liberty may even need the active intervention of authority to make it possible."

To return to my metaphor, we must guard against allowing the navigator to determine our destination, but we must allow him to steer the ship without amateur supervision of every turn of the wheel. A political leader is chosen because of his supposed qualifications for his job. If he is qualified, he should be allowed to carry it out according to his own best judgment. If his judgment is found defective by his electors, he can and should be removed. His constituents, however, must recognize that he has a duty to his office as well as to them and that their duty in turn is to fill the office but not to run it. We must distinguish between the functions of *representation* and of *government, requiring* our elected leaders to represent us while *allowing* them to govern.

It may well be questioned whether the enormously complex and slow-moving procedures of the United States Government are adequate to meet both the dangers and opportunities of our foreign relations. Too often, decisions of principle are postponed or neglected and opportunities lost because of the obstacles to decision imposed by our policy processes. The source of this malady is the diffusion of authority between and within the executive and legislative branches and the accessibility of all of these centers of power to a wide variety of pressures and interests. The problem is compounded by the durable myth of Jacksonian democracy, the view that any literate citizen can do almost any job and that a democracy can do without a highly trained administrative elite.

"Foreign politics," wrote Tocqueville, "demand scarcely any of those qualities which a democracy possesses; and they require, on the contrary, the perfect use of almost all those faculties in which it is deficient. . . . A democracy is unable to regulate the details of an important undertaking, to persevere in a design, and to work out its execution in the presence of serious obstacles. It cannot combine its measures with secrecy, and it will not await their consequences with patience. These are qualities which more especially belong to an individual, or to an aristocracy."

My question is not whether we might wish to alter our traditional foreign policy-making procedures but whether in fact we have any choice but to do so in a world that obstinately refuses to conduct its affairs under Anglo-Saxon rules of procedure.

The source of an effective foreign policy under our system is Presidential power. There are major areas of foreign policy—those relating more to long-term problems than to immediate crises—wherein Presidential authority is incommensurate with Presidential responsibility as a result of the diffusion of power between executive and legislative branches and within the latter. The foreign policy powers of Congress under the Constitution enable it to implement, modify, or thwart the President's proposals but not itself to initiate or shape policy. These powers, moreover, are widely dispersed within Congress among autonomous committees, each under a chairman who owes little if anything in the way of political obligation to the President.

The defects of Congress as an institution reflect the defects of classic democratic thought. These pertain primarily to foreign policy. In domestic matters, it seems to me, the Congress is as well qualified to shape policy as the executive, and in some respects more so because of the freedom of at least some members from the particular electoral pressures that operate on the President. The frequency of elections and the local orientation of party organizations, however, do not encourage serious and sustained study of international relations. Congressmen are acutely susceptible to local and regional pressures and to the waves of fear and emotion that sometimes sweep over public opinion. The legislator, in short, is under constant and intense pressure to adhere to the prevailing tendencies of public opinion, however temporary and unstable.

Public opinion must be educated and led if it is to bolster a wise and effective foreign policy. This is pre-eminently a task for Presidential leadership because the Presidential office is the only one under our constitutional system that constitutes a forum for moral and political leadership on a national scale. Accordingly, I think that we must contemplate the further enhancement of Presidential authority in foreign

affairs. The prospect is a disagreeable and perhaps a dangerous one, but the alternative is immobility and the paralysis
of national policy in a revolutionary world, which can only
lead to consequences immeasurably more disagreeable and
dangerous.

The pre-eminence of Presidential responsibility is in no
way an implied license for the legislator to evade national and
international responsibility and to surrender to the pressures
of local and parochial interest. I can find no better words to
define this responsibility than those of Edmund Burke in his
classic statement to his constituents at Bristol in 1774:

> Certainly, gentlemen, it ought to be the happiness and glory
> of a representative, to live in the strictest union, the closest
> correspondence, and the most unreserved communication with
> his constituents. Their wishes ought to have great weight with
> him; their opinion high respect; their business unremitted at-
> tention. It is his duty to sacrifice his repose, his pleasures, his
> satisfactions, to theirs; and, above all, ever, and in all cases, to
> prefer their interest to his own. But, his unbiased opinion, his
> mature judgment, his enlightened conscience, he ought not to
> sacrifice to you; to any man, or to any set of men living. These
> he does not derive from your pleasure; no, nor from the law
> and the constitution. They are a trust from Providence, for
> the abuse of which he is deeply answerable. Your representa-
> tive owes you, not his industry only, but his judgment; and he
> betrays, instead of serving you, if he sacrifices it to your opin-
> ion.

As a freshman Senator in 1946, I attempted in a speech at
the University of Chicago to define the proper role of the
legislator in relation to his constituents, to the nation, and
to his own conscience. After seventeen years I see no reason
to alter the views I then expressed in these words:

> The average legislator early in his career discovers that there
> are certain interests, or prejudices, of his constituents which

are dangerous to trifle with. Some of these prejudices may not be of fundamental importance to the welfare of the nation, in which case he is justified in humoring them, even though he may disapprove. The difficult case is where the prejudice concerns fundamental policy affecting the national welfare. A sound sense of values, the ability to discriminate between that which is of fundamental importance and that which is only superficial, is an indispensable qualification of a good legislator. As an example of what I mean, let us take the poll-tax issue and isolationism. Regardless of how persuasive my colleagues or the national press may be about the evils of the poll tax, I do not see its fundamental importance, and I shall follow the views of the people of my state. Although it may be symbolic of conditions which many deplore, it is exceedingly doubtful that its abolition will cure any of our major problems. On the other hand, regardless of how strongly opposed my constituents may prove to be to the creation of, and participation in, an ever stronger United Nations Organization, I could not follow such a policy in that field unless it becomes clearly hopeless. . . .

In conclusion, I should like to reiterate the theme of these remarks: Government by the people, despite its failures and shortcomings, remains the one form of political organization that offers the promise of fulfillment for our highest aspirations. Although we have been compelled to qualify the unlimited optimism of classic democratic thought, we remain convinced that the core of that thought—the belief in the moral sanctity of the free mind and the free individual—remains the most valid of human philosophies. In Carl Becker's words: "Although we no longer have the unlimited and solvent backing of God or nature, we are still betting that freedom of the mind will never disprove the proposition that only through freedom of the mind can a reasonably just society ever be created."

COMMENTS

JOHN COURTNEY MURRAY, S.J.

Editor, "Theological Studies," Woodstock College

SUBSTANTIALLY, Senator Fulbright put forth two essential theses. The first is that what he called "classic democratic theory" has today been proved false in its assumptions; and, furthermore, that as a theory or as a "mystique," it is presently completely impotent to direct either the people or the government in the construction of a viable, free, and just society, a political order, cultural order, and so on.

I do not think that this thesis today is questioned by any intelligent man. It is questioned only by those who are still victims of the fallacy of "archaism." I would add only two things. The first is that this so-called "classic democratic theory" was not "classic" at all in any classic meaning of the word "classic." I would use here a distinction that we use constantly in theology, the distinction between what is of the tradition and what is merely received opinion.

The mischief is caused today by the fact that "classic democratic theory" still is the received opinion. It has not yet been formally rejected. In the face of all the facts, we still think that our political institutions are being directed by the assumptions and the tenets of this theory. It is bad enough not to have a theory; it is far worse when you think you have a theory, which is not a theory, which is a no-good theory, and which in point of fact, although it is supposed to be an operative theory, is not operating at all.

The tenets of democratic liberalism, so-called, are all around us: Belief in the political sovereignty of the individual citizen; belief in the sovereignty of the consumer in economics; belief in the sovereignty of the conscience in religion and morals; belief in the wisdom of the common man; belief that there is no such thing as history, that there is only today; belief that the state is a work of art and not a work of history and of the genius of a people; belief that there is really no such thing as political philosophy, there is only the "art" of administration; belief that all problems that confront us are practical problems and that the resources of pragmatism are not only endless but also adequate. Finally, there is the belief that if the people temporal, the body politic, are subject to any evils whatsoever, the sure and sufficient remedy for them is public education that looks to the development of the free mind—not, mind you, the "liberal mind" of the tradition, but the free mind of the received opinion.

It seems to me that Senator Fulbright may possibly be a witness to the fact that "classic democratic theory" still is the received opinion among us. Am I wrong in thinking that he seems to share the nineteenth century hope that better public education will be the key to the development of the new political rationality that he so rightly wants, which he calls "man's capacity for rational moral choice"? Am I wrong in thinking that the Senator seems also to cherish the notion that the goal of education is not the liberal mind of the tradition, but simply the free mind of received opinion?

"Classic democratic theory" did not really become operative among us until well along in the nineteenth century. The tradition that was highly operative in the colonial and constitutional periods of our country's history did not say that only an educated people can be free. What it said was that only a virtuous people can be free. This is something quite else again. Early America did not hold, whether in politics or anywhere else, the Socratic paradox that knowledge is somehow virtue. Therefore, if it be true that the liberal tradition of the West is decadent among us, an important reason for its decay is the decay among us of traditional virtue, personal, social, and political.

I am not one to decry the values of education. I would like, however, to be a little sure whether or not public education today, even at its best, breeds conviction and, if so, what conviction? Based on what grounds? I am likewise not one to decry the values of the free mind. I would not, however, want it to be free of all conviction, for if it were, it would be a prey both to passion and to all the narrowness of intensity.

Senator Fulbright's second thesis concerned the need for the reconstruction of a philosophy of self-government, and here I can only say "hurrah." There is the problem of the relationship between power and freedom; the problem of rethinking the whole principle of "consent"; the problem of rethinking the principle of representation. There is the issue of the respective functions of executive and legislative. There is the problem of the structure of our machinery, especially for foreign policy-making. Finally, there is the role of the people in government, the ancient problem of participation. I think, here, that the big principle we must not get rid of is the one that is rooted in our tradition, in our real tradition—namely, that it is the right and the duty of the people to judge, direct, and correct the actions of the king. That is what they said in the Middle Ages. Today we would say not "king" but "government." This is a basic principle that one must never go back on. The problem is clear. It is to cultivate among the people the faculty of political judgment, and this means, above all, to lay down standards for right political judgment. This is a problem of ideas.

There is also the problem of institutions, institutions that will make the directive and corrective judgments of the people effective upon the actual policy and actions of government. I think that the prospects of democracy in the next decade or century are linked with our capacity to institute what I can only call a renaissance of Western history. The renaissance concept has always meant a creative return to the past, and this is not an idea that we like much as Americans. We are always reaching for the future; we are unwilling ever to reach back into the treasures of the past. But I think this is what we have to do now, a creative return to seize the principles of the past and then rethink them in the light of the contemporary fact.

CHARLES FRANKEL

Professor of Philosophy, Columbia University

WITH Senator Fulbright, I agree that inherited democratic theory badly needs revision. My own view is that although we do not behave very well, we behave a lot better than our theory leads us to suspect. Inherited democratic theory leads us to criticize as diseases in contemporary democracy what are often very effective adjustments to the realities. I do not believe that the old theorists of democracy were quite as foolish and certainly not nearly as optimistic as Senator Fulbright suggests. James Madison, as one example, took for granted that the perpetual problem in all political systems is the problem of continued disagreement, continued rivalry, continued competition between interests, between persons, between opinions. Marxist theory would like to imagine that there is some magic, some alchemy, by which, in a future good society, this could be done away with. But if one assumes that disagreement or factionalism is in some way or other a fundamental desideratum of all sophisticated human societies, then some way for modifying and regulating these disagreements reasonably and peacefully has to be figured out. I think that classic democratic theory held these views and in this respect was very far from utopianism.

With respect to Father Murray's remarks, I find myself in thorough agreement with his emphasis on virtue and with his astute remarks about the difficulty of defining the phrase "the people." I cannot resist saying, however, as one who happens to know some languages in which there are no definite or indefinite articles, no word "the" and no word "a," that it is hard to make a distinction between "the" tradition and "received opinions." "The" tradition is certainly a set of opinions received from the past. I am not quite sure by what political means commensurate with democracy we could define what "the" tradition is. I myself feel that I live in a society in which there are many traditions, and I choose my own received opinions. Occasionally, I have some of my own that are not received.

Let me turn to the word "elite." I would point out, in the first place, that in the context of modern specialized expertise, and in the context of large bureaucratically organized government, the word "elite" is not used in its classic form. The word in its classic form stood for a class, a class with a homogeneous background and presumably a common social outlook. But today we talk about the "elite" as people who acquire positions of authority or of great advisory importance because of some specialized knowledge or some specialized kind of experience, and in this talk we habitually make certain assumptions that, when brought to the surface, can very quickly be shown to be erroneous.

One of the questions, for example, that is often raised is why the people with their passion and their foolishness should be allowed to rule and to get in the way of those who know better. An assumption here is that technical experts agree. This is just not so. Technical experts do not agree. Perhaps the range of disagreement is a little narrower than it is for the rest of us, but it is not the case that those who occupy "elite" positions in modern society—these technical experts—can be held to hold some one position. This is partly why I find Mr. Walter Lippmann's book on *The Public Philosophy* a little difficult to follow. He seems to assume throughout that the elite groups governing foreign policy would have an easy way of coming to agreement. I believe that there would be elites holding different points of view and that we would still need some mechanism for determining which set of leaders would regulate our policy.

A second assumption is that the decisions made in the political field by so-called "experts" or the "elite" are technical decisions. They are, but within extremely narrow limits. I can think of very few important political decisions that do not involve the weighing and assessing of evidence from a wide variety of different specialists. This means that even those who are experts in one field quickly become laymen the moment they move into another field. The view that expertise is a prerequisite for holding competent opinions on public affairs is one that does not disqualify only *some* of us "people." It disqualifies all of us. No one today can be an expert in all the fields that he should ideally be an expert in in order to make public decisions. What is called for in making public decisions, accordingly, is not omniscience or omnicompetent knowledge but something closer to wisdom, and common sense, and an understanding of when and where and for what reasons to rely on the advice of experts. This is all the more true where questions of morals are concerned, as Senator Fulbright rightly pointed out and as I should wish to underscore. There are no experts in morals.

The crucial problem for all of modern society in the light of this competition among elites is to work out some system for regulated competition, some system for choosing leaders, to govern the process. From a pragmatic point of view, I believe democracy is the system for choosing those who will lead.

This brings me to the question of the electorate. Insofar as the mass of the people are effectively involved in the political processes of their country, they are already organized in groups and are usually led by professional leaders. The political process is not in fact a process in which "they" are opposed to "we." It is a process in which some groups with leaders are "in" and other groups with leaders are "out." The most important modification that I would add to this too simple formula is that there are also some groups that are "way out"; that is to say, they are not in the competition at all.

One of the great features in the evolution of democracy has been the growth of a political community in which more and more groups of people have moved to an organized status and have become legitimate members of the political community, with leaders who could effectively voice their interests. At the present time, the United States is fighting that battle over the Negro groups, which are seeking to gain legitimacy and to have the same voice as the white groups. There is also the problem of reaching the unorganized, the invisible. Old people in the United States, for example, do not have effective organized representation. The interests of the urban groups are not effectively organized. It is often necessary for democratic government to take the lead in organizing the unorganized, in providing the voiceless with a voice; the problem of the relationship of the electorate to the elite is essentially, I think, a problem of association and organization.

With regard to the competence of citizens for self-government, these are the questions that seem to me relevant: Have they the requisite ability to judge human beings? Are they shrewd enough to tell the genuine article from the charlatan? Are they shrewd enough to tell the demagogue from the honest man? The obvious answer is "certainly not always"; very often, "no." But, over the history of democracy, there is pretty good evidence that the people have not made all that many mistakes. Moreover, they can choose only between the programs presented to them by their leaders, they can choose only between the candidates presented to them by the elite groups.

The electorate need not understand the details of the issues, but it must understand the general spirit, temper, and drift of the issues. It has to have some understanding of history; it has to have enough understanding of scientific method, enough understanding of intellectual discipline, to be able to see that arguments have come out of a certain context and have a certain background.

If I were to identify the most serious defect of received democratic theory, I would say it is the tendency to suppress the significance of leadership in a democracy. The crucial question is the recruitment and distribution of leaders. Are the best people in a given society willing to go into politics? Do they find the public life a satisfying and rich one? Is it too punishing? Is the morality or the code of politics one from which they would retreat? What is the distribution of leadership? Is the leadership of labor unions as talented, as educated, as the leadership of great corporations? Where are the leaders for those who are voiceless? Where are the moralists? Where, if you will, are the poets?

To return specifically to the problems of participation, I think the crucial issue is the way in which voluntary organizations and —not to avoid a dirty word that is not as dirty as we might think it—pressure groups are organized. In the next ten years, it seems to me, we shall have to move very strongly in the direction of guaranteeing rights to individuals within so-called voluntary organizations.

Another important issue is that of decentralization. I do not think decentralization will come in the United States without a plan. I think that only coordination of plans at a center is likely to produce the necessary *de*centralization that can give individuals the chance to work on the local and regional levels for issues with which they are competent to deal. There is no intrinsic virtue in participation as such. People have their own personal lives to live. If they do not wish to participate, they should not be asked to or forced to. But the tragedy of contemporary democracy is that many people wish to participate but cannot find the channel through which to make their voices heard and their energies felt.

This requires the application of what is perhaps America's greatest creation in politics, the federalist principle. A recent article on Switzerland said the success of that country resulted from the fact that people's liberties, particularly in small things, were regarded. I myself do not feel disenfranchised because I am not present every day while decisions about Cuba or something else are being discussed. I want the chance to choose the leaders who will make those decisions and to try to throw them out if I do not like their answers. But I would certainly feel disenfranchised if in my own neighborhood or in my own professional association I could not get up and speak and, if necessary, walk out, slamming the door loud enough so that others would know I had left. The sense of impotence at the local level is the crucial issue.

PIERRE MENDÈS-FRANCE

Former Premier of France

IN stressing the importance of a satisfactory balance between public institutions, I shall not be telling my American friends anything new. Because democracy guarantees the individual's freedom of thought and action (provided he does not infringe on the freedom of others), it must avoid the monopolization of power; as soon as all power is absorbed by a single social group, class, or caste—or by a single man—grave abuses and disorders are inevitable.

Democracy demands the interaction of several institutions or political forces that counterbalance one another. Arbitrary tyranny and dictatorship, to cite Montesquieu's well-known formula, can be avoided only if "power checks power." The success and longevity of democratic institutions in the United States and Great Britain, despite the obvious differences in their political systems, are based on the fact that these countries have been able to preserve a proper balance between the various organs of government and that this balance is respected by all.

Democracy implies a dialogue; that is, it rests upon two essential and complementary functions that Mr. Walter Lippmann describes as follows: "The executive is the active power in the state, the asking and the proposing power. The representative assembly is the consenting power, the petitioning, the approving and the criticizing, the accepting and the refusing power."

This general pattern, based on a distinction between two kinds of public activities, is to be found in all truly democratic societies, irrespective of the specific type of their individual institutions. When the dialogue between the government, or the executive body, on the one hand, and the parliament, or the representative body, on the other hand, can no longer be carried on in a satisfactory way, it may be said that democracy is undergoing a crisis.

In the eighteenth century, American democracy was a typical regime of participation; the law of the land was made by the collectivity itself, by all the citizens in association. Decisions were based on the "sense of the meeting," arrived at by collective discussion. Reflection and deliberation were opened to all because the questions under debate were questions about which everyone could reasonably be expected to form an opinion—subjection to a far-off country or independence; monarchy or republic; extension of the educational system; problems of local administration, etc. Such matters could be debated in common.

Modern life has carried us far away from this pattern. Especially in economic matters, decisions must be based on reports that are often highly technical, and on expert knowledge and information that are not within reach of the layman. This state of affairs threatens to deprive the average citizen of the opportunity to participate truly and to help in making political and economic decisions that affect him profoundly. Government has become increasingly the business of professionals and experts. Many of the issues under debate and the measures decided upon have become more and more difficult for the general public to understand.

The danger implicit in this situation is that the relation between the people and public affairs will be determined either by emotional reactions, which are always oversimplified, or by the activity of pressure groups, which are necessarily tendentious and partial. Should the people, then, under these conditions, simply surrender its powers to one man or to a small group of men? I think not: Even if such men should be eminent experts—a hypothesis that is more than doubtful—to leave all concern for government in their hands is to strip democracy of all meaning.

Thus, it becomes necessary to devise new forms of consultation and debate based on specialized elites that will be both representative and responsible, professional and trade-union groups, intermediaries of all the types required by the complexities of modern economic life. Many of my compatriots are beginning to take a keen interest in such possibilities.

In the course of the last two years, I have made an interesting canvass of my country. I visited the most important cities and provinces, everywhere meeting the most representative men, leaders of economic life, of production, and of the liberal professions, trade unionists, high-ranking civil servants, leaders of the youth movements, university professors, scientists, etc. In spite of the inevitable diversity of their opinions, I found a very general desire to participate actively in public affairs (first of all on a local and regional level). The groups constituting what in France have come to be called *"les forces vives de la nation,"* the professional and cultural associations, the unions, etc. show the greatest eagerness to help in framing the decisions affecting the development and progress of the country.

The tendency to demand greater local and regional responsibilities has its parallel in a characteristic feature of American public life—namely, the importance attached to democracy "at the grass roots."

Refusal to resort to violence, respect for law, continual and sometimes difficult consultations among men and groups, "multilateral decision-making," the democratic system of checks and balances, civil liberties, recognition of the rights and functions of the opposition—all these are not only valid in relations among men, professions, and social classes, but equally applicable, and for the same reasons, to relations among peoples.

But is the Western world prepared, has it the courage, to integrate its actions on the level of international solidarity? Hitherto these actions have been isolated, disparate, and sometimes contradictory. Our governments persist too often in pursuing more or less selfish national aims, sometimes in disregard of the common interests of our whole civilization. However, everything argues the necessity for a policy elaborated and pursued in common; for despite secondary divergencies, the true and broad objectives of the Western countries are the same. The Western world requires a continuous, coordinated, constructive policy, regardless of what name we may give it, of what international body carries it out, and of the degree of discipline expected of each participant country.

During the war, an enormous increase of efficiency was obtained by an interallied rational organization. Can it be that such a rational organization is possible only in times of mortal and immediate peril? Can it be that our enormous unutilized or poorly utilized capacities can be mobilized only in cases of immediate threat to our survival—and not voluntarily, for long-term peaceful objectives?

This I am unwilling to believe. I continue to hope and trust that the free peoples and their governments will succeed in organizing their cooperation on solid foundations.

In every sector of political action, in our domestic as well as in our foreign policies, the time has come to reject the conviction, which is, alas, only too common, that the situation is hopeless, that man is incapable of surmounting the difficulties of our century, and that in consequence every social group, or every nation, must "muddle through" by its own means. There are, in our public administrations as in the world of business, in our governments as well as in our international institutions, men who, in the last analysis, "countenance only as much order as comes into being of itself." Where the stakes are as high as they are today, such an attitude of resignation is disastrous and unacceptable.

We know that we must adapt our traditional conception of democracy in such a way as to make it capable of mastering a complex development—at once technological, economic, and social—of ensuring the harmonious and well-balanced expansion of our industrial countries and also the swiftest possible growth of the new countries. This implies an adaptation, a modernization, but not an abrupt break with the past. It does not call for the substitution of a new set of principles for the old democratic principles, as certain socialist writers of the past century supposed. These writers believed the economic and social factors of modern life to be incompatible with democracy. Today it has become clearer to us that this assumption was erroneous. In fact, what we need is to extend to new fields—particularly to economic and social life and to the realm of international relations—the principles of democracy that have lost none of their truth or virtue.

Our aim is to build a world in which technological progress and efficiency will not be ends in themselves but will serve the cause of human freedom, dignity, and happiness through democratic processes.

JOSEPH S. CLARK

United States Senator from Pennsylvania

THE expansion of government in the twentieth century has been the inevitable result of revolutionary economic, social, and political forces which so threaten civilization that their control becomes essential to human survival. The size, range, and complexity of government increase—and will likely continue to do so. There seems no other feasible approach if civilization is to survive.

It can be argued, of course, that the increasing role of government is undesirable. But even though the argument may be moot, I would defend the proposition that this expansion is good—not bad. Surely we have reached the point where we can say, for our time at least, that Jefferson was wrong: Government is *not* best that governs least. The eighteenth century's aversion to tyranny has become the twentieth century's anti-totalitarianism. In fact, they are much alike, but our democratic reaction is different. We now know—as Britain and Germany know and as France has just discovered—that to be effective in today's world a national government must be capable of strong action and have strong leadership.

Otherwise, democracy cannot survive. The fallacy in Jefferson's argument is the assumption that the expansion of government leads to the curtailment of individual freedoms. This is just not true. Despite the moans of those who thought

Lincoln a tyrant, Franklin Roosevelt a dictator, and now the Kennedys a dynasty, the history of personal freedom in this country is one of which we can be proud.

Where the civil liberties of our people have not been adequately protected, as in the case of Negro Americans, the failure is one of government inaction, not of government action. There are, to be sure, blots on our escutcheon from the days of the Alien and Sedition Acts to the reign of Joe McCarthy. But on the whole the force of government has been on the side of the Bill of Rights and of a free individualistic society.

That nightmare of "federal control" which haunts the dreams of our conservative friends is an hallucination. I cannot think of one example of the "heavy hand of the federal government reaching out into our private lives" that has actually been restrictive of our personal freedoms or detrimental to our economy—if, that is, one accepts the concept of the police power (always to be distinguished from the "police state"), the income tax, and the need for organized society!

The federal government has been subsidizing education in this country ever since the Northwest Ordinance of 1784. No harm and much good have resulted. The same is true of social security, housing, urban renewal, and government plans for health care for the aged.

The real question, of course, is not the power of the government itself, but how that power is used to promote justice and national well-being. The influence in our essentially free economy of the corporation and the big labor unions with their potential concentrations of economic power requires the countervailing pressures of a forceful, democratic government as a watchdog. It is this sense of government as a third force, representing the public interest at home and abroad, which in my view is required to protect both freedom and democracy. It is accordingly as salutary as it is inevitable.

The need for further cooperative international action to prevent political, social, and economic chaos is so great and sensible, and intelligent men from all countries are becoming so used to working together for international advancement, that creative control over world problems will be substituted for the essentially amoral international doctrines of the past. And, alas, the recent past.

Thus, I would hope to see the role of government increase in five major international areas in the next ten years:

1) General and complete disarmament, verified by an international disarmament organization, enforced by an internationally recruited and commanded peace force. International controversy will be settled by international judicial peace-keeping agencies with adequate budgets and power under world law to enforce their decrees.

2) An international agency, perhaps an outgrowth of the present United Nations, adequately financed with funds saved from the armament race, to assist underdeveloped nations to that "economic break-through" which is necessary to enable them to raise living conditions within their borders to standards acceptable in the modern world.

3) An expansion of the powers and activities of the World Bank and the International Monetary Fund in order to establish a world currency as the medium of exchange for international transactions.

4) An extensive development of interlocking regional agreements for the orderly conduct of world trade, including the stabilization of raw commodity prices and the reduction of impediments to trade such as tariffs, quotas, and the like.

5) An international attack on the population problem.

If even some small part of these developments should occur, the role of government in the world economy will surely increase substantially.

The foregoing discussion may well seem to some unrealistic

because the words Communism, Russia, and China have nowhere been mentioned. It is obvious that the difficulties placed in the way of the achievement of these five goals by the present policies of the Communist nations are substantial. But these difficulties are not insuperable. There can be no lasting progress on a world-wide scale unless and until we can either come to terms with, or overcome, the Communist menace to democracy and freedom. But this major problem, with all its intricacies, requires an even greater intervention of free governments into the world economy than would otherwise be the case.

On the national scene, fiscal policy is being taken out of the realm of morals, where it had languished ever since Ben Franklin's lay sermons on thrift two centuries ago. We treat it today as an economic matter. This is a revolutionary change in policy. Only three years ago, the budget was still treated as a moral document. A balanced budget was prudent, honorable, sound, and good; a surplus was even more so; a deficit was imprudent, profligate, spendthrift, and bad. The terms were those of moral judgment. Today, with a remarkable bipartisan consensus, fiscal policy is couched in the language of economic consequence.

The next question is: Are our democratic governmental institutions adequate for the responsibilities that these extraordinary social, political, and economic forces are thrusting upon us?

We have inherited from our forefathers a governmental structure which so divides power that effective dealing with economic problems is cumbersome. Local, state, and national governments each have their responsibility in housing and urban renewal, in the appropriate uses of water, in transportation, labor-management relations, and education. At each level, the responsibility for appropriate action is divided between the executive and the legislature, and the judiciary is prepared to step in at a moment's notice to declare unconstitutional whatever action the other two may decide upon. Under the circumstances, it is extraordinary how much we accomplish under forms of government heavily weighted against any kind of action, particularly that which will alter significantly the status quo.

Of course, inaction is what the Founding Fathers intended —inaction until such time as an overwhelming consensus was prepared for action of some sort, inevitably a compromise. They were right in their day.

But they are wrong in ours.

How, in fact, do our many different governments, with power split three ways both horizontally and vertically, manage in the modern world? On the whole, better than we have any right to expect. Local and municipal government has revived since the war. State government is the weakest link in the chain; but our governors, many of them struggling under obsolete state constitutions that hamstring the executive at every turn, are, for the most part, increasingly aware of the need for their states to play a more effective part in the growth of the regional economy of which they are a part. Respect for the office of President of the United States, whatever one's politics, has been justifiably high among serious students of government in the years since the depression of the early 1930's. The courts, state and federal, have played on the whole a wise and statesmanlike role in adjusting ancient jurisprudence to modern needs while protecting essential civil liberties.

It is in the third branch of government, the legislative, that things have gone awry. Whether we look at the city council, the state legislatures, or the Congress of the United States, we react to what we see with scarcely concealed contempt. This is the area where democratic government tends to break down. This is where the vested-interest lobbies run riot, where conflict of interest rides unchecked, where demagoguery knows few bounds, where political lag keeps needed action a generation behind the times, where the nineteenth century still reigns supreme in committees, where ignorance is often at a premium and wisdom at a discount, where the evil influence of arrogant and corrupt political machines ignores most successfully the public interest, where the lust for patronage and favors for the faithful do the greatest damage to the public interest.

As a former chief executive of a large American city, as a member of the United States Senate, as a public servant who, in both capacities, has been obliged to know a good deal about the workings of state government, I have no hesitation in stating my deep conviction that the legislatures of America, local, state, and national, are presently the greatest menace to the successful operation of the democratic process.

There is another almost equally serious defect in our democratic system, which may well result in government's failing in the role required of it in the next ten years. We are not enticing into government at all levels the high calibre of individual we must have. The rewards of government service are inadequate, the punishments too severe. We leave the choice of careers far too much to the higgling of the marketplace. We make far too little effort to induce our able young people to fill the places where they are needed to advance American and, indeed, world civilization. In short, we are not adequately staffing that part of the army which must fight for freedom through governmental action.

Finally, the effective conduct of the regulatory agencies, local, state, and federal, is quite definitely unfinished business. This, too, is closely tied to the problem of recruiting adequate personnel. Without adequate regulatory agencies, the economy can, on the one hand, be strangled through red tape and foolish administration or, on the other, come under the domination of powerful special interests, whose unchecked greed can destroy competition and, with it, free enterprise.

Thus, I postulate that whether government will play its proper role in the next decade is part of a larger problem: Can we equip democratic government with the framework, the tools, and the men necessary to enable us to perform adequately the whole role of government?

What is necessary to staff freedom more effectively? A few suggestions may be offered:

1) *The executive should be strengthened at the expense of the legislature.* Perhaps De Gaulle has shown the way. A constitutional amendment increasing the term of representatives from two years to four, decreasing the terms of senators from six years to four, and holding all congressional elections in Presidential years would help to give greater authority to Presidential policy and increase his ability to get it enacted. It is usually five years between elections in England, yet democracy is not in jeopardy. We need not fear executive tyranny in this country merely because the legislature is more responsive to executive recommendations.

Far too many executive appointments require legislative confirmation. Under the Philadelphia city charter, the Mayor makes all appointments without councilmanic approval, except for that of the City Solicitor, who is also the lawyer for the Council. This precedent might well be extended to state and national governments to permit the executive to select his own agents without the need to satisfy legislative parochialism.

Governors and mayors should be entitled to succeed themselves and should serve for four-year terms. They should have executive authority over the whole range of government instead of having wide areas of executive action controlled by boards and commissions whose members are not directly responsible to the elected executive. New state constitutions and city charters are badly needed in most states and many of the medium-sized and smaller cities. And, finally, executive pay should be adequate to enable the executive to live in comfort and to send his children to college.

2) Legislative customs, manners, traditions, rules, and procedures should be reformed in the interest of expediting action. Among the practices that render legislatures unresponsive to democratic pressures, as distinguished from plutocratic or political-machine pressures, are the following: The selection of committee chairmen by seniority rather than on ability, as determined by secret ballot, and all such outmoded procedures as the filibuster in the Senate, the requirement that committees can meet while the legislature is in session only by unanimous consent, and the "pickling" in committee of bills strongly recommended by the executive.

A provision requiring that legislation recommended by the executive be brought to a vote on its merits would be helpful, as would rules requiring that proposed legislation be reported out of committee favorably or unfavorably on the motion of a specified number of committee members.

Sensible budgetary procedures similar to those presently existing in many well-governed cities would be a big help at the national level. For example, there should be a sharp distinction between capital and operating budgets and adequate advance budgetary planning.

3) Reapportionment of legislative districts, now well under way, should help.

4) Living conditions, pay, expense accounts, and working schedules of all public servants should be reviewed, with a view to creating the prequisites that will attract talent.

5) The sinister influence of political machines, whose power derives from patronage and the ability to get legislation enacted or defeated, or administrative action taken or denied, at the behest of party contributors, must be destroyed. This can best be done by rigorously enforced modern merit-system legislation, by carefully devised and rigorously enforced laws dealing with political contributions, and by tax inducements to small contributors in the hope that the frightening cost of modern political campaigns can be met without reliance on "fat cats."

6) We must somehow create a climate of public opinion that stops deriding politicians as second-class citizens. To be sure, this is to some extent the problem of which comes first, the chicken or the egg. Politicians must have thick skins. They want, on occasion, to "dish it out," so they must be prepared to "take it." But they are entitled to a presumption of integrity to the same extent as the doctor, the lawyer, the banker. Fear of smear is still a deterrent to the entry into politics of many good citizens.

These are not drastic reforms. They merely modernize our existing governmental structure. Nor, if enacted, will they usher in the millennium. But they should help to make it possible for government to play adequately in the next decade the role that a continuation of democracy as the most just form of government would seem to require.

COMMENTS

ROBERT C. WEAVER

Administrator, U.S. Housing and Home Finance Agency

I AM in complete accord with Senator Clark's statement that the state has a basic role to play in planning and urban metropolitan problems and that it is not meeting it. The projected increase in the urban population of the United States in the 1960's is about 39 million compared with 29 million in the last decade. In order to meet the housing requirements of the new households and to eliminate more than 3 million dilapidated housing units by 1970, we will have to produce 2 million new non-farm housing units per year by 1970. That is about 40 per cent over the increase in the 1962 level, which was appreciably higher than the level in 1958–59.

Furthermore, based on projected income levels and housing costs, an estimated 15 per cent of the required housing units would have to be partially subsidized in order to meet the needs of those families who would not be able to afford them in the ordinary operations of the market.

It has been estimated that in a 22-year period ending in 1980 $108 billion would be needed for water supply and treatment and sewerage collection and treatment. This will require an average level of expenditure of about $5 billion in construction expenditures alone, approximately three times the level in recent years.

A conservative estimate of investment needs in urban mass transportation facilities during the current decade is $10 billion for ways and structures, rolling stock, and other equipment needs and maintenance facilities. I might add that this is of basic importance to our cities because unless we are able to move people and goods our cities will be choked. Someone has said very dramatically that if all of the people who come to Manhattan Island during the rush hour drove their own cars—about 80 per cent of them now arrive on some form of mass transit—the solution would be easy: All Manhattan south of 60th Street could be a parking lot, and then there wouldn't be anything to come to!

A total of $4 billion for urban-renewal grant assistance has already been authorized by the Congress. These funds to defray two-thirds or three-fourths of the net project costs are now reserved for local agencies at the rate of some $700 million per year. Distribution of these expenditures is running only about half of this because the lead time in the program is extremely large. However, the private redevelopment that is related to urban renewal is generally several times as great as the public expenditure, so that in a few years redevelopment expenditures related to urban renewal expenditures will total $3–5 billion per year.

So much for background, which I have gone into in order to point up the mammoth problems that government—at all levels—faces. Our policy has always been to put primary reliance for planning upon the local agency and the local government. But the trouble is clear: What we have is metropolitan areas without metropolitan government. There is a void. I hope, with Senator Clark, that the void will be met increasingly by intelligent, sympathetic, effective action on the local and state level. Insofar as that happens, the federal government will withdraw because we are in the cities now only by default, only because local people have for so long been incapable of influencing local affairs.

The reason for this is that they have had no rights except what they could get from the states, and the states have been so often dominated by their rural sections. This should improve with the recent movement towards reapportionment, which a single Supreme Court decision has brought about much more quickly than anyone expected. The only danger is that it may not be done well, that it may become a stifling rather than an implementing instrument for those cities which have so many problems.

ADOLPH W. SCHMIDT

Vice-President and Governor, T. Mellon & Sons

I AGREE with many of Senator Clark's comments about the executive and the legislature, as well as the future role of the politician in our country. I know that we share strong convictions on the need for better and more comprehensive forms of planning. I have done a lot of it both on the local and on the state level. I regret only that many things do not turn out in the way we had hoped. I am sure that we might all agree as a result of observing the planning process that governmental wisdom in these matters is not infallible.

As for Senator Clark's suggestion that fiscal policy is now properly becoming an economic rather than a moral matter, I must point out that the commandment is still "Thou shalt not steal." And this is a moral precept. Whoever disobeys it, individual or government, must pay the penalty. One of the penalties the Latin American countries have been paying during the last decade is a flight of capital from their shores of $500 million, in spite of severe restrictions against such export. This is one reason the entrepreneur in the United States is reluctant to invest his own private funds in these areas.

From what I have heard at this Convocation, I would have to conclude that the prospects for democracy during the next decade and in the years thereafter are actually not very good. We must remember, I think, that no democracy of other civilizations has lasted beyond 200 years. We are about the oldest. The great hope is, of course, that we can do better, and I do not think we should despair.

I do not know why historians in our universities today are such detractors of the cyclical theory of history. I think, on the contrary, that we should devote much thought to what people like Spengler and Toynbee are trying to say to us. We are the first generation in history to have two great syntheses of history before us. No such thing was available to previous civilizations. In these comparisons, we are told some of the things we should avoid if we want our democracy to continue. The greatest challenge, of course, is war. Incessant warfare in the latter days of a civilization created such attrition upon the small leadership group that eventually the society could not continue.

We always say that we can cure all these matters by education; but, as a result of some experience in this field, I believe, at least for the present, the American people are not interested in education. I know they are interested in marks, grades, examinations, diplomas, credits, credits, credits, because all these produce degrees and obtain jobs and afford a certain amount of social status to which some individuals aspire. But this is not what I mean by "education." Our future lies in *liberal* education, because all people who have the vote and must carry on our democracy must know what the issues are, so that when the next crisis comes it can be discussed or thought about intelligently. This cannot be given by technical education or vocational education. We can agree with Jefferson that democracy can only be carried on by an educated citizenry, but we sometimes forget that he meant a liberally educated citizenry, not a technically trained one.

I cannot go along with Senator Clark on his world solution. I do not believe that we can merge democracy with dictatorships, whether they are of the Soviet or the Latin American variety; but I do believe that we have great hope in the Atlantic, and I believe that this is the next step we must take. The only stimulus to our economy that will accomplish the growth rate we all want will come through a joining of the Common Market of Europe through Britain and Canada with the United States to form a great new Atlantic Common Market.

Think of what 450 million of us could do in concert! But we must first decide which we choose of two impulses that are growing out of our situation. One impulse is toward unity, and the other is toward parity, parity meaning what the State Department calls the "dumbbell theory"—a ball in the United States and a ball in the Common Market joined by a bar of partnership. My own opinion is that the parity theory and the unity theory are irreconcilable. We must decide which one we are going toward because I firmly believe that if the Common Market stops at the borders of Europe, even if it includes Britain, it can become one of the most divisive factors in our lives. I would like to go forward in the Atlantic, like peoples sharing alike, and I believe this could lead to what in previous days was called the "Golden Age."

VISCOUNT HAILSHAM

Minister for Science, United Kingdom

I AM glad to take part in a conference that is proceeding upon the assumption that the outcome of the present struggle for the allegiance of mankind will be permitted to be determined not by the accidents of nuclear power, but by the conscious choice and rational wisdom of ordinary human beings determined to control, and not to be controlled by, their environment, or to become the victims of their own technology. This may seem a big assumption to make, but unless we make it, it is hard to indulge in rational speculation about the future.

We must understand the technological revolution if we are to discover the answers to the problems and some gleams of hope and wisdom. The first thing to understand about it is that it has killed classic Marxism stone dead. Apart from the fact that Marxism, like many of our own political ideas, is tied to a pre-Darwinian explanation of human development, its truth depends on the belief, now wholly untenable, that the industrial revolution meant that the rich must continually grow richer, and the poor poorer, until in intolerable agony they rose, broke their chains, and seized absolute power.

Whether richer or not, the rich have become more numerous. But the poor have also become much richer too, and even show signs of ceasing to be poor altogether. In other words, society is far more homogeneous. The chains of the worker have indeed been broken, but by increasing wealth and radically improved education, and it is the inherent logic and dynamic of the technological revolution itself that has created the rise in education and the improvement of living standards in the working class. Indeed, the characteristic achievement of the revolution is to have demonstrated that the time may not be far off when whole societies may create an adequacy of material goods that, coupled with an adequate education for the many, destroys for the first time in human history the distinction between the elite and the electorate.

This could, and on two conditions almost certainly will, be done. Of these, the first is that we manage to avoid the disaster of nuclear war; the second, that the threatened disparity between world food production and world population, which so preoccupies Aldous Huxley in his essay for the Center, "The Politics of Ecology," is avoided or controlled. I do not wish to enter into that particular debate except to say that I do not accept either his pessimism or his neo-Malthusianism, and I am quite sure that he has not accurately analyzed either the psychological motives underlying the current population explosion in underdeveloped countries or correctly stated the contrast here in the West by attributing our lower birth rates solely to the practice of contraception.

Here I am on quite a different tack—to establish that the inner logic of the technical revolution itself, left to itself, unimpeded by military aggression or internal subversion, is to drive human society, exactly in proportion as it becomes fully industrialized, to a form of democracy that is transformed and perfected by the nature of the revolution itself.

If what you have in America is the affluent society and what we have in Britain is the welfare state (in fact, we have different degrees of each in both), and if each in a sense can be described as a society of the common man, the society I am seeking to anticipate and whose characteristics I wish to capture I would christen the society of the qualified man, the educated society, or—for it is the obverse of the same thing—the fully responsible society.

The traditional objection to democracy both in theory and in practice, ever since Plato and Thucydides began to notice its defects in the fifth century B.C., has been exactly the contrast between the elite and the electorate, the classes and the masses, as they used to be called. The contradiction has been that the complexities of administration and the maintenance of adequate civilized and cultural standards demand the existence of a class of men enjoying amenities and leisure and education up to age twenty-four or above, whereas the facts of life have been that the means of production are adequate to support such a class only on a limited scale, and thus in a state of privilege over the majority. The mere existence of such a class therefore presupposes a contrast between rich and poor, between elite and electorate, between those who actually carry the responsibility of government and administration of all sorts and those who are governed, a contrast that it is said a democracy will never continue to tolerate for long.

I have not the leisure to demonstrate how far the various criticisms of the democratic thesis, the fear of mob rule, or the experience of the more sordid side of electioneering are really all variations upon this single theme. My case is that both the requirements of the technological society and the potentialities of modern production virtually drive society forward toward a fully educated society in which the contrast between electorate and elite has virtually disappeared—not because men will necessarily have moved any closer to equality of achievement or of reward, but because quantitative production has provided the means, and the requirements of technology the necessity, to train or educate human beings without regard to wealth, birth, color, religion, or race to their limit, and to reward the remainder for their services, if they are prepared to work, to the limit of *their* capacity.

I am not describing a society in which everyone is equal, and I am certainly not describing a utopia. I do not claim to have discovered an antidote to original sin, which seems to me the only doctrine of the church for which there is ample empirical evidence a posteriori. I do not claim that such a society will be particularly agreeable, particularly moral, or even pleasantly secure. All I have said is that this is the logic of modern technology, that it is a development of democracy and not of Communism, and that it is something that the democrats of today would do well to further and to bring about precisely because it eliminates the inner contradiction of elite and electorate that has been the destruction of so many democratic regimes in the past.

The essence of my thesis is that it is Communism and not democracy that will be destroyed by its inner contradictions, contradictions, I may say, that become more and more apparent every day. Yet even this destruction could happen by evolutionary means. No nation, not even Russia and far less China, has willingly embraced Communism, and only fear, force, or fraud holds nations within the Communist embrace. As education and wealth and modern industrial techniques progress there, the logic of the technological revolution may be expected also to produce comparable results.

It needs no less to be said that the democracy I am seeking to describe, although a legitimate development of existing democracies, is something that will involve a transformation not less radical and even revolutionary than anything contemplated on the other side of the Iron Curtain. Although the early glimmerings of the educated society are to be seen in America, in Britain, and in other developed countries, we shall not see it complete in our lifetime. And until it is complete, until it is the standard human society, until, indeed, the human societies so created can be integrated into a harmonious world order, its development will always be in danger, always capable of being overthrown by ignorance, force, or fraud, always capable of breaking down into something degenerate and less satisfying.

As it exists today, democracy is not so much a system of government as a principal power and a means of changing political and economic systems without war. The differences between democracies are as important as their resemblances. Their material apparatus and their institutions can be efficient or inefficient, and their efficiency or inefficiency can be as decisive of their success or failure as the sincerity of their intention to abide by their moral and political purposes. These are issues that require prolonged, systematic, and scholarly discussion and thought.

I shall deal first with the amateurism of the elite. When democracy is first installed, it generally inherits from aristocracy a fine tradition of amateurism. It is the Caesars who produce the professional governors, the Chinese and the Roman Emperors, the Indian Civil Service, Napoleon's *carrière ouverte aux talents,* Pharaoh's appointment of Joseph as his Grand Vizier.

Yet, of course, it is clear enough that without a degree of professionalism no modern regime can exist. In the middle of the nineteenth century, Britain discovered that her Indian possessions had copied the mandarinate from the Chinese Empire and, by a second act of plagiarism, imported into the homeland a career civil service recruited by examination, administratively competent, incorrupt, and politically neutral, whose size and importance in Britain today possibly makes for a more fundamental difference between American and British democracy than the absence in the United States of a titular monarch and a hereditary peerage.

Does America need a mandarinate? I suspect that it is acquiring one with great speed. Yet even now it is strange to an Englishman to observe the number and the relatively low level of the appointments that require to be changed in

Washington with the coming and going of consecutive administrations of different political color. But neither in America nor in Britain does the professionalism of the mandarinate extend to the real occupants of power—the President or the recipients of his confidence in the United States, the Prime Minister or the members of the British Cabinet in Britain.

In Britain, there is a strange blend of amateurism and professionalism in parliamentary life and the Cabinet system. There is, no doubt, great value in the representative or senator, in the member of Parliament or local councilor, who does not pretend to work whole time and has outside interests. But for five hundred years, the solid core of British governments has been distinctly professional; indeed, their professionalism has been handed down by a sort of apostolic succession. Macmillan served with Churchill, Churchill with Asquith, Asquith with Gladstone, Gladstone with Peel, Peel with Canning, Canning with Pitt, Pitt with colleagues of his father, and so back in uninterrupted succession to the great Elizabethan secretaries of state and beyond.

With all that, it is worth saying that, apart from the professional civil service, professionalism in British government at the top is distinctly empirical. If there is anything to be learned, it is learned in the course of a general education, experience of life, electioneering, the parliamentary struggle, the grinding toil and hidden conflicts of actual administration. It is not the subject of systematic study. It is like a family business handed down from father to son, with a good deal of traditional know-how. But at the end of the day there are no graduates from the Harvard Business School or the Massachusetts Institute of Technology. Indeed, it is worth remarking that there is no Harvard Business School and no equivalent in Britain of MIT, and I venture to suggest that on neither side of the Atlantic is government as such taught on the same scale as business administration. If it were, I can-

not see a democratic electorate treating its degrees with anything but hilarity or its graduates advertising their qualifications amongst those likely to enhance their chances of
election.

To this extent, therefore, we are back where we started. A
modern society requires that it be governed by professionals;
in fact, it entrusts its confidence to semi-amateurs, whose
know-how is at best empirical and who must rely for the more
technical business of administration on a career civil service
to do their bidding. Nor is there the smallest reason to suppose that the business of government could in fact be carried
on by political neutrals. An element of sheer amateurism is
an essential characteristic of democracy if democracy is to be
given effective choices of policy; the politician who forgets
his grass roots in order to become a professional administrator
will both lose his seat and deserve to do so.

It is, however, at this stage that one must look at the electorate that sends us to power. It is not, of course, principally
preoccupied with politics—except when things go wrong, and
after they have gone wrong. But is it as foolish, is it as emotional in its judgments, is it even as self-interested as one is
sometimes tempted to think? For myself, I think not. I do
not think it is a bad judge of men, though I feel certain that
its tendency is to judge measures very largely through its
judgment of the men who carry them out.

The essence of democracy is, of course, one man, one vote,
and it is the perpetual terror of its critics that this principle
will swamp the educated, pull down standards, set aside
morality, devalue civilization. As a mere matter of history,
this has seldom happened at the ballot box. The real instances of mob rule have been the result of violence or usurpa-
tion, not manhood suffrage. The weakness of democracy in
the past has lain more in the capacity of the electorate for
self-deception than in their violence. But this is no more
than to say that the real logic of democracy is universal educa-

tion, and this means something different in character nowadays from the minimum schooling of the past.

Two important further questions now emerge for discussion. The first is the part played by party in the democratic process. Side by side with the formal apparatus of government, President, Congress, and Supreme Court, Queen, Lords, and Commons, about which our constitutions are explicit and elaborate, and our constitutional lawyers enthusiastic and occasionally eloquent, there exists another set of organizations, Republican and Democrat, Whig and Tory, Conservative and Labour, about which most books on constitutional law are either strangely reticent or, when not actually silent, frequently most uncomplimentary. Yet I suppose that without a close scrutiny of our party institutions a visitor from Mars would go back with a strangely incomplete picture of democracy.

I have often been puzzled by the extremely bad press that parties have often had at the hands of writers. I can suppose only that this is because each party abuses its opponents and all are believed. I will not delve into the ancient authors, but literature is stuffed with lampoons by reputable writers, ancient and modern, on the absurdities of the party system. In his life of Disraeli, Froude calls it a concealed form of civil war, and it would not be difficult to multiply quotations pouring scum on the party politician, his electoral behavior, his supposed shiftiness, the instruments of his will, the whips, the party discipline, the organizations and programs, indeed the whole paraphernalia of party warfare.

Without denying that party, like other forms of human behavior, is a fit subject for satire, it is necessary to insist that the survival of party is a necessary condition of any form of freedom. "You can have no parliamentary government," said Disraeli in the House of Commons, "if you have no party government." Burke and Macaulay alike have issued their defenses of the party system. Even if they had not, the fact remains that freedom consists in the free ventilation without physical violence of different political opinions, that where-ever men have debated politically they have formed themselves into parties, and that parties, properly organized, are the only—or, at least, the most effective—means of uniting public opinion in war and of providing the electorate with effective choices between viable alternatives in peace.

This does not mean, of course, that party is not capable of abuse. The worst, of course, is the one-party state (by which I mean a state in which there is one official party and all others are frowned upon). It is worth pointing out that the evils of the one-party system can exist locally even where there are two vigorous parties existing in the nation as a whole. Both in America and in Britain, there are constituencies, indeed there are whole districts, where this is the case. This is in-evitable and must be borne. But I cannot but notice a distinct falling-off in the standards of political life and public service where this happens, a degeneration of political debate into personal squabbles, a tendency to caucus rule, a considerable public apathy, and, ultimately, scandal and personal corrup-tion. A healthy democracy is one that has two parties, but, I would add, an efficient democracy is one that has not many more than two great parties. The electorate, like a computer, works best on the binary system, and parliamentary elections are best fought on the law of contradiction.

The modern organization of party is something that has grown up gradually. It fell to my lot for something over two years to be responsible for the affairs of one of our great parties. I would not seek to generalize unduly from this ex-perience. Indeed, in some ways, I should be extremely foolish to do so, for some of the most characteristic of British political organizations—the ward, the constituency associa-tions, the convention—were, I think, directly borrowed just after the middle of the last century from the United States.

I would, however, make two or three points about a modern party that are not usually emphasized, but that I regard as important to its health. Although you never read much about party in a manual of constitutional law—by definition a party is an unofficial organization for capturing the official machinery of government—a degree of professionalism is essential in a national party if it is to achieve either consistency of purpose or even fundamental integrity of character.

Apart from the usual organization for this purpose, three institutions are essential. It is, of course, inevitable that a party has to send round the hat in order to finance an election. But this is a very bad way of raising money. To my mind, it is an axiom of good organization that the party fund should be raised continuously between elections and that no money should be accepted that has strings visibly attached.

The second essential is an independent research department. By independent, I mean that its organization should be separate from that of the party machine and its conclusions uninfluenced by it, though the questions asked are naturally sometimes stimulated from within. The function of the research department is to pursue genuine social studies —to check party dogma constantly against social realities, to conduct a little market research, to put into the party program some consistent intellectual content, and to take out of party program ideas that are doctrinaire, obsolescent, or plain wrong. The whole essence of this group is its professionalism and the continuity of its work from one election to another.

The third feature is the function of political education—again paid for out of party funds, again independent of the formal party machine and of the research department. The function of this institution is to educate party workers and to allow party workers who participate in the scheme to communicate on an intellectually adventurous level with the leadership.

Finally, I am convinced that although the local organizations and their national convention must be democratically controlled and organized, the national leadership must keep permanently in existence a small central office of professional experts concerned with the health and reputability all over the country of the party machine, complete with regional and central advisory services, to assist the formation and organization of local parties, a sound political library, and a small public relations organization. I believe that a party reputably organized in this kind of way and representing genuinely one of the two or more main strands in current political thinking is not only an adjunct to democracy but one of the essential means by which democracy can be made to work.

My last problem, which in a sense is far more serious than any I have discussed so far, is the relationship among democracies and the effect of their relationship upon the control of the elite by the electorate. At first sight, this presents no difficulty. The control of the electorate is exercised by the election of representatives. Chosen representatives meeting together with those of other democracies arrive at agreed solutions, and, in turn, these solutions come back to be criticized and to have judgment passed upon them by the democratic electorate. But it is not as easy as that. The electorate is able to exercise its control spasmodically, once every so often at an election. In the meantime, a more delicate but indirect control must be exercised continuously by Congress or Parliament. Yet the very inadequacy of national institutions to meet the political demands of modern life means that, in practice, the executive governments of groups of nations must negotiate package deals with one another and, precisely because these are the results of something like horse-trading, must leave their own assemblies to accept or reject their bargains as a whole.

I cannot at this late stage of the argument pursue the fundamental question that every democrat must face about this issue: whether or not a world order based on democracy and consisting of independent sovereign states is really a possibility. My consolation for this omission is that I am quite certain that a definitive answer to this vital question has not yet been found. Yet I must just append a note of warning to American statesmen on the more workaday, yet no less important, question of the risk that managing a democratic alliance places upon the leader, usually the most powerful ally—the risk, that is, of destroying the independence, and therefore the democracy, of the other allies to whom she is bound, as did Athens in the Delian League of the fifth century B.C. During his election campaign, if I mistake not, your President described his future position, if elected, as Commander-in-Chief of the forces of the free world. Yet this is precisely what he is not if the allies to whom he is bound are not to be deprived of the very independence for which they are prepared to unite.

The superiority in numbers, wealth, and strength, and therefore in influence and initiative, of the United States is not in question. Nor is its integrity of intention or generosity of character. Yet it is precisely the most valuable features of her predominance that the rest of us must watch most closely if we are to avoid an inequality of status that will surely, if it be admitted, destroy the alliance. I believe this to be generally recognized, but, of course, administrative convenience and commercial advantage are allowed too often to override political principle.

I can understand American impatience with the small scale of some of the advanced industries in the Western camp compared with their own, and I am not for the moment concerned with either of these as such. But have Americans paused to reflect that an alliance in which all the advanced and sophisticated technologies were left to one of the partners, in which the rest of the partners were permitted to supply only conventional arms, Scotch whisky, or compact cars, would not ultimately succeed in retaining the loyalty of European electors?

An independent deterrent in the sense of a wish to engage in or threaten nuclear war apart from one's allies is, I hope, desired by nobody—least of all, I hope, by the United States of America. But an independent deterrent in the sense of an independent contribution to a joint deterrent, some essential part of advanced technology in peace or war that all can produce or share jointly in its manufacture—a supersonic aircraft, a rocket, a reactor, a guidance system, yes, and a warhead too—these may be conditions of a healthy relationship among allies of equal status, though of unequal strength. Therefore, I would say to all Americans: Beware of allowing administrative convenience or commercial advantage to drive British, French, Dutch, Italian, or German technology off the market in any field. Your freedom and independence may well depend on your willingness to order from European countries a navigational aid, a missile, an airliner, or any of the more sophisticated pieces of equipment that have become the marks of advanced technology. Be warned of the folly of belittling democratic allies or disregarding the pride of those who are smaller, less numerous, poorer, or weaker than yourselves.

I conclude with two reflections. I have seen too much in my lifetime in the way of social advance and in the way of the defeat of evil by smaller and weaker forces to be drawn into pessimism regarding the future of democracy. But I have seen too many supposedly unassailable positions taken—taken because of the negligence or treachery of the defenders—to be capable of overoptimism. It is in these circumstances that the voice of reason can be most valuable in discussing the weaknesses and the strengths of the intellectual base from which we fight.

4.

Concentrations
of Private Power

ADOLF A. BERLE, JR.

Lawyer, author, former Assistant Secretary of State

In the eighteenth century from which the United States sprang, power was assumed to dwell in governments or in government-favored ecclesiastical organization. The church and the state were the dangerous power-holders. Private property—especially in the mercantile classes—existed, but only in marginal amount. Land, with undisputed primacy in production, was ultimately traceable to, and in most parts of the Western world controlled by, the crown or its feudal successors. Colonial life here had weakened state control over land to the point of disappearance—a nation of small landholders liked it. If, it was thought, men could enjoy private property, manage their own affairs, and buy and sell in a free market, freedom would be preserved.

This odd and untenable theory is still current in the United States. A brilliant recent volume by Professor Milton Friedman of the University of Chicago, entitled *Capitalism and Freedom,* is dedicated to two propositions: first, that a private market economy is the primary bastion of protection of freedom, meaning thereby the capacity of men to determine their own lives; second, that government intervention in free market operations directly threatens that freedom.

Yet the fact was, and is, that the free market, left to itself, is self-destructive. Even when land was the chief instrument of production, private concentration of land-holding could and did take place to a point where freedom was threatened. The industrial age, organized by corporations that could and of necessity did grow to unparalleled size, emphasized the problem. This problem was unknown to Adam Smith, partly, perhaps, because when he wrote *The Wealth of Nations* corporations had been virtually outlawed in England for half a century. Left to the tender mercies of the concentrations of wealth that resulted from complete individual freedom to deal, and of a legal order that permitted corporations as a normal way of organizing business matters, the industrial market presently became a monopoly market in some lines, an oligopoly market in others. The plutocratic age regnant in the United States at the turn of the century proved the fact. To restore the conditions thought to have been endemic in the free market, the state was forced to intervene. Thence came the Sherman Antitrust Act, later the Clayton Acts, the Federal Trade Commission, the Patman Act, and the continuous and close supervision of the Department of Justice. Paradoxically, it came to this: If there was a government powerful enough and willing to intervene, it could maintain a variety of free market.

And this is what the American state endeavored to do by continuously tightening the mechanisms of the antitrust laws and by continually expanding the conception of "restraint of trade or monopoly." By bringing at least one antitrust suit each week (there were sixty-five in 1962), by outlawing a growing range of private agreements, and by other devices, the government has been able to maintain, in perhaps half the American economy, a sector of so-called free market activity.

But by now it must be apparent to anyone that the free market is no longer a natural condition of economic life. It is a device, maintained and used by the state, to maintain certain conditions in certain fields considered useful to the American economy. It is, in its way, as much a piece of governmental mechanism as is, for example, the Interstate Commerce Commission. Unless the essential goods and services needed by the American public are produced by a host of small units competing with one another, the market will remain such a statist device. Should the paternal hand of the federal government be removed, markets will become more monopolistic than they were in 1901, when President Theodore Roosevelt first began to enforce the antitrust laws.

Also, what resulted was not the classic "free market" eulogized in song, story, and nostalgic, not to say romantic, economics. We got, and now have, oligopoly—two, three, four, or perhaps five large corporations supplying the bulk of services or goods in most lines. These are surrounded by a considerable number of small enterprises in the same line that live within the shadow—and the price range—of their big brothers.

In agriculture and in the labor market, the conception was frankly abandoned. For a free production and price system, the United States substituted a maintained price and a degree of production controls. The results of free competition by laborers against each other to sell their skill was so bad that labor unions, at first almost illicit, later became recognized as essential protection. The concept of "collective bargaining" protected by the federal state was substituted for that of free competition. Public utilities, communications, and transport, of course, have not been operated under the free market system for half a century.

In result, we have a series of power pyramids in industrial production, in public utilities, in agriculture, and in labor. These, taken together, dominate the American economic scene where it is not primarily dominated by direct government operation, as in defense industries, atomic energy, and scientific development. Were it not for the governmental use and application of the free market, power concentration would be far greater—as, in fact, it was (save in agriculture) when, in 1910, the United States challenged the existence of the Standard Oil Company. Let us, therefore, in the name of elementary reality, have done with the nonsense that a free market, unaided, maintains freedom of individuals to live as they choose—if indeed it ever did, which the writer, like Charles Dickens and Karl Marx, strongly doubts. That occurs only when the state maintains free market conditions by restricting in large measure the very freedoms of contract and property that the free market is assumed to provide.

The Sherman Antitrust law when passed represented a decision to maintain more or less free market conditions. In the context of technical development and of the institution of corporations, that decision automatically set up the possibility for so-called private—that is, non-statist—concentrations of power. Now, there is an inescapable law of political science: Property aggregated becomes power; conversely, power fragmented and reduced to possession becomes property. The eighteenth century revolution against concentrated governmental power, trusting itself to the institution of the free market, went almost full circle. By mid-twentieth century, it fled from concentration of power in non-statist institutions to the power of the state to protect against those concentrations.

All this did not, I think, mean that the new power pyramids were evil. In point of fact, they came about largely because technical development, mass demand, and public requirements called for them. Productivity, based on our power-pyramid system, is the highest in the world. Distribution of income and product on the whole has not been bad. It is steadily improving, despite certain glaring areas where better distribution of income and opportunity is clearly needed. The instinctive desire to fragment power pyramids indulged in some quarters has never been pressed, chiefly, I think, because no one wished seriously to interrupt the current of productivity. It is true that the United States Supreme Court, in the Brown Shoe Company case, maintained that the Sherman and Clayton Acts committed the United States to a regime of competition and that, therefore, the country had chosen to accept the increased costs, wastes, and instability involved in it. But this seems to have been an intellectual exercise by the Supreme Court; the American public has never been presented with a calendar of wastes and costs. Obstinately, its labor likes an organization able to pay stable wages, and its consumers will buy wherever they can get the product they wish most cheaply. If a vast corporation can provide it, that corporation gets the labor and the trade.

There is, of course, a way of restoring small unit production and competition and of eliminating power pyramids. That way is simply to outlaw corporations, as they were outlawed after the South Sea Bubble Act. If, in each business enterprise, each individual is obliged to provide its capital and assume personal liability for its debts, business operations will once more be reduced to the scale of operations that can be carried on by an individual or a family. But to do that would be to revolutionize—backwards—American production. No one would remotely consider it. Nobody wants Ebenezer Scrooge or *Bleak House* back. Faced by a choice between great productivity and distribution of income with high concentration of power and low productivity and bad distribution without it, Americans have steadily, and intelligently, chosen the high production.

Our problem, therefore, is not that of destroying concentrated power. It is that of assuring that concentrated power only fulfills the wanted economic functions but also does not inhibit or invade the freedom of the individual or of American democracy to pursue the good life and the good society.

The restraint of power, and not the elimination of it, is the problem of a democratic society. It makes little difference whether the power-holder is an elected politician or a cor-

poration president—except that we have constitutional norms
for restraining the elected politician, while we are only feeling our way towards restraints on the corporation president,
the trade union leader, or the dispenser of bank credit.

How do we go about the task?

First, I think, we need a reasonable definition of the area
in which the protection is needed. And here we can appeal
to both history and practice. The American Revolution posed,
and the American Constitution and its Bill of Rights under-
took to protect, the two main conceptions—the conception of
a man and the conception of democratic process. The man
was assumed to be the ultimate concern of a democracy—free
to seek his God or his conception of cosmic order (hence,
freedom of religion), to seek education and information
(hence, freedom of speech and discussion), and to be free
from the deprivation of his life, his liberty, or his property
save by "due process of law."

These same protections were also needed to protect the
democratic process; this was the massive contribution made
to American constitutional law by the late Chief Justice Har-
lan Stone. Hence, freedom of assembly and of political organization and of voting and political action. In all matters
not invading these protections, utmost weight must be given
to any law duly passed by the federal or the state legislatures.
But where such laws limited, threatened, or invalidated the
capacity of a man to have knowledge, to use that knowledge
freely, and to employ it through speech or vote in choosing
his government, then the most jealous protection must be
extended.

Constitutional protections—civil rights—historically were
designed to be limitations on the power of government. Now
that the history is changed, are they also limitations on the
power of private concentrations?

In this respect, American practice is well advanced, though

American law is somewhat retarded. Lawyers are still debating whether the civil rights guaranteed a man by the Constitution can be invoked by him against a bus driver or a restaurant manager as they can be against a bureaucrat or a policeman. The state trooper is an officer of government; admittedly, the Constitution tells him there are many things he cannot do. The highway gas station is nominally an independent contractor working under franchise from Texaco or Gulf or Standard Oil of New Jersey. Supposedly, it can do what it likes with its own. Yet, in fact, a string of gas stations or chain restaurants on a superhighway by denying service, let us say, to a Negro, by denying him essential gasoline or food, can limit the Negro's freedom almost as effectively as the state trooper. A labor union—perhaps the tightest power pyramid controlling the livelihood of its members and, indirectly, the services needed by the whole public—is nominally a private organization not affected by the Constitution. The state university or school system is public and (certainly under the segregation cases) is constitutionally limited.

But from the point of view of the man denied employment because of his color, the need for protection against his labor union is no less great than his need for protection of his right to education against denial by a government school. He is not impressed by historical legalisms. You may patiently explain to him that the Bill of Rights was intended only to protect him against a Bourbon monarch (Louis XV), an English king (George III), or the transposition of similar government abuse into the United States. You can point out that independence came in 1776, that the Bill of Rights was promised him in 1787. Now tell me, he will ask (as did Mr. Justice Marshall), whether the Constitution set up a government or merely enacted a monument to eighteenth century history?

The modern fact is that, within limits, private concentrations of power in business, in labor, and in finance can restrict a man's freedom to earn a living, to live as he chooses, to vote as he pleases, and, in extreme cases, to reside where he wishes. Likewise, they can, to a limited extent, invade the freedom of the democratic process, as anyone in the state of Mississippi well knows. If these restrictions and invasions occur with increasing rarity in most parts of the country, the reason is that holders of private power choose not to exercise that power. When I was young, a Negro could not buy an orchestra seat in a good theatre, but was relegated to the peanut gallery. Twenty-five years ago, I made an appointment to meet a Harvard schoolmate, principal of a local high school, at an Atlantic City hotel. I discovered that I could only meet him at the freight entrance and talk to him in a waiter's dressing room. Practice rather than law has changed the customs in most of the country's theatres and, I hope, in the Atlantic City hotels. Even so, though business practice is ahead of my lagging profession of the law, it has a very long way to go.

Lest it be thought I am flogging a dead horse, let me indulge in a bit of economic science fiction—perhaps not too far removed from reality.

The population of the United States increasingly lives on consumer credit, administered through a number of credit or perhaps card systems. Ninety per cent of automobiles are so bought, and most household appliances and a great amount of soft goods are thus handled. Let us suppose that these credit systems have a central clearing office. Nominally, they are judging credit risks—whether the credit user or cardholder, or an applicant for these facilities, can be trusted to pay the debts he incurs. Perfectly right. Now let us suppose that a power-hungry operator—perhaps a Fascist or Communist—becomes head of the credit clearing association. He directs that inquiry be made whether cardholders are Republicans, Democrats, or Socialists, Roman Catholic, not Roman Catholic—or what you will. Cautiously, he allows it to be known that if you are in a disliked category your credit card will not be renewed or your application will be denied. Or any variations on that theme. (This is not altogether fanciful. Not so long ago private banking systems as a rule denied mortgage credit to most Negroes attempting to buy or build houses, and were adamant in refusing credit if the Negro bought in locations of which they did not approve.)

It seems clear, then, that our fictitious Fu Manchu, manipulating the consumer credit system, if unrestrained, could make himself a dangerous threat both to individual men and women and to the democratic process. Have we not indeed seen the thing done on more limited scales by fascist labor leaders in Europe and Latin America—not to mention some power-hungry banker politicians in the past century and, more recently, labor czars in the United States? If our Fu Manchu were a Communist organizer, his abuse of the credit-card power would be a foregone conclusion. Would we need to await that moment before using our juridical tools?

Elsewhere I have argued that power, and certainly corporate power that the state permits to reach the point where it can invade personality and the democratic process, automatically is limited by the Bill of Rights. That idea is attacked by my good friend and colleague, Professor Herbert Wechsler, of the Columbia Law School. These protections should be, he thinks, extended only by new legislation. He may be right. But then he thinks of the American Constitution as a set of "neutral" rules, thereby reducing the possibility of judicial fiat having the effect of legislation. But for that matter, a Supreme Court once held in the famous bakeshop cases (*Lochner* v. *New York*) that the Constitution forbade any legislative interference with the classic free market. That decision caused Justice Holmes—dissenting—to say, tersely, "The Fourteenth Amendment does not enact Mr. Herbert Spencer's social statics" (see Professor Robert G. McCloskey's comment in the *Harvard Law Review* for November, 1962). History, like time, implacably moves forward. As it does so, it imports new premises.

I here suggest that the premises have been basically altered to a degree yet unrealized. They are only just emerging in general knowledge. The American state is not merely a political democracy. It is also an economic republic. It has been so declared and recognized as a matter of law. No other interpretation can be given to the Employment Act of 1946. Its primary institutions have been brought into existence. It is not a protected aggregate of individual enterprises or of private uses of property in production. It is not an aggregate of disparate money-making ventures. It is not a collection of labor unions with guaranteed organization and representation rights and strike power. It is a choate whole, whose continuous operation is relied upon to produce the goods and services necessary to provide at least a minimum, and professedly more than the minimum of goods and services available to the humblest. The economic republic is intended to provide (so goes the federal statute) maximum employment and productivity. Increasingly, its politics deal with the results to be obtained by and from non-statist enterprises. Its budget, its banking, its transport, its taxation, its welfare legislation, to mention only a few, are means to that end.

Few, if any, parts of this vast machine can operate independently of any other part. Not merely the conditions under which each part works but the substance of their being, their money and labor conditions, their transport and credit, work within the functioning of an integrate economic republic. This, in turn, is both assisted and guided, encouraged and controlled, by the democratic process functioning at all times through public opinion and, when necessary, through the political state. Some applaud and others condemn this fact. Yet in either case it seems to be the fact, and the central fact, of our current political economy. Is it rational to suppose that no Bill of Rights, no protection, no safeguard for individuals and the democratic process, runs against private concentrations of power, created by state governments or by the federal system, sanctioned by law and practice, and used for purposes of creating and maintaining a federal economy? Is it either safe or sane to assume that they lie outside and apart from the ultimate concern of economic democracy—that men and women are free to learn and develop a democratic process operating without duress?

Already we know that private economic concentrations are not likely to pass away. Nor do we desire them to do so; they came in response to a set of conditions, social, economic, and technical, that required them. In certain areas, indeed, they will grow in strength. Increasingly, the line between government and private enterprise ceases to have meaning. The line barely exists in defense industries or in those using atomic energy. Only a few months ago, there was organized in the District of Columbia a corporation in which the federal government and the American Telephone and Telegraph Company were chief partners to launch and operate the Telstar communications system. Increasingly, great industries work together on great and new areas of scientific research and development, two-thirds of which is paid (the amount runs into many billions of dollars) out of the federal budget. In entire industries, notably housing and construction, a federal hand or guarantee guides the essential investment stream toward their achievement. From federally developed and chartered atomic reactors, electric power begins to flow into the American grid—and another power-pyramid development crosses the government-private line. These are not the results of "creeping socialism." They are the flood tide of the twentieth century, moving implacably toward a new plateau of production and distribution.

My conclusion can be brief: America has not changed her basic conception. The American economic republic, like the political state, is based upon—indeed, is the achievement of —free men, protected in freedom, working together in a political democracy. Protection of that basic ideal has been, and will continue to be, the great and ultimate guarantee of progress. Already its results relegate to the past the achievements formerly considered great, but in retrospect puny, of the nineteenth-century free market. Already it has made obsolete the Communist enthronement of statist monopoly of economic power.

Its conception of a free man and of a free self-determining society is anchored in hope as well as in history. By applying the old protection to the new alignment of power, we may, in sober confidence, expect to conquer the present century's mountain-danger more successfully than we mastered the foothills of the past.

WALTER REUTHER

President, United Auto Workers

KHRUSHCHEV believes that our free society is composed of competing and conflicting and irreconcilable economic pressure groups that are incapable of achieving a common denominator and a sense of national purpose in the absence of a total threat of war. He knows that we have had 3 recessions in 8 years; that in the last 62 months, as the Joint Economic Committee of Congress reported, more than 7 per cent of our work force has been unemployed; that in the last 10 years we have lost 23 million man-years of potential economic production because of mass unemployment. He looks at the tragic underutilization of our productive capacity and our failure to achieve adequate economic growth. He looks at the problem of more than one million young Americans both out of work and out of school—and Mr. Khrushchev says to himself: We do not need to defeat America, America will defeat itself.

He believes that the powerful economic-concentration, pressure-group structure of our society has so fragmentized us that we are incapable of harmonizing our separate private interests and making them compatible with the needs of the whole of our society. He believes that we are incapable of rising above this fragmentized power structure and of harnessing our economic potential and achieving full employment and full production in peacetime. He believes that we are incapable of working out our national priorities and the allocation of resources to the practical fulfillment of those priorities.

I believe that we can prove Mr. Khrushchev to be wrong. The problem does not lie in the fact that our system of freedom is unequal to the challenge; it lies in the fact that we are not trying, that we have not fully comprehended either the character or the dimensions of the challenges that we face.

Freedom can prevail over tyranny, but it will prevail only as we find a more effective way to deal with the central problem, which is the improvement of the quality of our society. We will be judged not by what we have, but by what we do with what we have. We will be judged not by the brightness of the chrome on our new Cadillacs, but by the worth and the quality of our whole society; not by how great is our technical progress or our material wealth, but by our sense of social and moral responsibility—through which a society is able to translate material wealth into human values and technical progress into human progress, happiness, and dignity.

When the Founding Fathers wrote our Constitution, they were dealing essentially with the concentration of power represented by an absolute government. The new forms of private power had not yet been created. These new private-power centers are not the product of evil men. They are the product of a technological revolution. General Motors is the product of the gasoline engine, of automation, of the electronic computer; and the United Auto Workers is the product of General Motors.

We cannot displace or dismantle these new power-concentration centers, except as we are prepared to expand greatly the power of the central government. No matter how tempting it may seem that the answer lies in making little power centers out of big ones, this approach flies in the face of the realities of the technological revolution. I share the view, therefore, that we must learn to live with bigness; we must meet the problems of the growing concentration of private power by developing new concepts, new procedures, and new democratic mechanisms through which we can discipline the decisions that flow out of the private power concentration and make them more responsive and more responsible to the public need.

We need to revitalize the free market-place of ideas, so that together we can intensify the search for new ideas and new concepts and new approaches, because the problems of to-morrow will not be solved with yesterday's tools. The free market-place of ideas in America has been eroded. Joe Mc-Carthy is gone, but his impact has left its tragic imprint upon American society. We now have the John Birch Society—these little men filled with fear and frustration who are try-ing to repeal the twentieth century. We must be prepared to judge the merits of new ideas not by their source but by their substance.

To start with, I want to talk about the labor movement. The modern labor movement has new status and new power and, therefore, new responsibilities both to its individual members and to the whole of society. My particular union, the UAW, has 1.25 million members. Although we have made, through the years, a constant effort to improve its democratic structure and to refine the democratic procedures by which a member has his rights protected, we are fully conscious that a union—like other human institutions—de-velops a bureaucratic structure and that too often the union as an entity, rather than its membership, becomes the end purpose of its efforts.

I share the view that a modern union like the UAW must assume a kind of quasi-public function and stature and must be prepared to subject its leadership decisions, as they bear upon the individual's rights, to public scrutiny. Therefore, several years ago we created a "Supreme Court" within the democratic structure of our union, which we called the UAW Public Review Board. It is composed of seven outstanding citizens from the United States and Canada. It has an independent budget and an independent staff, and it has the constitutional authority to review any decision of the International Executive Board of our union bearing upon the rights of the individual and upon the proper discharge of our duties in terms of the Ethical Practices Code of the AFL-CIO. The board has the right to review, support, set aside, or modify, and to make the final and binding decision upon any matter that comes within its jurisdiction.

We created this board because we believe that as our technology creates larger and larger private concentrations of power, the only way those who exercise that power can escape being exposed to the greater discipline of government compulsion is by showing their willingness to respond to self-discipline and by voluntarily creating the mechanisms to control their power.

With regard to "collective bargaining," the UAW believes that when we sit at the bargaining table—as I have done for twenty-seven years—we share a responsibility to our membership as its legally designated representatives, and the corporation officials sitting on the other side of the table have their responsibility to the stockholders. What we both must always keep in mind is that although we have our separate responsibilities, we also have a joint responsibility to the whole of society, which of necessity must transcend our separate responsibilities. Neither labor nor management can hope to remain free except as each gives priority to that joint responsibility in all private economic decisions.

One of the problems of collective bargaining is that too often those who participate in it sit together only when a contract is about to terminate and therefore come together under the most adverse conditions, when positions have been deeply entrenched and rigidified. This is not the climate in which objectivity arises very easily.

The recent development between the Steelworkers Union and the Kaiser Steel Corporation in creating a joint committee, with public members, to have a continuous review of mutual problems and mutual responsibilities has very great promise. It has two distinct advantages. First, it means that problems can be dealt with long before they become critical, because the bargaining process is one of continuous review rather than a periodic coming-together of the power blocs. Secondly, the role of the public members is to help both management and labor to find answers not just to their separate problems, but to the joint problems that might affect society as a whole.

The collective bargaining process too often is an irrational process. We need to find a way to make it rational as well as more responsive and responsible to the public need. The only way this can be done is to have collective bargaining based upon economic facts and not upon the exercise of economic power. How does one get these facts into the bargaining process? What the process should entail is a rational, joint exploration and evaluation of what the facts are, so that the resulting decision will contribute to the working out of the competing equities of workers, stockholders, and consumers. Only as these three groups share in the equitable distribution of the greater wealth that our developing technology makes possible can our economic potential be fully realized.

The UAW has suggested the creation of a public pricing agency to function in those limited areas of our national economy where powerful corporations and powerful unions dominate an industry and essentially have repealed the market forces in the economy and adopted a system of administered prices. The studies made by Gardiner Means indicate very clearly that most of the price movements in our economy in the past have been "triggered" by a few key industries in which prices are administered.

This public pricing mechanism would work roughly as follows: If the General Motors Corporation wanted to raise prices, it would have to give notice to the pricing board sixty days in advance. During that period, the board would hold hearings, and the corporation would be obligated to defend the economics that justify and support its decision to raise prices. General Motors could still raise prices, but the American public would know the facts because the public board would make them available. If the UAW demanded a wage increase or a combination of wage increases and fringe-benefit increases that General Motors felt would necessitate a price increase, then not only would the UAW have to defend its demands before the board but the public would know these facts as well and escape the crossfire of competing propaganda. Enlightened public opinion is the only rational way to mobilize moral persuasion and to discipline private economic decisions in the areas where they bear upon public good.

The next point I should like to make is that it is highly unrealistic to believe that one can find a rational way of harmonizing all the millions of private decisions flowing out of the exercise of power in the absence of some practical, workable, democratic national planning agency. Therefore, I believe we will eventually have to create some mechanism to bring a rational sense of direction into private decisions. It seems to me that only a national planning agency can provide this direction. Somehow we must get over the notion in America that private planning for profit is good but public planning for people is subversive. The Common Market nations, the Scandinavian countries, and England are all proving that democratic planning is compatible with a free society.

One of the great American tragedies is that Adam Smith is still a part of current economics when he ought to belong to ancient history. The answer to America's problems will not be found in Adam Smith, any more than it will be found in Karl Marx. The genius of our society grows out of our ability to find practical answers to practical problems. We cannot master the complex problems of the twentieth century, or realize its great economic potential, or create opportunities for human fulfillment if we rely solely and exclusively upon the blind forces of the market-place.

Tomorrow's problems will make even the problems of today look simple, because the revolutionary forces that propel us forward will pick up increasing momentum in the period ahead. Just as one example, our present technology is based essentially upon the electronic computer with an impulse cycle of three-tenths of a millionth of a second. Now on the drawing boards is a new computer with an impulse cycle of three-tenths of a *billionth* of a second—a thousand times faster. When this is fed into our technology—as it will be—its impact will create economic and social problems that we must prepare ourselves to deal with rationally and effectively.

My last point concerns the impact upon the democratic process of the disproportionate leverage that the concentration of economic wealth exercises politically. We in the UAW have suggested a more rigid limitation upon contributions for political purposes. We have much to learn from the British system, because as the cost of political campaigns pyramids, the disproportionate effect of concentrated wealth and power upon the electoral process must also pyramid. This problem must be faced, and it must be solved.

I have unlimited faith in the capacity of free men and free institutions. I am confident that we can find ways to harness the special competence, the special contribution, that the power centers can make to our free society, and bring the exercise of private power into harmony with the needs of our whole society. I believe that we can realize the bright promise of undreamed-of economic progress and the opening of whole new frontiers of opportunity for human fulfillment.

COMMENTS

ARTHUR F. BURNS

President, National Bureau of Economic Research, Inc.

WE HAVE heard a good deal at this session about the excesses of business power. We have also heard a little, and we might have heard more, about the excesses of labor power. I am inclined to believe that the more flagrant abuses of business power can be eliminated by more stringent enforcement of the antitrust laws and that this could be done without loss of economies of large-scale production. I am also inclined to believe that the more flagrant abuses of labor power can be eliminated by limiting the size of trade unions and that this could be done without injury to the interests of workingmen.

It is clear, however, that neither Professor Berle nor Mr. Reuther wishes to follow this classical route of dispersing private power. In the first place, they seem to see economic disadvantages to our nation in doing so. In the second place, they are convinced that the giant corporation and the giant trade union are, in any event, here to stay. I shall accept their premise because I am realistic enough to recognize that it may be right in the existing state of political opinion.

How then is our democratic society going to meet the problem of concentrated private power? Professor Berle's answer is by imposing restraints on private groups through a broad interpretation of the Constitution or by new legislation. This would unavoidably mean an enlargement of governmental power. It may also involve some damage to free markets, which constitute our nation's greatest economic asset. Nevertheless, if Professor Berle is right that giant private groups are here to stay, then I feel—as he does—that their ability to limit the freedom of individuals to earn a living, or to live where and as they choose, must be controlled. Once Professor Berle particularizes the bill of rights that he seeks, the chances are that he and I can travel a considerable distance together.

With regard to Mr. Reuther, it is clear that he also seeks an expansion of governmental authority over economic life. Perhaps the most far-reaching of his several proposals is the suggestion of a governmental price board that would prevent the larger corporations from raising prices until, to use Mr. Reuther's language, the facts behind the proposed increases had been assembled and made public.

This proposal seems defective to me on several grounds. In the first place, it would not subject wage increases demanded by trade unions to the same scrutiny as price increases by corporations. True, Mr. Reuther would sanction a review of wage demands if a corporation claimed that it planned to raise prices because of labor's insistence on higher wages. But suppose that the corporation felt able and willing to absorb an increase of 3 per cent in wages, but not one of 10 or 15 per cent. In that event, the corporation could not announce whether, or by how much, it planned to raise prices until the problem of wages was already settled.

Or suppose that it were beyond any dispute that a particular corporation could afford to pay a particularly high wage increase demanded by the union. In such a case, it would obviously serve no purpose for the corporation to have its affairs investigated by the price board. If, however, the corporation yielded to the union's pressure and granted the wage increase, the union's action would again escape scrutiny by the price board. This would happen no matter how large the wage increase was or how much economic trouble it might cause by establishing a new wage pattern to which the less prosperous firms in the same industry or region would need to adjust.

A second criticism of Mr. Reuther's proposal is that it would not in practice remain confined to any narrow list of corporations or industries. But even if events took that improbable turn, the price board would soon be swamped with hearings on the prices of many hundreds or thousands of commodities—each surrounded by all sorts of complexities of technology and finance, to say nothing of requiring the wisdom of a Solomon. I do not like to think of the long delays that would follow, or how the spread of uncertainty in the business community would impede commitments on the new investments that our economy needs if we are to enjoy full prosperity.

In the third place, if Mr. Reuther's board really accomplished his purpose of restraining price increases through public review and criticism, it would in effect become a price-fixing board. If, on the other hand, its so-called fact-finding reports were in practice flouted with any frequency, the next logical step would be to seek compliance by applying sanctions. In all probability, the ultimate result would therefore be a vast network of price-fixing by the government, and—sooner or later—of wage-fixing as well.

The spread of such regulations over prices and wages would severely limit the freedom that Americans have traditionally enjoyed. To be sure, once the scope of business decisions on prices and wages is curtailed, businessmen will make fewer mistakes. That does not mean, however, that government officials will make better decisions than would the businessman immediately concerned. Nor does it mean that when economic mistakes are made, they will be corrected as promptly by government officials as they would be by businessmen. The latter are always subject—even in oligopolistic industries—to competitive market forces and pressures.

One unavoidable effect of a proliferation of governmental controls over economic life would be a redirection of the energy of business executives. More and more of their finest hours would be devoted to cajoling government officials or to contesting or circumventing governmental edicts, instead of to developing new markets or to experimenting with new processes or with new or improved products—activities that alone serve to build a nation's economic strength. Efficiency, therefore, would suffer, and the higher rate of economic growth to which our country aspires might well remain an elusive objective.

If this analysis of Mr. Reuther's price board is anywhere near the mark, I hope that he will reconsider his advocacy of it. I also hope that he will re-examine the factual premises of his proposal. The causes of inflation during recent times are many, and it is simply not true, as Mr. Reuther would have us believe, that the large corporations have been solely or mainly responsible for it. Surely the policies of our government and of our trade unions have also contributed heavily to inflation. There can be no escape from the fact that between 1947 and 1961 labor compensation per hour in our private non-farm industries doubled, while the increase in output per man hour rose only 42 per cent. If the increase in wages had been closer to the increase in productivity, the price level would now undoubtedly be lower than it is.

Economic power has many dimensions, but the one that underlies Mr. Reuther's proposal for reviewing price advances is an alleged ability of corporations—or at least the large corporations —to appropriate an excessive share of the community's income. I am sure that well-informed and reasonable men will agree that instances of this sort exist. But I deem it a duty to point out that the power of corporations to earn a profit, when viewed in the aggregate, has declined sharply during the postwar period. At the peak of the business cycle in 1948, profits before income taxes were 22.6 cents out of every dollar of net corporate output. At the next cyclical peak, in 1953, they amounted to 20.5 cents, at the peak in 1957 to 18.0 cents, at the peak in 1960 to 17.5 cents, and in the first half of 1962 to only 17.4 cents. This steady and substantial decline in the share of corporate profits reflects, of course, a rise in the share of other groups—namely, corporate employees and the government. In fact, since the tax rate on corporate profits is high and substantially above what it was in 1948, the share of output available to stockholders has been much lower, and the deterioration of profits has been even more serious, than the statistics I have cited may suggest.

This deterioration of corporate profits is, in my judgment, the most serious obstacle to attaining the high rate of economic growth that our nation requires to achieve and maintain full employment. I am afraid that unless profits improve—and improve materially—business investment in new and better tools of production will remain retarded, and so also will the number of jobs and the flow of better wages for our working people. Let us not forget the simple but profound lesson that other countries have learned from our nation's history and that even some socialistic countries are now using to conspicuous advantage. The lesson is simply that, whether we like it or not, financial incentives are a powerful force in economic life. A nation that aspires to great economic achievement should be practical enough to hold out the prospect of attractive rewards to enterprise, to innovation, and to investment.

Finally, I want to express sympathy and agreement with Mr. Reuther's objective of reducing the impact of technological change on the lives of individuals. Experience has demonstrated that this can often be accomplished by careful planning. This is an area in which some management and labor groups have been doing constructive thinking and experimenting. It is also an area in which effective cooperation between corporations and the representatives of their employees can and should be widely extended.

W. WILLARD WIRTZ

Secretary of Labor

WITH RESPECT to the responsibility of the corporate members and the union members, I am intrigued by Mr. Reuther's statement that the UAW shares the view that although both unions and management have separate responsibilities, they both have a joint responsibility to the total community, which of necessity transcends their separate responsibilities. I am frank to say that I see comparatively little sense of this public responsibility in connection with any of the particular disputes that develop. I have an idea that this is much more clearly expressed at something like the monthly meetings of the President's Labor-Management Advisory Committee.

My second point perhaps shows an equal degree of cynicism— or of practicality, depending on how you view it. There have been references here to the effective expression of the public interest and to enlightened public opinion. I am frank to say that twenty years of attempted representation of the public opinion leave me with a not very encouraging view of the effectiveness of the forums for the expression of public opinion. I refer to the establishment in the New York newspaper strike of a Board of Public Accountability. It would be the dictate of necessity to recognize that this group did not contribute materially in any way, so far as I know, to the conclusion of the dispute. This was very possibly because of the nature of the particular circumstances; but, beyond that, I think we fool ourselves when we seem to count on any effective expression of the public interest in a particular crisis.

There are several reasons for this. Public opinion is unorganized and unidentified. It is also almost exclusively couched in terms of the settlement of a particular dispute and does not go substantially beyond that. Fifteen years ago, the nation was in an agony of concern about the problems in the coal industry. There was a strong feeling on the part of the public about these problems. But there has been almost no public expression of concern about the problems of labor relations in the coal industry since 1950, the date of the last strike. I do not suggest that there is reason for concern, but the public does not know whether there is or not. It was concerned when there was the problem of interruption of work, and that was the beginning and end of it.

The most promising answers to the problems we face lie in the area of increasing private responsibilty in matters where there is no difference between the private interest and the public interest. This is a very broad area. Most decisions seem to be dictated by a kind of "iron law of economic necessity" rather than by reference to the public interest as a whole, and yet surely there is increasing evidence of an identity between private and public interests. The problem gets distorted when we think of the public interest as being separate and apart from the other two interests in a labor dispute. I see the answers more clearly if I think in terms of a *common* interest rather than of a public interest.

I would like to enlarge a bit on Walter Reuther's discussion of the experimentation going on in the Kaiser Steel Company with the steelworkers. I suggest something interesting about some of our recent major disputes in this country—the steel industry fight in 1959, the airlines problems of 1961 and 1962, and the longshoremen and the New York newspaper cases of 1962–63. In all these disputes, there has been a central emphasis on the imperative necessity of working out better procedures for the future. In the newspaper case, for example, one of the issues on which there was substantial agreement was that there should be some kind of unity of collective bargaining among the various unions and the newspapers involved in the troubles. In the dock case, there was firm agreement that the problems of automation, job security, and manpower utilization in that industry must be the subject of a two-year study and that the findings of the study would enter into the agreement of the next contract period. There is tangible evidence that the private parties involved in these disputes intend to follow better defined lines of responsibility.

ROBERT L. HEILBRONER

Consulting Economist

I WANT to itemize three problems having to do with the overall problem of the concentration of power, which to my chagrin have not been mentioned.

The first I would put under the rubric of "assault upon the individual" emanating from private concentrations of power. This takes the form of a change in the way a man in this society thinks of himself. There was a time—and now it seems to me a long time ago—when an average person in our society thought of himself, first and foremost, as a citizen. Today I believe that an average person thinks of himself, first and foremost, as a consumer. One of the extraordinary aspects of our society has been its capacity to invent and distribute the world's most powerful instrument of mass education and then to convert it into means for the disposition of goods. I cannot but wonder at the fact that my children, looking at the great silver screen, already "mock" that stentorian and phony seriousness with which products are sold to them and measure their disbelief in what a man says against the so-called "sincerity" with which he says it. This is not, of course, solely and wholly the problem of the concentration of power, but it is surely intimately tied up with the existence and perpetuation of large, aggregated economic power.

My second point has to do with the degree of approbation, if you will, with which we look upon the system as a whole. "All things considered," we say, "it is not a bad system." Dr. Berle even gives it the name of a kind of economic republic, the creation of free men. I know precisely what he means because I am the product of that republic and have received its benefits. I daresay there is none among us who does not also share in the vitality and growth and creativity of that republic. And these benefits can be traced to our massive aggregations of power with their curious mutual coexistence and the ensuing outpouring of goods.

But I suggest that there is another republic in this nation, of whose existence we have only recently become—again—alerted. It is, of course, the republic of the poor. There was a period in our recent history when all of us, myself included, were so infatuated with the success of the "upper public" that we tended to forget about the "lower public." This is as true of those in the labor movement as of those in business and in the "groves of academe." But recently a rediscovery has taken place, and we have come to realize that a fifth, a fourth, perhaps two-fifths of our nation lives in another republic.

I am not sure what the connection is between the two republics—the republic of the poor and the republic, if you will, of the great and successful power aggregations. But I suspect there is a relation, and I suspect there is, and should be, some responsibility. Since this problem, which seems to me of considerable importance, was not raised, I tack it on the wall.

My third problem was also left untouched. There seems to be a consensus among us as to the prospects before us. We will "muddle through." But a great deal of our capacity to make progress, whether or not we do something called "marching forward," depends on the ability of men in power—business power, private power, government power—to think in new frames of reference. We live in a world that is clearly in ferment. We live also in a national community that is disastrously undereducated and yet is forced to cope with formidable problems. In a word, we are faced with that dreadful cliché of our times, "challenges," which has become the contemporary synonym for the nineteenth-century word "opportunity." Usually we talk about the "challenge" only in order to say, after a certain amount of lip service to the difficulties, that we will of course surmount them. But I submit that the challenges are real challenges in the sense that they may not be surmounted. The revolutionary world presents us with problems of adaptation, not all of our own choosing, which will strain to the hilt our ability to formulate new methods of international operation. The coexistence of two republics at home, in the face of a world grappling with technology and revolution, presents us with the question of whether we can be content with a semieducated and overentertained electorate.

We cannot simply say, with a kind of bland assurance, "Well, all has gone well in the past, and therefore all will go well in the future." The stimuli that have often impelled us to great social changes are not present today. We do not have a depression, nor do we have, thank God, a war, the two great agents of social change. If change is to take place, if adaptation both at home and abroad is to take place, it will depend on the capacity of those in power to change their minds, to make up their minds. It will depend, in a word, on the ideology of those who are at the apex of private power.

I have tacked three problems on the wall. Since I am in the happy position here of being only a critic, I do not have to solve them, nor am I sure what solutions I would find. But these are the kind of questions whose purpose is to stimulate a democracy, to stimulate the adrenal glands in a body politic. It seems to me that our adrenals have been running very low these days, and I hope that the questions I have posed will do something to make us all think more painfully.

5.

The Responsibilities
of the Mass Media

NEWTON N. MINOW

Former Chairman, Federal Communications Commission

I HAVE made the conscious choice here of concentrating on broadcasting in the United States, more particularly on American television.

The word "television" does not even appear in federal legislation providing for the regulation of broadcasting. What Congress did was to create the Federal Communications Commission with regulatory authority, under the standard of "public interest, convenience, or necessity," over all forms of radio transmission, in order—in the words of the Supreme Court—to keep "a grip on the dynamic aspects" of this new means of communication.

"Dynamic" is too weak a word to describe television. Americans now own 55 million television sets. There are more television sets in American homes than bathtubs. On an average day, television in this country will reach an audience of 100 million people, and American children under 12 will spend about 70 million hours each day in front of television receivers, more time than they spend with their teachers—and, in some cases, with their parents. Today, the estimates are that there are about the same number of television receivers in all other countries as there are in the United States alone. But after a study of current television growth around the world, Richard Cawston of the BBC concluded, "One thing is certain: Two new television stations opened today. And two more will begin tomorrow."

The year 1907 is a watershed date, because in that year DeForest's invention of the triode vacuum tube led to broadcasting. In these terms, we are still at the beginning of television. Even Telstar, with its present technological sophistication, is but a crude vision of what will soon be the everyday, global marriage of sight and sound. I believe television is now having an impact on society as great as, if not greater than, the printing press had over the course of several centuries.

Are we rising to the profound challenges that television presents? Is our free society keeping what the Supreme Court called "a grip on the dynamic aspects" of this new communications medium? Where is television going these next ten years? How should it get there?

I would like to set out the present principles from which the next decade's developments in the United States will spring. The single most important principle is the availability of broadcast channels to as many commercial and noncommercial broadcasters in as many communities and areas as is technically possible. We are opening all available channels with the commitments that broadcasting is a medium of free expression and that the government will not censor any programs. We have chosen that system on fundamental libertarian grounds. We have sought to encourage many *diverse* sources of broadcast programs. Our broadcast system rests on the same premise as does the First Amendment—"that the widest possible dissemination of information from diverse and antagonistic sources is essential to the welfare of the public, that a free press is a condition of free society" (*Associated Press* v *U.S., 326 U.S. 1, 20*).

As a corollary, we have also opted for the maximum number of local stations—to serve as outlets for local expression. There are now roughly 4,000 radio stations in over 2,300 communities in the United States. In television, the figure is 625 stations in about 300 communities; and our present allocations policy contemplates the possibility of 2,229 TV stations in about 1,200 communities. We believe the public interest is best served when the broadcast bands are available as an outlet for all the interests of a local area.

We think this a wise policy, especially when we realize what is happening with newspapers. Since 1945, the daily newspaper *circulation* has increased from 40 million to 60 million; in the same period, the number of cities with dailies under competing ownership has decreased from 117 to 58. Only forty years ago, 552 United States cities had competing daily newspapers. And in the nineteenth century newspapers were numerous and comparatively small, so that almost every significant shade of opinion and every variance of a local difference were represented. For example, when Hartford, Connecticut, had 13,000 people, it had thirteen newspapers. Today—and this is typical—in an area population of roughly half a million, there are only two newspapers in Hartford. Present trends, therefore, point toward fewer and fewer people deciding what more and more people will receive from the print media. Our basic principles should point us in the opposite direction for television.

The present television system in America is a mixed one, comprised of a limited number of advertiser-supported competitors, located mainly in the larger communities, and a smattering of non-commercial educational stations. Its performance is likewise mixed. In 1960, President Eisenhower's Commission on National Goals concluded: "Thus far, television has failed to use its facilities adequately for educational and cultural purposes, and reform in its performance is urgent." The Commission also said:

> The American system of broadcasting is deeply entrenched and is founded on the rock of freedom from government interference. It is not, however, beyond critical examination in the light of its performance. It is too easy to say that people are getting what they want. The fact that large audiences are at-

tracted by fourth-rate material does not acquit the broadcasting companies or the government, which has ultimate responsibility for the use of this valuable and scarce resource, from asking whether the public interest is being adequately served.

Although I believe there are signs of improvement in television's performance, I also believe that our television system has serious flaws. Because of the television industry's present structure, the forces of commercial competition undeniably tend to limit the range of programming—particularly in the evening hours when the largest audiences are available. Those whose tastes and desires in entertainment are not shared by overwhelming majorities are often shortchanged. So long as this is true, our system may not be a failure, but it is certainly not a success.

Suggested plans for reform have generally tended in one of two directions. The first assumes that there is something wrong with our basic principles and that competition—particularly commercial competition—must necessarily result in the disregard of minority tastes in favor of more profitable majority-taste programming. We have rejected this assumption, and are going in the opposite direction. We believe that our problems stem not from too many voices but from too few. We believe that competition has not yet had a fair chance to show what it can do with television. In 1947, the Commission on the Freedom of the Press recommended "that government facilitate new ventures in the communications industry." That recommendation is the basis of our plans for the future. Our main hope for healthy growth rests on two bases: UHF television development through the all-channel TV receiver law and methods of financing television other than through advertiser support.

In 1952, the FCC assigned enough channels to television to accommodate more than 1,900 commercial stations and 275 educational stations. Twelve channels (Numbers 2 to 13) were assigned in the VHF (Very High Frequency) range and 70 channels (Numbers 14 to 83) were assigned in the UHF (Ultra High Frequency) range. The plan provides for 591 VHF and 1,362 UHF commercial stations. Yet today we have only 543 commercial stations, 458 in VHF and 85 in UHF.

In large part, the failure of UHF broadcasting to develop alongside VHF has been a chicken-and-egg problem. Since there were few receivers capable of receiving UHF signals, advertisers, networks, educators, and other groups shunned the UHF station; but without viable UHF stations presenting programing, the public had little incentive to purchase the so-called all-channel receiver.

The basic solution, we believe, stems from Congressional enactment of the all-channel TV receiver law. Under this legislation, the FCC has directed that a television receiver manufactured after April 30, 1964, can be shipped in interstate commerce only if it can receive all eighty-two channels, not merely twelve. With the anticipated purchase of some 5–6 million new sets each year, the sets in the hands of the public will become almost entirely all-channel within a period of roughly eight years.

We believe that lighting up eighty-two channels—and not only the twelve VHF—will lead to four new dimensions of television service to the public:

1) It will make possible a truly nationwide educational television system through a network of stations devoted to classroom instruction during the day and to broad, cultural adult programming in the evening. The future of educational television is clearly geared to UHF, for fully two-thirds of the channels reserved for educational television are UHF channels. A first-rate educational network could be the most significant programming development in the broadcast field in the next decade and perhaps the next half-century. Free

from commercial inhibitions, it could provide the experiments and discoveries needed in the medium.

2) Lighting up eighty-two channels will make possible nationwide pay television. In its simplest terms, the argument of pay television proponents is that if a minority part of the audience could pay directly for the programming it wishes, then its informational and entertainment needs could be met without detriment to the advertiser-supported TV system aiming largely at majority audiences. We have decided that pay-TV deserves a fair trial in a competitive setting. For that reason, we have authorized pay-TV experiments in Hartford, Connecticut, and Denver, Colorado. If pay-TV passes its tests, the logical place for it would be in the UHF channels. This, again, would enlarge viewer choice.

3) Lighting up eighty-two channels will make possible a fourth commercial television network appealing to higher rather than lower common audience denominators. Until now, a fourth network had no chance to find a local outlet simply because the UHF channels lay fallow. With UHF, an alternative, national program service may emerge.

Such a new network might concentrate on serving the interests or programming areas not now met in content or time periods by the three present networks. There are some imaginative men in commercial television who are fully aware of the mounting cultural interests in this country, and I believe that the commercial broadcaster will find it profitable to venture into this relatively unexplored territory. A new network might well direct its programming to this emerging audience, which many thoughtful observers think is larger than most present broadcasters believe. And a new network, by aiming consistently at higher levels and standards for less than a majority audience, could stimulate the entire industry to lift its sights.

4) Finally, more channels will make possible new stations to meet local needs. In some areas, it will provide a first

TV outlet. A candidate for local office in Allentown, Pennsylvania, a proponent of a local school bond issue in Atlantic City, New Jersey, a local educator in Battle Creek, Michigan —none now has a local television station to carry his views. It is our hope that as a result of the all-channel law many communities will be able for the first time to turn to a local television station.

These are our plans—our ideas and goals for broader television service during the next decade. The list is not complete; some of the plans may have to be revised or scrapped and new and better ideas found to take their place. But I doubt any change in the bedrock on which they are founded, the enlargement of the citizen's range of choice. Let me stress, however, that our goal is not simply to enlarge the citizen's range of choice of *teleivsion channels*. We will have accomplished little if by twisting the dial to perhaps five channels instead of two, the viewer's real choice is unchanged. Is the viewer only to be able to choose Tweedledum or Tweedledee or Tweedletwaddle? Is his selection to be among five old Hollywood movies or six new Westerns?

Additional channels are a means, not an end. The goal must be true diversity of choice offered by the additional channels, a challenge that Henry David Thoreau anticipated more than one hundred years ago when he wrote:

We are in great haste to construct a magnetic telegraph from Maine to Texas; but Maine and Texas, it may be, have nothing important to communicate. Either is in such a predicament as the man who was earnest to be introduced to a distinguished deaf woman, but when he was presented, and one end of her ear trumpet was put into his hand, had nothing to say. As if the main object were to talk fast and not to talk sensibly. We are eager to tunnel under the Atlantic and bring the Old World some weeks nearer to the New; but perchance the first news that will leak through into the broad, flapping American ear will be that the Princess Adelaide has the whooping cough.

In addition to the possibilities of UHF television that I have discussed, what can be done in the next ten years, through existing and new television channels, to use this medium more wisely and completely? There are many pressing needs for the next decade. I should like to suggest several which seem to be of surpassing importance.

One crucial need is the provision of a sound economic base for educational television. Presently, *all* educational television stations in this country spend less on programming in a year than the three commercial networks spend in a week. In writing about an educational network, Walter Lippmann once said:

> No doubt, this network would not attract the largest mass audience, but if it enlisted the great talents which are available in the industry, but are now throttled and frustrated, it might well attract an audience which made up in influence what it lacked in numbers. The force of a good example is a great force, and should not be underrated.
>
> We should not, I believe, shrink from the idea that such a network would have to be subsidized and endowed. Why not? Is there any doubt that television is a mighty instrument of education—education for good or education for evil? Why should it not be subsidized and endowed as are the universities and the public schools and the exploration of space and modern medical research, and indeed the churches—and so many other institutions which are essential to a good society, yet cannot be operated for profit.

Private philanthropy has started to meet this need. The new educational channel serving parts of New York, New Jersey, and Connecticut is a great step. Plans are underway to bring educational television to Los Angeles. The last Congress for the first time authorized federal grants for educational television. Over seventy educational television stations are now broadcasting in the United States. Education is at last beginning to catch up with the communications revolution.

But really to advance, educational television must undertake great projects, great challenges. To do this, it must secure an adequate economic base of support. And it must do this in the next decade if it is to do it at all.

Another pressing need that must be met in the next decade is ensuring fair access to the broadcast channels by candidates for public office. Ways and means to finance the use of broadcasting during political campaigns will be an ever growing issue in the next decade. Political broadcasting in 1960 cost almost one and one-half times more than it did in 1956. Our FCC reports indicate that in 1960, from September 1 through Election Day, total broadcast charges were $14.2 million with adjusted totals of $7.5 million for Republican candidates, $6.2 million for Democratic candidates, and $431,000 for all others. In the 1962 election in New York, 40 cents of every political campaign dollar went to television, New York stations receiving more than $1.2 million.

In the simpler society of Athenian democracy, a candidate could reach all the electorate by raising his voice in a large open-air forum. Today, broadcasting over the public airwaves, an unparalleled avenue to the voter's mind and heart, is in danger of being limited only to the wealthy candidates, or to the not-so-wealthy candidates who are willing to become dependent on special interests to finance their campaigns. Our democracy cannot afford the commitments, the hostages, as it were, that a politician sometimes assumes if he is going to raise the necessary money to win. A solution must be found to reduce the financial burden by offering some amount of free time to candidates, enough time so that during the campaign they are free to raise more issues and less money—and during their term of office free to vote their inner consciences instead of their overdue obligations.

Finally, much remains to be done in ensuring that broadcasters live up to the obligations that their licenses impose. Among our present inquiries is whether the public in some

areas is receiving adequate local community television service. We also question whether enough thought is being given
to the needs of children and the special impact television has
upon their world. In 1961, I proposed a joint venture in this
field by all of the television networks, and the Attorney General of the United States indicated that the antitrust laws
would not bar a joint attempt in good faith to serve the needs
of the nation's youngsters. The networks chose to respond
individually, rather than together, as is their right. And, at
least, heightened efforts are presently underway to use television to stretch a child's mind and imagination.

One of broadcasting's main duties is to inform the public
about the issues of our time. As Fred Friendly once said,
"What the American people don't know can kill them."
Broadcasters are doing an ever better job in covering "hard"
news. But in today's complex world, as the Commission on
the Freedom of the Press pointed out in 1947, "it is no longer
enough to report the *fact* truthfully; it is now necessary to report the truth about the fact." Hence, an increasing amount
of depth reporting with news analysis is appearing on radio
and television. Moreover, American broadcasting has trav-
eled a long distance since that disastrous day in 1935 when
Alexander Woollcott's "Town Crier" was tossed off the air
because a sponsor complained that Mr. Woollcott had criticized Hitler and Mussolini and thus might have offended
some listeners. Today, we encourage broadcasters to offer
opinions every day, believing that the public will be the
beneficiary of clashing views and attitudes.

We believe that broadcasting in the 1960's should be encouraged to become even more interested in controversy, to
help feed and shape public opinion. This does not mean tip-
toeing with issues like greener grass, milk for children, and
canoe safety. It does mean the presentation of such vital national issues as tax policy, disarmament, and race relations;
and it also means presenting strong points of view on local

problems such as a school bond issue, teen-age driving and drinking, and local reapportionment. The clash of conflicting opinions and attitudes is the true dialogue of a democracy. Television has unique powers to nourish the viewer's mind and to inflame the viewer's spirit—and thus help him decide whether Monday's villains are Friday's heroes.

But the presentation of controversy on the air carries with it serious obligations. In dealing with controversy, the law wisely requires that the broadcasters "afford reasonable opportunity for the discussion of conflicting views on issues of public importance." Ensuring that fairness is the responsibility of the FCC. Perhaps no agency can adequately meet that staggering duty. At the very least, it presents extraordinarily difficult problems, both to broadcasters and to their government. In this part of our work at the FCC, we are engaged in the most sensitive relationship possible between government and its citizens. Many actions we take in this area and others—or even public utterances we venture—are immediately labeled as intrusions on free expression, government censorship, attacks on freedom, and worse. A former FCC Chairman, James Lawrence Fly, said at one time:

> Bear in mind there is one man at the transmitter, one man free to speak; but there are millions who are listening—the very people freedom of speech is designed to protect. Their interests are paramount. The station owner has a monopoly or quasi-monopoly over a wave length, but that wave length is licensed for use only in the *public interest*. If you conceive of free speech as a right of the listener, then you cannot take the position that the operator of the broadcasting station can do whatever he chooses with the powerful instrument he has been licensed to use.

The search for solutions to these knotty problems is often discouraging, but our efforts to find sensible answers will go on. The principle of full and fair exposition of controversial issues on the air is too indispensable a part of our free society to be discarded because we lack the courage to protect it. Controversy watered down to avoid offending pressure groups would offend the largest and most important group of all— the mass of our citizenry who, by implication, cannot be trusted to make up its own mind.

More freedom to engage in controversy, the sensible financing of political broadcasting, and the growth of educational television are but a few challenges of the next decade. I have tried to set out here the basic principles guiding present government regulation of broadcasting and to offer some suggestions for the future. In so doing, I have become even more deeply conscious of our needs for outside criticism and an independent review of our policies.

More than eleven years ago, one far-sighted United States Senator proposed a citizen's advisory board for radio and television. Senator William Benton, on October 20, 1951, invited the nation's attention to the television revolution. He said then:

> With the imminent unfreezing of nearly two thousand television channels and their allocation into private hands, the entire future of television, the future of what I call the most extraordinary communications instrument ever devised, surpassing the invention of printing, the invention of the motion picture, or any of the other great strides forward in the possibilities of communication between people, might be crystallized, and possibly irrevocably crystallized, for generations to come.

The board then proposed by Senator Benton would have issued an annual advisory report to the Congress, to the Federal Communications Commission, and to the public, reviewing the year's progress, or lack of progress, in the public service rendered by radio and television, and made suggestions as to how such public service could be developed. The board was never created. I think it should have been. It is not too late.

At the FCC, we are trying through a variety of means to stimulate a greater degree of public participation in decisions about broadcasting. The public is becoming more aware of its rights, and I believe broadcasters are becoming more aware of their responsibilities. But are all of us doing enough?

The technological explosion in communications leaves those of us concerned with its day-to-day operations with little time to grasp its deeper meaning. I have not even attempted here to discuss the implications of international television. In 1962, the United States exchanged live television programs with Europe through the miracle of active space communication satellites. In so doing, we achieved something more enduring than launching a man into space. We launched an idea into space—an idea to use communications to build, not a wall sealing in ignorance and prejudice, but a window opening toward truth and freedom.

Are we wise enough to sustain that idea?

As Father John M. Culkin has said, "It is still early in the history of the new mass media, but we are already on the brink of simultaneous global television. Someone must assume responsibility for ensuring that these media fulfill their promise as instruments in the service of the mind and the spirit. If not us, who? If not now, when?"

LORD FRANCIS-WILLIAMS

Critic and Journalist

LET me begin by two statements that no one, I think, will seriously challenge. The first is that civilization depends upon communication—upon the ability of men to communicate with each other by means more subtle and more durable than those open to primitive communities. The second is that democratic civilization requires that much of this communication shall be in a form and at a level that will gain the acceptance of a mass audience and enable that audience to keep itself regularly informed on, at any rate, the major issues of the time. Not only informed, indeed, but stimulated to an awareness of its own involvement. And, if possible, to a sense of the importance of participation.

Having given these two propositions, may I add a third that, I imagine, will also be generally accepted. It is that the history of democracy is bound up with the history of the press. A free press is an essential instrument of democracy, and, on the whole, over the past two hundred years, it has served its purpose well, although not without some faltering on occasion nor without a good deal of resistance at times from those in command of political, social, and economic power.

The question before us is whether it is likely to serve this democratic purpose equally well in the next decade.

Let me say right at the beginning that I do not regard

radio or television as a substitute for the press. This is equally true whether television and radio are run as a nonprofit-making public service, like the BBC, or as profit-making commercial services as in America and on the Independent Television channel in Britain. Radio and television can extend in many ways the services offered by a free press. But they cannot replace them. This inability lies in their nature. It arises, in part, from the fact that although a newspaper can be read and if necessary reread at any hour of the twenty-four that is convenient to yourself, and at your own pace, a radio or television program must be heard when it is transmitted. You have to be there at a particular hour of a particular day. And you have to absorb what is being offered at the rate at which it is being given to you. You cannot skip and you cannot turn back. You have to take it as it comes. Broadcasting is, in many ways, the most pervasive means of communication in the history of the world. But it suffers from one grave defect. It lacks durability.

The history of mass communication is the history of development along two parallel tracks, one concerned with space (the area of coverage), the other with time (durability). When men first learned to paint on the walls of caves and then to write, they added to communication a new dimension —the dimension of time's permanence. With the invention of printing, they added another—space, the ability to duplicate what was worthy of record and disseminate it over an area far wider than was possible with the spoken or even the written word. Radio and television have conquered space, making it possible to communicate simultaneously to immense audiences, but they have done so at the cost of the other vital theme in the history of communication, time, the quality of permanence. There is nothing as transient as a radio or television report, especially a report on current affairs. You must catch it on the wing or lose it for ever.

This impermanence in the means of communication is particularly important in the realm of ideas—without which civilization, particularly democratic civilization, cannot survive. The most potent ideas, like the most enduring expressions of the creative spirit, are rarely capable of being grasped in all their implications at one hearing. They need to be read and reread. And I toss out, in passing, the sobering thought that in television and radio—these masters of space and enemies of time—the only element that commands the durability denied to all else is advertising, for it alone is permitted the gift of constant repetition.

I do not deny the importance of radio and television as a means of communicating information and ideas—in some ways, the most significant means in the whole history of communication. It would be foolish to do so, particularly for one like myself who is at present involved through the medium of a new cooperative enterprise, Television Reporters International, in endeavoring to make television reporting in depth on issues of current international importance simultaneously available to many countries and more especially to the emergent new nations of Africa and Asia, where illiteracy is one of the great problems of communication. But the element of impermanence in all such media is one we cannot ignore. It makes the responsibility of the press—of the written word that can be considered at leisure, weighed, and analyzed —not less but more important in the conditions of our time.

How far is the press as we know it capable, in fact, of meeting those responsibilities, how suited to meet the challenges of democracy during the next decade?

In the past history of democratic advance, the role of the press has in every country been of immense importance. Indeed, I would go so far as to say that democracy is impossible without a free press: The existence or nonexistence of a free press is one infallible touchstone of the claims of any society to be democratic. I stress the word "free" because the historic role of the press has always been two-fold—or perhaps three-fold. It has first, of course, the responsibility to report, collect, and print news as an essential munition of democracy whose importance has never been more crisply expressed than in a phrase of Rebecca West's: "A community needs news for the same reason that a man needs eyes. It has to see where it is going." But the press also has the responsibility to interpret and comment on the news and thus make its own unique contribution to that continuing debate which is at the heart of the democratic method. And finally, and certainly not less important than either of its other functions, it has a responsibility to watch authority. The great seal of authority always has two sides; it looks different according to where you stand. It is the function of the press to look at the face of authority from below, from among the governed not the governing; its role is to be dangerous to those who rule even when they rule with the best intentions. Its business is to establish a minefield through which all authority, at whatever level, must walk with care.

It was not some irresponsible hell-raiser of yellow journalism but one of the greatest papers in the world, *The Times* of London, at the height of its power and responsibility just over a century ago, that proclaimed in words as significant now as then: "The press lives by disclosures." And surely it is as true now as then that "the dignity and freedom of the press are tramelled from the moment it accepts an ancillary position. To perform its duties with entire independence and consequently with the utmost public advantage, the press can enter into no close or binding alliances with the statesmen of the day nor surrender its permanent interests to the convenience of any government." The responsibilities of the journalist do not alter. They remain today, as they were then, "to seek the truth above all things and to present to his readers not such things as statecraft would wish them to know but the truth as near as he can attain it."

The democratic need for a press that stands aside from all established forms of authority, holding an independent position as a reporter of and commentator on the news, is likely to grow not less but greater in the next decade. The freedom of the press is not a privilege of newspapers but a right belonging to the public, and it is one that becomes more, not less, important as societies become more sophisticated. We have to recognize that if external pressures to confine or diminish the independence of the press seem to be on the increase and call for our active vigilance at home and abroad, the greatest threat to the traditional position of the press now comes from inside itself. In what shape now is the modern press to perform its classic role in democracies? In what shape is it likely to be during the next decade if certain tendencies —and some of them are already more than tendencies— continue?

Journalism is a profession, with the historic responsibilities of a profession to those it serves, the historic and well-established obligations of a profession upon those who serve it. But it is a profession inside an industry, and the industry is in danger of swamping the profession.

Historically, the ability of the press to perform the functions required of it in a democracy has always depended upon the existence of a variety of newspapers. It is only where there are many voices representing many interests that a completely free press can be said to exist. Indeed, the whole premise upon which the long argument for press freedom was based and which eventually brought it to success was that a democracy required means by which every substantial interest should be able to express itself. The press does not merely depend on competition to thrive; competition is its heart's blood—the competition of ideas, of information, of disclosure, the challenge of controversy, the assurance that what ought to be printed will get printed because even if one paper ignores or suppresses it there are plenty of others that will publish.

Newspapers have neither the right nor the ability to claim a judicial role in society. They lack both the power and the discipline of the law to sustain them in any such part; their judgments are, of their nature, arrived at without any of the rules the law imposes to ensure that those who sit in judgment shall give due weight to all relevant evidence and only to what is relevant. Never trust the newspaper that claims to be wholly objective and impartial. The newspaper with a reputation for impartiality is the most dangerous of all. In a partisan world, it is foolish to expect that newspapers alone shall be nonpartisan. Indeed, those that set themselves up to be so are likely to make not only uncommonly dull newspapers but also dangerous ones. For the qualities that inspire the good newspaper are, and ought to be, much more akin to those of the advocate than of the judge.

The values of the press do not call for impartiality. What they do call for are the qualities of the honest advocate: that facts shall not be suppressed or distorted to bolster up a bad case—or even make a good one stronger; that argument shall be related to evidence, and that it shall be presented with honesty towards those attacked as well as those defended. And above all, they require that all sides shall be presented and that there shall exist a sufficient number of papers of differing interests and publics to see that they are. There cannot be a good press—there certainly cannot be freedom of the press in any complete and genuine form—unless there are an adequate number of newspapers to make sure that every significant fact in every important public issue is put before the public and every significant point of view allowed expression. The freedom of the press is not a freehold. The press is the trustee not the owner of the estate, holding such authority as it possesses solely in a representative capacity on behalf of its readers. This authority needs constantly to be invigorated by the loyalty of deliberate choice on the part of those who buy and read one newspaper rather than another. A newspaper's readers are its constituents. They cast their votes for it each day they buy it. To deny them the right of choice is as inimical to the proper process of democracy as to deny the right of choice in popular elections.

The concentration of press power is a threat to the democratic method of the same order as concentration of political power, for although it is true that in a democracy the general direction of government is decided by public opinion—by electoral choice—the issues by which a modern government when elected sets its course are subtle and complicated, and the modern administrative machine is vast and anonymous. It grinds on its way, regardless. The power of the ordinary man to influence it is infinitesimal unless he can find a public voice to speak for him. He must have—this indeed is an integral part of the case for press freedom—a choice of voices to appeal to. The solus newspaper is as contrary to the true principles of democracy as the single voting list.

This is well recognized by all believers in the freedom of the press when the concentration of the press into a few channels flows from political action as it does in totalitarian countries. But I suggest that the end results are not less contrary to the true values of democracy when this concentration in the field of information and the press follows from the commercial exploitation of the press as an industry without due regard to the responsibility of the press as a profession. Yet in the last decade, by the process of mergers and amalgamations, the deliberate maintenance of high cost structures by unions and managements alike, which have had the effect of driving all but the strongest out of existence, and by the aggressive exploitation of mass-circulation positions to make it progressively more difficult for those serving medium-size publics to survive, the concentration of press power in fewer hands has already reached dangerous proportions and in the next decade may well become one of the most serious of all internal challenges to democracy.

The process of press concentration has not yet gone quite so far in the metropolitan press of America as it has in Britain, but the development of the solus newspaper outside metropolitan areas has gone much further in the United States than it has even with the British press, where it is serious enough in all conscience. I regard the solus newspaper —the single paper with virtual exclusivity in a great community—as one of the greatest dangers to press freedom in its full sense. Not because such newspapers are necessarily politically biased but because their almost inevitable tendency is to seek to become all things to all men, to blur the edges of controversy although controversy is essential to communal health, to avoid disclosing what is unpleasant, to become eunuchs of journalism, unready and unable to generate that spirit of constant scrutiny and debate which the democratic method above all else calls for.

Democracy, which of its nature derives from and exists by the mass, cannot live by its peaks alone, valuable and sustaining though those peaks are. Its health depends not on the exceptional but upon the average. And it needs to be said that although the press is a business, it is and always must be more than a business if it is to fulfill its democratic purpose. The freedom of the press, long fought for, secured by the struggle and sacrifice not of journalists alone but of men and women of infinite variety and courage in the armies of democratic advance, is not the private possession of newspapers or their proprietors or editors, but belongs to the community. It does not exist in order that newspaper owners should grow rich or that those who work for newspapers should be able to live pleasant lives—desirable as both these propositions may be. It exists because this freedom is a necessary instrument of democracy and without it democracy cannot survive.

A newspaper must sell to live. But it cannot claim that what sells easiest and most is by that fact alone justified. Those who own or write for newspapers cannot free themselves from their obligations to the past or the present, and still less from their responsibilities to the future. They have no more right to claim immunity from the historic responsibilities of their office because those responsibilities may sometimes seem to them to stand in the way of easy commercial advantage than have members of Parliament or Congress, or judges, or educators. And indeed their position is analogous to that of these others, just as the independence of the press was won in the same struggle as that for free parliaments, an independent judiciary, and freedom of knowledge. The journalist is not buttressed by constitutional safeguards as the legislator and member of the judiciary are. His status and the principles that should govern him in his professional conduct are less firmly rooted in tradition than is theirs or the university professor's. Unlike them, he is a hybrid, a Janus with two faces, a two-purpose beast. He has commercial obligations, perfectly legitimate ones, which they do not have. But his obligations to society are not less than theirs and are of the same order. He cannot divest himself of them for any purpose of commercial advantage or private interest whatever without failing in his trust.

A free press depends, and must always depend, upon a three-fold partnership of those who own newspapers, those who edit or write for them, and those who read them, the public. Newspapers cannot survive in freedom unless the public insists that they do so, and unless it has confidence in their purpose. They cannot secure that confidence unless they deserve it by the manifest evidence of their independence, their integrity, and their responsibility. As the great newspaper owner and editor, C. P. Scott, of the Manchester *Guardian,* declared: "A paper which has grown up in a great community, nourished by its resources, reflecting in a thousand ways its spirit and its interests, in a real sense belongs to it. How else except in the permanence of that association can it fulfill its duty or repay the benefits it has received?"

Of course a newspaper must by energetic management and efficient administration pay its way. There is no bonus for democracy in a subsidized press. Of course it must entertain. To entertain as well as to inform is part of the traditional functions of the press. Of course it must hold up the mirror to life in all its aspects—the trivial as well as the serious, the scandalous as well as the reputable, the sensational and the temporary as well as the permanent march of events. But if it does any of these things at the cost of its essential purpose as a vital instrument of public information and an irreplaceable factor in the democratic debate, then it cannot be surprised if it loses the confidence of the public that can alone sustain it. When newspapers fall in public esteem by excessive triviality, by arrogance, by intrusion, by a total disregard for the rights to privacy of ordinary people, they diminish not only their own authority and their power to command public support in what is important to their public independence but the stature of democracy itself. When newspapers find what they believe to be vital to the freedom of the press under attack, it is into their own hearts that they should look as well as into the state of the society of which they are a part.

The journalist is perhaps subject, more than most, to one of the great temptations and dangers that it seems to me besets our modern society in many of its aspects: the temptation to become so immersed in the satisfactions and excitements of technique as to lose sight of the ultimate purpose of what one is doing. I see this as one of the gravest ills of our enormously exciting and expanding technological era, in which men find it easy to persuade themselves that the immediate satisfaction of proficiency in difficult and interesting techniques and the status to be gained from that proficiency absolve them of the need to consider the deeper purpose of their lives. It is a temptation that has always beset the journalist pursuing a good story or absorbed in the technical problems of make-up and presentation and the beguiling art of persuasion, for he sometimes finds it difficult to stop and ask himself where he is going.

More than ever at this stage in our democratic advance we need to ask ourselves where we are going. It is particularly the responsibility of the journalist to do so. To ask it of himself and of his society. He is one of those who must help to set the signposts. He cannot do so unless he is informed, educated, independent of mind, and staunch of purpose. He needs to be better informed and better educated than at any time in history, for he must find his way as a pathfinder for the public.

It is inevitable in the process of political and social development that an increasing amount of the material of which the public needs to know in the field of politics, of science, of industry, will come from centralized sources and come with an authority and expertise that only those men can challenge who are trained and disciplined in the examination of evidence, with knowledge and assurance to find other balancing sources of information, and with sufficient confidence in themselves to take nothing at its face value. Yet challenged they must be. It is the task of the press to fit itself more and more for this formidable expert responsibility in many new fields in the future.

I would like to see universities and institutions of higher studies helping it to do so by looking at the problems of mass communication in these areas and considering the development of graduate courses of a new and broadly based kind for, as a start, newspapermen proposing to specialize in politics, in public administration, in defense, and in science writing. I should hope that these basic studies could be supplemented by regular refresher courses to keep newspapermen abreast of the newest thinking in their fields and in touch with the most eminent independent authorities available. If the press is to do its democratic job adequately in the future, we must bring about a marriage between journalistic skill and expert and disciplined knowledge in more and more crucial fields of public concern. A companionate marriage—perhaps. I am not suggesting we should try to turn journalists into Nobel Prize winners. What we do require in this new age is that they shall have at their disposal the means to bridge the gap between the expert and the ordinary man and—which is no less important—to keep the claims of official administrators, official scientists, official defense departments, under constant, informed, and independent scrutiny.

Yet basically the obligations of the press in the coming decade remain what they have always been: to report honestly, to comment fearlessly, to let no interest—even its own—stand in the way of the public interest. Let us hope that all of us who are concerned in any way with this dangerous, exhilarating, profoundly demanding, and democratically irreplaceable business of independent public communication will be faithful to our trust.

COMMENTS

BARRY BINGHAM

Editor and Publisher, Louisville "Courier-Journal" and "Times"

I AM in almost complete agreement with both papers, but I must defend that eternal whipping boy "press monopoly." I think both of these gentlemen are tilting against windmills on this point, and, further, I think that they have given the wrong diagnosis for a major illness of the press in this country and elsewhere. The tendency to monopoly ownership is inevitable, and it is here to stay whether we like it or not. We are up against a law of economics, which I fear cannot be denied, no matter how we feel about it.

As an example of how this works, let me select the twenty-two cities in the population class of Louisville, the city in which I live—cities between 300,000 and 500,000 in population. Every one of those twenty-two cities used to have several competing newspapers. In my own city, when it was half the size that it is now, there were nine competing daily newspapers. Now there are only two, and both are under one ownership. This is absolutely typical. Of the other cities, there now are only six in which there are competitors, and nobody can say how long competition will last even in those cities. The only way I can imagine competition arising in these places would be through some form of government subsidy, or perhaps by subsidy on the part of one of the great foundations. Most of the critics of the press shy away in horror from such a suggestion, but I do not know how else competition can be provided in these cities I speak of.

In 1961, the *Saturday Review* asked a cross-section of deans of journalism in this country to name what they regarded as the top fifteen newspapers in this country in terms of responsibility and living up to their ideals. Of the fifteen, four were under solus ownership. To put it another way, there were four major cities in the United States whose newspapers did not appear on the list at all. Those are all cities in which there is very lively press competition going on. With regard to the four solus ownerships, perhaps we got there despite our interesting condition, but we *did* get there. I suggest only that the monopoly situation was not the key to it, nor was competition the key to the fact that the other newspapers did *not* get on the list.

In my own city, readers are constantly crying "monopoly" at us. Whenever they see something in the newspapers that they do not like, they immediately say, "This town should have another newspaper." They will no doubt start crying "solus ownership" when that phrase penetrates through to Kentucky. I suggest that these phrases are shibboleths and that they replace intelligent thought. They are a too easy way to explain everything that is wrong with the press. Of course, there is no such thing as a real monopoly of communications in American cities of any size. Louisville, for instance, has three television stations and nine radio stations, all constantly grinding out news as well as rock and roll. Monopoly, I say, is less a threat to press excellence than monotony. There are highly individualistic newspapers that are flourishing in solus ownership situations. At the same time, there are newspapers dropping from the presses all over the United States that are as alike as sausages coming out of a grinder. I don't think this is a healthy tendency.

Monopoly has its dangers. But there are also grave dangers in cutthroat competition, which is the kind of competition that flourished in these cities when there were additional ownerships and that still flourishes in some of our metropolitan areas. I make bold to suggest that monopoly ownership even has certain limited virtues. It relieves the pressure of advertisers on the owner; they cannot be effective in pressuring one newspaper. Monopoly also reduces the temptation of ownership to sensationalize the news. In my town again, which is typical, 95 per cent of our circulation is by home subscription and only 5 per cent is by street sales. It can easily be seen how that reduces the temptation for big headlines and for sensationalized news to sell against your competitor. A responsible owner of a solus newspaper can give his readers more serious news and can give them bolder and livelier opinions than the man who is running in hot and deadly competition with a rival.

All of this applies to television as well as newspapers. Mr.

Minow evidently believes that television would benefit inherently from a proliferation of channels. I doubt the validity of this belief. He himself made the perfect comment when he said that if "lighting up eighty-two channels" gives a further choice only among Tweedledum, Tweedledee, and Tweedletwaddle, it is not helping anything very much.

What the press and the other communications media need is more owners of papers and stations who regard their ownership as a public trust, more owners who consider service first and profits second. As a newspaper owner, I admit, of course, that newspapers must sell to live, but I would maintain to my dying breath that we must not live to sell. We need more owners with the peculiar passion for communicating thought and not just communicating a welter of facts. The public can help us to achieve excellence in our operations, but in order to do so it must give us intelligent, insistent criticism, well-informed criticism, based on an understanding of what we are trying to do and what we are able to do. It is a great mistake when readers are led astray by the theory that all the faults of journalism are caused by monopoly, because they are then spending their precious forces fighting against an inevitable phenomenon, one as inevitable as those grim twins "death and taxes."

SYLVESTER L. WEAVER, JR.

President, McCann-Erickson Productions

THE MASS media represent today the powering or fueling element in our modern society as they extend and galvanize and alter our incentive society. When an individual is shown through the mass media what he can get for himself and his children by harder work, by more work, by more intelligent solving of problems, his response is immediate. The big changes that are taking place really come not from basic industry, not from technology, but from the massive effect on people of our incentive system as demonstrated by the mass media. Let the people of Japan and Australia, of Brazil and Mexico, see in programming and editorial matter and advertising what can be theirs if they will work for it, and you get a quantum jump in their attitude and their condition overnight.

The individual reaction to promises from the mass media

about a better life is surpassing all the other reactions of men to the disciplines under which they have always lived—family, church, community, and so on. This revolution can be understood by examining the five quintiles of American society. The top quintile—or fifth—has always been in good shape in this country, and in the last twenty-five years the second and third quintiles have moved up tremendously in prosperity and in culture. The bottom quintile is a disgrace, and, in my opinion, more corrosive to our society than slavery was to our grandparents because we have knowledge that they never had. We are not ignorant. We should know better than to allow the bottom quintile to remain in its present condition. The poverty of the fourth quintile is also a stigma against a democratic society. Such poverty, such suffering, is unnecessary. The best way of overcoming this kind of problem is to have the mass media really involve these people meaningfully in the same incentive-system operation that is going on in the top three quintiles. People who are poor, who are barely educated, who are sick, who are old—or too often only because they are colored—do not believe in our incentive system because they know it is not really for them. When it becomes true that the media deliver promises that realistically involve them, they will react exactly the same as the second and third quintiles have reacted in the last twenty-five years, and they will move up with the rest of us where they belong.

The mass media, in other words, can make people work miracles if the rewards that are pictured are realistically attainable. The management of the mass media should mount a major offensive against this poverty and against the other great crimes of ignorance and stupidity and bigotry and fear. The mass media should focus their reporting and exhorting powers on the potential of each individual across all the quintiles of our society. We are moving up. It can be seen in book sales, in record sales; we spend more money for concert tickets than baseball tickets; television audiences for years have been 25 to 30 million for cultural programs, information programs, nonfiction programs, when they are well-managed, well-produced, and well-scheduled. We should want all people to join the literate and civilized world of the elite, to become involved in our common future, and we can do this only by exposing all of them to all the cultures and the knowledge and the adventures of man.

All the media are aiming at this individual in transition, and we must give him the whole spectrum to meet his needs. We have many things on our side. We have the new technology, which is increasing the number of available channels, the delivery of audio-visual material over more stations, more educational TV and pay-TV; we also have the large screen, stereo and sound, the kind of group-sharing equipment that is giving greater impact to material seen in schools and churches; and now we have an optical system—and an electronic system will follow—where cartridges delivered in the home will give you a program when you want it because you will be able to record it from the air or you can just rent it and have it delivered to you. Tomorrow, the show you want, when you want it; equipment that you can speed up to scan it, or slow down, or freeze, or repeat endlessly if you want to see all the nuances.

With this kind of technology and this kind of responsibility, the mass media must move ahead. We now have world interconnection by satellite; we will have cartridge programming. The media have an unexampled opportunity and, of course, an unavoidable obligation. They must make man's knowledge, his achievements, his cultures, available to everyone anywhere on earth at the push of a button and at the speed of light.

WILLIAM BENTON

Publisher, Encyclopaedia Britannica, and U.S. Ambassador to UNESCO

I do not complain because the entertainment programs of American television reflect the present level of majority tastes in entertainment. This I agree TV must seek to do—in entertainment. I complain only because TV is so concentrated on this. If the submerged, enslaved nine-tenths of the Athenian population, who could not be reached by the human voice to which Newton Minow referred, had suddenly been made free and affluent, what would they have then demanded for entertainment? Wouldn't it be the equivalent of our TV Westerns—perhaps a serial about the adventures of a Greek frontiersman in Asia Minor?

I continue to complain only because television, the most marvelous instrument of communications ever devised, so consistently fails to provide programs for those substantial minorities whose needs are well understood by Mr. Minow, those whom he calls "short-changed." I shall continue to complain that we as a people have not sufficiently developed the means to encourage the more serious minorities. Only thus, I fear, can we lift the level of the majority.

Lord Francis-Williams has set forth in masterly fashion the responsibilities of the mass media as he sees them. He has chosen to concentrate on the printed word, noting the relatively impermanent and transient effects of information and ideas conveyed by broadcasting. As a publisher of books, I too am impressed with print. Further, I recognize the devitalizing effect on the democratic dialogue of those tendencies in the press which Lord Francis-Williams analyzes so well. Nevertheless, a vast diversity of materials remains in the medium of print, despite the trend toward the "solus position" in newspaper publishing. This is a diversity lacking in broadcasting.

One reason I emphasize broadcasting in my comments, rather than the press, is that I see more clearly the paths toward its improvement. Television is still young, flexible, growing, sensitive to criticism. It exists by the approval of the public, which owns the airwaves and must decide, through its constituted agencies, who is to use them. Even if its programs lack permanence, and often must fail thoroughly to inform the public on major issues, TV has demonstrated that it can stimulate the public's awareness, its sense of involvement, the need for its participation.

Mr. Minow has told us how we may move toward greater diversity and independence in television. If our television thus provides more of a Forum and less of a Circus Maximus, to use Clinton Rossiter's phrase, the quality of the mass media as a whole will be improved—and perhaps Lord Francis-Williams will agree that this will even have its impact on the press.

The next few years may show that Mr. Minow's greatest accomplishment as Chairman of the FCC has been his sponsorship of the new all-channel receiver law under which all TV receivers turned out after April, 1964, must be equipped to receive signals on eighty-two channels. As he suggests, one consequence should be the creation of a great nationwide educational network, with perhaps as many as 200 stations. How is this to be financed? He has pointed out that the seventy educational stations now precariously on the air—he refers to them as a "smattering" of stations—have less money to spend on programming in a year than the three commercial networks spend in a week.

I share Mr. Minow's view that the second great hope for the

future of TV is the development of "methods of financing other than advertiser support." Yet I do not believe these educational stations can do an adequate job with only government appropriations or private gifts. I believe most of these stations at least some of the time—presumably in evening hours when they are beamed to adult audiences rather than to the schools—should operate on a subscription basis, charging viewers who have special and serious interests for special and serious programs. This can provide the "sound economic base." Further, I happen to believe that these educational stations should be permitted, perhaps with some limitations, to accept commercial patrons or sponsors. Finally, the universities or civic groups interested in them should be permitted to operate them for profit, which would open up the possibility of partnership with able private individuals who are attracted by the profit motive. This was the pattern established by the General Education Board when it established *Parents Magazine,* and by the University of Chicago with the *Encyclopaedia Britannica.*

As to a fourth commercial network, supported by advertisers, appealing, as Mr. Minow hopes, to "higher rather than lower common audience denominators," I applaud this also. There are many sponsors who could be attracted to programs that deliver a high-level audience at a low-level cost.

I want to praise Mr. Minow especially for one other among his recommendations. I now speak as one who has campaigned for public office. A way must be found, he says, to reduce the financial burden on candidates by offering them some amount of free time, so that they are free, as he puts it, "to raise more issues and less money." I have myself proposed in the United States Senate that the federal government finance a limited amount of free, well-spotted radio and television time during campaigns for federal office, as in Britain. The idea of federal support for political campaigns was first publicized by Theodore Roosevelt.

Finally, I am delighted to hear the man who has been the principal officer of our government in the field of broadcasting say, a decade later, that the citizens advisory board that I advocated as a United States Senator should have been created then, and that it is not too late to do so now. Senators Bricker, Hunt, and Saltonstall joined me in this proposal, and three days of hearings were held on it in 1952, all devoted to proponents of the idea. We urged that the Congress should create, and the

President appoint, a board of distinguished citizens who would undertake to appraise and report every year on the state of broadcasting. This would have been a board with no other power than the respect its findings could command. Perhaps Lord Francis-Williams will agree that the British Royal Commissions are a suitable model. I have since urged the creation of a privately constituted board, affiliated with a university.

How can we get such a commission appointed? In advocating such a commission—public, private, or both—I have for the last dozen years been quarreling with a state of affairs in which the only highly organized, systematically focused pressure on TV, the FCC, and the Congress has been that exercised by the commercial interests. This has resulted in television's being abandoned almost exclusively to escapist entertainment. It is much as if our printing presses were abandoned to the novel. We do not object to the novel, or to entertainment. We object to its virtually exclusive pre-emption of the airwaves. This inevitably produces the short-changing.

The existence of an advisory commission or board would give a powerful voice to those who view radio-TV as an instrument for "the public interest, convenience, or necessity," the great phrase of the early Congressional Act. Now the voice largely heard by the broadcasters is heard only as the audience, singly, tune their sets on, off, and around. There are those, of course, who call the resulting TV rating systems "cultural democracy." I wish these apologists, or cynics, would ask themselves whether the TV ratings mean that the American people would rather watch horse operas than build peace. Would they rather watch mysteries than educate their children? Are they more interested in comedians than they are in freedom and justice? I deem not. There is a high common denominator in our people, as well as a low one, and among the same men, women, and youngsters. Television has taken the low road and ignored the high.

On the average, every man, woman, and child in the United States today is said to command the equivalent of eighty-five slaves. With the help of slavery, Athens was able, for a century or so, to endow those among her population who were free citizens with the leisure that made Athens the greatest enterprise in adult education the world has yet seen. The citizens turned their free time into leisure—that is, into learning. The Greek word for learning is akin to the word for leisure. Do we know how to do the same with the free time created by the new technology? Can we yet learn how to use the potentials created by technology, an opportunity most dramatically exemplified by television, to apply Greek practices on a grand scale?

6.

Education:
For What
and For Whom?

LORD JAMES of RUSHOLME

Vice-Chancellor, University of York, England

PERHAPS the greatest of all teachers, Socrates, made his most significant contribution by forcing us to examine with scrupulous care the resounding words and phrases that we use to conceal our ignorance and the imprecision of our thought. There are few fields where such words and phrases are more commonly used than in education, and among them few are in more constant use than the phrase "a democratic education."

The most superficial examination will show its essential ambiguity. It may, for example, mean an education that is administered democratically, one that is organized democratically within individual institutions, or one that is designed to produce democratic attitudes, or fit individuals for life in a democratic community, and all these are distinct meanings. But even if we postpone consideration of these interpretations, we must at the start recognize that the common use of phrases such as this by implication acknowledges the existence of a close relationship between a democratic form of social organization and the kind of education that its citizens receive. At the most obvious level, any form of government will survive in the modern world only if it can compete in knowledge and skills with its rivals. In the conditions of modern life, the rule is absolute: The nation that does not value trained intelligence is doomed.

We must never forget that the first and inescapable obligation of education is to teach people; to see that they are good chemists, or lawyers, or engineers, and this obligation is at least as real a part of education for democracy as the more abstract and idealistic approaches that we usually associate with the term. An educational system that does not teach a boy or girl as much as he is capable of learning is failing both the community and the individual.

But beyond this quite fundamental aim, democracy makes other demands on education. It presupposes an educational system distinguished by the sheer quantity of education available to the citizens. Such an extensive system is demanded both by the need for knowledge and expertness as elements in survival and by another and deeper need. The citizen of a democracy will increasingly claim educational opportunity as a right, for he will see it as a means to social and cultural advance. This demand gives rise to one of our most difficult practical problems: Granted that education is on all grounds a prerequisite for a successful democratic community, how much of it can we afford? I am not thinking primarily of actual money, although this is clearly enormously important. It is, indeed, an urgent question for the national economy to decide what share of the national income should properly be devoted to education in competition with other fields of valuable expenditure.

Educators frequently refer to education as a national investment, and would claim for it a preferential place compared with, say, housing, automobiles, or even hospitals, because it is itself the prerequisite of other kinds of advance. There is clearly an important field for further study here. But in addition to the purely financial question, there is another still more intractable—that of manpower. The ultimate limitation on the amount of education that we can provide is fixed by the number of people who are both able and willing to teach at the various levels we require. If, for example, we expand our higher education too lavishly, we denude our schools of ability so drastically that the education they give becomes jejune and ineffective. It is on these questions of fixing priorities in the use of money and manpower that a free society is most clearly at a disadvantage compared with authoritarian regimes that can control and direct, and in no field is that more obvious than in education. A great obligation rests on us to explore every means of using our educational manpower most effectively. But in the last resort there is a question of the ultimate values of society. A community that, by the inducements and the prestige it offers, channels ability into entertainment or advertising rather than into the task of educating its citizens will ultimately decay, and it will deserve to do so.

There is yet another very important way in which education must serve the democratic state. This is both the most fundamental and the one that differentiates most clearly the role of education in a democracy from that in other kinds of society. Whatever our formal definition of democracy, at the heart of it must lie the ideas of citizens who participate as fully as their abilities allow them to do, and of decisions that are reached after discussion. Education has, therefore, a special role. It must not only produce competent specialists; it must produce individuals with interests as wide as their abilities permit.

Here we reach a most difficult and technical area of discussion—that of the curriculum. The problem with which the educator is faced in this context today is simply this. The rapidity of the growth of knowledge—the dominant feature of the intellectual history of our time—forces on him an ever greater specialization. The needs for an informed citizenship demand an even greater breadth. The reconciliation of those conflicting demands is one of the crucial problems that we have to face. My own view is to believe that our higher education must have a core of specialized studies, but that by every device of stimulus and encouragement and by letting them live in educative communities we must lead our students to the efforts of continuing self-education without which they cannot hope to be prepared for the world in which they will be living.

But whatever experiments we try in the fields of general education, one task is of supreme importance: Our education must aim at strengthening their critical faculties so that our pupils may have some hope of withstanding those mass suggestions and imposed and unexamined assumptions that today assail them with such force. There is no more urgent task for our education than to produce this constant critical awareness, and perhaps its most intractable problem is to combine this with an underlying faith in the validity of those beliefs about the human personality on which alone democracy can rest.

I have so far tried to indicate the supreme importance of education for the survival of democratic communities both in quantitative and in qualitative terms. I want now to say a little more about the *kind* of education that is particularly fitted to nourish a democracy. There is, of course, an initial difficulty in the ambiguity that surrounds the word democracy itself. It has quite clearly come to mean more than a form of government, especially when used in educational contexts. It has become one of those inclusive words which embrace within themselves a set of attitudes toward society and life. But whatever the precise meanings we attach to it, it is obvious that the word democracy implies a belief in the liberty of the individual.

The great eighteenth century revolutions from which sprang so much of the thinking that today we call democratic included the word liberty as one of the most prominent elements in their professions of faith, and it is through the idea of liberty that democratic thought has made its most obvious impact on education. Two centuries ago, Wesley could write, "Break the will, if you would not damn the child. Whatever pains it costs, break the will." Today such a sentiment shocks or ought to shock any intelligent teacher. Instead of coercion, he has persuasion; instead of authoritarianism, he has put libertarian methods. If he is asked to define his objectives, he will quote the Declaration of Human Rights and say that a democratic education involves the full development of the personality. And there is no doubt of the good that has resulted from such attitudes. Our schools are far happier places today than they were fifty years ago. It is pure gain that fear has given place to cooperation and that we regard the child as an individual with a personality of his own that must be respected.

Yet we must recognize certain dangers in an excessive libertarianism in education, and a threat to democracy if it is associated with too permissive attitudes. It threatens first the basic necessity of learning certain skills; it endangers the idea of maximum intellectual effort both as a good in itself and as a prerequisite for the prosperity of the community. In so far as it uses such devices as school councils and the like, trivial though they may be, it presents an oversimplified picture of what democracy really is, making it appear as a simple matter of control by majorities. The teacher in an overlibertarian environment may be so afraid of indoctrination that his teaching will lose all authority and all inspiration, lost in a grey wasteland of benevolent neutrality. The teacher who aims at producing citizens of a democracy must certainly strive to inculcate habits of independent thought, but he will not do so by giving the impression that one view is as good or true as another, that every man's opinion is as worthy of respect as every other's, or that tolerance is the same as indifference.

One of the central difficulties of that excessive libertarianism that is so often held to be democratic is that the authority of the teacher is replaced by that of the herd. In fact, we may be substituting one tyranny by another that is often more cruel, more capricious, and less informed, and these qualities are particularly evident in youth when conformity is always valued. Yet, if our education is to be truly democratic, it must be capable—if not of producing nonconformists, since perhaps no education can do that—of not crushing them, at any rate.

Here one of the central problems of a democratic society finds a particularly clear expression in an educational context —the search for a proper source and weight for authority in a society that claims to be free. If we consider a little more closely the aim of the libertarian to develop the full personality of the child, we can see its inherent difficulty. Do we really want to develop *all* sides of the personality, for is it not one of the deepest elements in human experience that not all sides of our personality should be developed? And if we answer, as we must, that it is the *good* sides that must be developed, we arc at once postulating the need and the ability to judge what is good. It is a dangerous and ultimately fatal tendency of much democratic education to remove this authority from the teacher and find no substitute for him except the prejudices of the majority. Yet in much that concerns education, and most importantly in judgments of value, the views of majorities are very often wrong. If democracy is not to move towards degeneration under the Rabelaisian motto, "Do what you will," it is necessary for its teachers to realize that they should speak with the authority of that educated minority whom Coleridge called the clerisy.

How is this belief in the necessity for authority to be reconciled with the demand that we should be prepared in our education to encourage heretics? In fact, there is no real contradiction, if we remember that moral and social education, like all kinds of education, must be adapted, in the familiar phrase, to the age, ability, and aptitude of the child. With the young, the not very intelligent, and the insecure, the teacher can and must be definite and clear in the standards that he tries to inculcate. With the older and the more intelligent, though making his own position clear, he must be prepared for discussion, and even disagreement. This is such a truism that it would not be worth saying were it not that so many of our democratic educators, in their desire for an affirmation of libertarian principles, have failed to take account of the different responses called for by different circumstances and the varying needs of different individuals. A doctrinaire permissiveness that implies an underlying denial of objectivity in judgment will, so far from strengthening democracy, prove its greatest enemy.

Let us now consider the actual control of education within a democratic community. Who, in the last resort, ought to run the schools and universities? Who should decide what goes on within them? This is clearly a matter of great importance and great difficulty. Education is one of the principal means by which a society seeks to perpetuate its values; it is through education that it produces the workers of various kinds on whom its prosperity depends; it is partly through education that it will seek to maintain or alter its social structure. On all these grounds the state, in one or another of its manifestations, cannot be disinterested in the educational system, and to many writers who would claim to be thinking in democratic terms in a democratic community all education must be under the control of the state. Nor is this interpretation of democratic sentiment the only force tending to increase the power of the state in education. The quantity and quality of educational provision demanded by a modern community increases the cost to a point which the state alone can provide. It is inevitable that the community will demand ever increasing control over the education which it subsidizes. This is a weighty additional reason why, to many people, a democratic educational system means one in which the agencies of education, whether they be schools, or colleges, or universities, are under the control of the democratic state itself, whatever that phrase may mean.

On the other hand, it is possible on democratic grounds to fear and resist this intrusion of the state into activities concerned ultimately with the mind and spirit. It is this fear of a monolithic state system, crushing individualism, which led some nineteenth century writers like J. S. Mill and Spencer to oppose state education altogether and which today leads many democrats to favor the continued existence of private educational institutions, at any rate in competition with those of the state. Here we have one of those not infrequent examples of the way in which holders of beliefs that spring from common democratic sources may be led to completely contrary conclusions. The necessity for compromise that usually follows is the source of both the strengths and weaknesses of democracy. In this particular case, the compromise has led in democratic countries to the bewildering variety of educational systems with which we are familiar. In England, the institutions range in independence from completely private schools to others completely administered by local education authorities, a transition that includes schools partially controlled by religious denominations and others directly under the central government, while the universities guard jealously an autonomy that remains nominally unimpaired by the fact that by far the greater part of their income comes from the state.

In the conditions of the modern world, it is inevitable that more and more educational power should pass to the state, almost certainly in the form of central government. I should say frankly that this does not fill me with the alarm felt by some of my friends. For sixteen years, I was head of a school financed by central government. No greater freedom than I possessed would have been proper, even if, indeed, it had been conceivable. But such a happy state of affairs is only possible if certain conditions are observed. If our interpretation of a democratic educational system means increasing control over educational institutions, we must examine with the greatest care what the limits are to the power that the layman should wield over the practitioner. The layman, whether he be an elected representative or other, represents the needs and aspirations of the community, which in any case supplies the money. Some control he must have. Yet if he attempts to prescribe, say, the content or the methods of teaching, he will not only be speaking from ignorance and, therefore, often be wrong, but his interference will enervate or frustrate the professional whose work is involved.

The role of the expert provides one of the most interesting problems for a democracy, whether the expert be civil servant, scientist, or other professional. It is one that we must solve if we are to be efficient enough to survive. And in no field is it more difficult than in education. This difficulty arises partly from the fact that nearly everyone regards himself as knowledgeable about education. Men who would hesitate to express views on nuclear physics, or medieval French, or selling shoes speak with confidence and definition about education. And to some extent this is healthy, for it recognizes that education is a wider matter than what goes on in schools. And, indeed, the term expert is a most ambiguous one when used in educational contexts. In my own view, we are in danger of giving too much authority to the educationist and too little to the teacher. But, whatever the difficulties, I believe that if our educational system is to be at once more democratic and more efficient, we must put more rather than less faith in the experts, whether they be civil servants, teachers, or administrators, and reserve to the majority of laymen control only over the widest and most general matters.

In the long run, the safeguards for the proper liberty of those who practice an art or science lies much more in a quality of personal relationships than in the formal machinery of control. Nevertheless, machinery is necessary, and it must be such that the professional feels that he has the responsibility and the freedom that his expert knowledge justifies. There is no essential conflict between such freedom and ultimate control by a democracy, though a state of tension will always exist. To work out the details of particular solutions will call for greater wisdom and tolerance than we have often shown. In so far as a democracy shows, as it sometimes does, an almost pathological fear of government on the one hand and the expert on the other, it is weakening its sources of loyalty, knowledge, and proper authority.

If a belief in individual liberty is a characteristic element in democratic thought, an adherence to the idea of equality is no less important. It is an idea which is both immensely powerful and essentially ambiguous. For Tocqueville, it was the central and most characteristic element in the democracy that he analyzed with such unparalleled skill. For Acton, the idea of equality was essentially inimical to that of liberty. For Bryce, it was the source of "half the errors which democratic practice had committed."

Certainly there can be no doubt that the desire for equality in some sense is one of the strongest elements in democratic societies today, and it may well be held that the greatest of all the problems that face democracies in the years ahead centers on the interpretation of the word equality and its reconciliation with other democratic ideas.

It is certainly true that the idea of equality has particularly clear relations with education. It will obviously affect very directly the organization of the educational system. Further, education can be one of the most powerful agents tending towards a greater degree of equality in society. Two quite distinct meanings can be attached to the term in educational contexts. On the one hand, we can assert that although all men are manifestly not equal, we must as far as possible treat them as if they were and do all in our power to play down the difference between them. Such a view we may call equalitarian to distinguish it from the other view, which interprets equality as meaning equality of opportunity—which aims, that is to say, at recognizing and accepting the differences between individuals, and seeking to give them the opportunities appropriate to their particular talents.

The equalitarian view has colored a great deal of educational thought and practice, particularly in the United States, though it is now growing in strength in England. If we adhere to it, we will be opposed to differentiation between kinds of school. It is the voice of equalitarianism that speaks when Conant says, "We could not, if we would, separate into different school buildings those who wish to enter the profession via the universities and all others." In so far as it leads to a greater concern for the average child, an equalitarian attitude has accomplished great things: It is a fatal weakness to a democracy for a considerable body of citizens to feel disinherited. In this particular direction, English education has learned much from the United States, though it still has some way to go. But having said that, I would be remiss if I did not express my misgivings as to the long-term educational results of an equalitarian educational philosophy.

By seeking to minimize the differences between individuals, the equalitarian philosophy is actually opposed to that important element in democratic thought which regards the individual as having supreme value by very virtue of those attributes which make him unique. In practice, we see the results in classes with far too great a spread of ability for the best to be extended or the weakest encouraged and helped. We are committed to aim at the mean. There is, moreover, a dangerous if more subtle tendency to equalize in esteem kinds of ability and subjects of study. If calculus is manifestly too difficult for the majority of pupils, it is easy for the equalitarian to maintain that it is just as good to be good at carpentry. And the effect of such a doctrine is a curriculum with too many soft options and a resultant decline in standards, and ultimately an impoverishment in culture, for it is but a step to saying that Jerome Kern is "just as good as" Mozart, if not, indeed, better, since more people like him. Nor can the comprehensive high school be justified on the very grounds that commends it to equalitarians—that it promotes social cohesion. Drawing as it must on a limited geographical area, it is actually very often far more socially stratified than a school that is intellectually selective.

But perhaps the most practically important argument concerns the supply of teachers. The number of those able and willing to teach the most able will always be very limited. If the most able individuals are to receive the kind of educational stimulus they need, both in their own interests and in those of the community, the efforts of those teachers must not be diffused: The academically gifted child must be brought to that minority of teachers capable of instructing, of stimulating, and of educating him. If the educational needs of democracy are to be met, if democratic societies are to be viable culturally no less than economically, if their individual citizens are to receive the kind of education fitted to their individual needs, then democracies must learn to recognize, to value, and, if necessary, to make a special and separate provision for excellence and ability.

It is clear that for me equality means equality of opportunity, and I do believe it to be true that unless they foster that conception, democratic countries will not survive. But, having said that, we must analyze more closely than we sometimes do some of the difficulties concealed behind that phrase. If we go through the slums of one of our cities and compare the lives of the children playing in the gutters with those of their contemporaries in a good suburb some miles away, we see the initial difficulty of giving reality to the idea of equality of opportunity. There are three considerations that follow: The first is that in seeking to equalize opportunity we must beware lest we infringe upon proper liberties. Thus, where we see one child enjoying the privileges of an expensive independent school we are tempted to say, "Let us abolish the independent schools." It may conceivably be right to do so, though I do not myself think it is, but let us be aware that what we are doing is to say to parents, "You may spend your money on cruises or automobiles—but not on the education of your child." Here again two democratic sentiments—that for equality and that for liberty—are opposed to each other.

But even if by some miracle all schools could be equalized, a greater source of inequality remains, the home. Every teacher knows that in some ways the home is more educationally influential than the school. How can we equalize opportunity between the home that provides books and conversation and the one with perpetual "telly," that takes the *Guardian* or the *New York Times* rather than the *Sunday Pictorial*? It was when faced with this problem that Plato produced the most impracticable part of the *Republic*, the idea that children should be removed altogether from the contaminating influence of home and environment. We must take warning from him that the pursuit of equality of opportunity, noble though that ideal be, must not lead us down a slippery slope of social engineering that regards human beings as specimens in some vast laboratory experiment rather than as ends in themselves.

In the same way, the school that seeks to remedy deficiencies in opportunity may be led outside its proper function. Every teacher worthy of the name must have concern for his pupils outside the classroom and must attempt to remove obstacles to his development whether they be financial or social or domestic. But how far is that to go? There is the danger that the school may neglect its real function of teaching and become, as Bestor says, "a home, a church, a work-shop and a doctor's office rolled into one."

The fact is that a consideration of the difficulties implicit in the phrase equality of opportunity forces us to realize that education is but one among a multiplicity of social factors. We often expect too much from it; we lay upon it inappropriate tasks that weaken its main mission—the intellectual development of young people. If democracy is to make the best of its educational system, if for some it is to make real education possible, it must realize the necessity for rapid advance on all fronts, in housing, in health, and in general social welfare.

Our democratic education, as I envisage it, with its emphasis on equality of opportunity, must not become a rat-race with some "room at the top" as the only prize in life. If democracy involves the creation of an elite, not of birth or wealth but of merit, we must see that this new elite has the virtues that at its best the old aristocracy often possessed, the virtues of a sense of obligation, of service, of that respect for the rights of individuals which rests on a perception that in some sense all men *are* equal. Here our very belief in equality may be an obstacle. We are so afraid of admitting that anyone is better than anyone else that we hesitate to bring home to our ablest pupils the responsibilities that go with ability and power. There is no more important task for democratic education than this: to recognize that the existence of leadership is not only not undemocratic, but a vital prerequisite for the continuance and the flowering of democracy. If much of our educational effort is to be devoted to the average, let us also remember that on the opportunities that we give to the best—opportunities intellectual and moral and spiritual alike —the future of the average does itself depend.

To the problems of a democratic education, then, there are no easy answers. There is nothing for us but the unspectacular road of finding more money, of making better schools, of producing better teachers. We must avoid the short-cuts that believe we can educate for democracy by providing soft options of life adjustment rather than the hardest intellectual effort of which each person is capable. Above all, it is with faith in his mission that the educator must react to the new world of affluence, of scientific discovery, and of mass media. If by education men cannot be made a little more rational, a little more tolerant, a shade more sensitive than they would otherwise be, then the teacher has no real justification for his existence except as an instructor in techniques. He may see the dangers of a new technology and a new equality for the values that he holds. There is, indeed, a very real danger that the kind of civilization that science and democracy between them will create will be what Hoggart calls a candy-floss culture, and it is easy enough to see the signs of this happening. Nevertheless, the teacher, of all men, must believe that he can resist it; he must have faith that experiences of the highest value are not necessarily corrupted and debased when they are made more widely accessible. He can, indeed, with a good deal of justification argue that his efforts are having a profound effect, that the "decline in standards" about which so much is spoken and written is outmatched by their general elevation in many ways. There is plenty of evidence that he can produce to show that the majority of men are more tolerant and have better taste and are even more rational than their ancestors.

But if his faith is to be justified, his teaching must be informed by certain attitudes. He must be determined that what he gives to his pupils is, in fact, the best of which they are capable. It must be appropriate to their capacities and their needs, but it must never be a soft option that demands from them anything but their greatest efforts. He must quite consciously set out to arm them against the irrational pressures of suggestion, which seek to make them simply acquiescent recipients of bread and circuses, and this will actually be the most effective kind of "education for citizenship" that he can do. Above all, he must not doubt that there are judgments of value that depend on a surer foundation than the tastes and preference of a majority made vulnerable by the techniques of mass-persuasion. In the last resort, in answer to the taunt that he is seeing himself as a Platonic Guardian, an authoritarian figure who claims to know best, he must admit the charge, for he must believe that he speaks for the best that has been thought, written, or created, even if his own perception of it may be very imperfect.

The teacher's vision of democracy must be one that sees it not simply as a matter of majority votes, although in some spheres of life these are appropriate enough, but rather as a process of taking decisions after discussion based on knowledge. His view of liberty must not be simply the ability to think and do as one likes, for that surrenders the freedom to do the best of which one is capable in order to do what is easiest or what the pressure of social conformity dictates. His view of equality must not be that all individuals have identical needs or talents or potentialities, but that every individual has a nature of his own that makes him an object of respect and value. Because democracy demands in practice such difficult reconciliations, between liberty and authority, between majority decisions and the perceptions and rights of minorities, between the sense that all men are equal and the necessity to give unequal weight to their judgments, it is the most difficult of all forms of government. Because it is the most difficult, the responsibility that it lays upon the educational system is correspondingly heavy, and it is in the educational system that the ideals that inspire democracy can be most clearly seen. And because, in the last resort, the quality of education depends on the quality of the men and women who are concerned with it, it is fundamental to democracy that they themselves should be inspired with its spirit and with a determination to understand it more fully.

Let us end by quoting yet again from Tocqueville, whose study of the greatest of democracies enabled him to see with unexampled clarity the dangers and the hopes of democratic ideals:

> We have not to make ourselves like our progenitors, but to strive to work out that species of greatness and happiness which is our own. . . . I am full of apprehension and of hopes. I perceive mighty dangers which it is possible to ward off— mighty evils which may be avoided or alleviated; and I cling with a firmer hold to the belief that for the democratic nations to be virtuous and prosperous they require but to will it. . . . Providence has not created mankind entirely independent or entirely free. It is true that around every man a fatal circle is traced, beyond which he cannot pass; but within the wide verge of that circle he is powerful and free: As it is with man, so with communities. The nations of our time cannot prevent the conditions of men becoming equal; but it depends upon themselves whether the principle of equality is to lead them to servitude or freedom, to knowledge or barbarism, to prosperity or wretchedness.

routines in certain places, because the routines may not be there and they may be living in other places. The aim of education has to be so to develop intellectual power that the individuals and the communities that are made up of these individuals will be able to face and solve problems now totally unforeseen.

I therefore reject the suggestion advanced from very high quarters that the object of education is to produce marketable skills. There may be no market for these skills, or they may be taught the wrong skills for the markets that are available.

I reject the suggestion that the aim of education is adjustment to the environment. We need to improve the environment, not to "adjust" to it. The rate of change means that we have no idea what the environment will be.

I conclude further that education is now, and always ought to have been, a lifelong process, and that all modern developments confirm this future for education. A steady reduction in the hours of labor is in prospect. We may have an opportunity to become the first full-time citizens since the Greeks. They were full-time citizens because of their slaves. We can be full-time citizens, if we will, because of our technology.

It is necessary, therefore, to overcome the belief that education is a children's disease like mumps, measles, whooping cough—having had it once you need not, in fact you cannot, have it again. The task of life is learning, and the man who stops learning is as good as dead.

All signs point to the necessity of universal lifelong liberal education, and all metaphysicians hold that what is necessary must be possible. Even apart from metaphysics, I believe that this is practically possible in the affluent, technical societies of the West. It has been estimated that the United States can now produce annually $60 billion more of goods than it can sell. This abundance can be coped with only through a steady reduction in working hours, a steady increase in the leisure of the population. What it takes in order to produce the kind of educational system that we need is clarity and resolution.

HYMAN G. RICKOVER

Vice-Admiral, USN

AN EDUCATED man is one who understands the basic fundamentals that make the world around him intelligible to him. He is a man who can accept new ideas, think about them, impart something of himself to them, and come up with something new. This is the mark that distinguishes men from animals. An uneducated man, on the contrary, as a famous philosopher said, is like a seal who sleeps for a minute and a half, wakes up, takes a look around him, goes back to sleep again. He just reacts; he doesn't think. Or, one might say, he is like a mirror. Ideas are not absorbed, they are always reflected. Now this is a very simple definition. There are many definitions, and I believe there have been a number of philosophers who have tried to coin definitions of an educated man, but this is my stab at it.

What can we do to have educated people, and particularly educated children? I thoroughly agree with Dr. Hutchins that the object of education is *not* salable skills; the object of education is to develop the intellect. There are three basic things I believe we can do.

First, we must turn education back to the true educators, the teachers. The United States is the only country in Western civilization where the enterprise of education is conducted by administrators or businessmen. Obviously, when you have any large organization or institution, you have bureaucracy and hence administrators. But these people should be assistants to those running the enterprise and not run it themselves and act as if teachers were their hired help. For this I blame the so-called educational organizations such as the National Educational Association. I call them the NEPA—the National Educational Protective Association. It is composed largely by, and for the benefit of, school administrators. It is time that the teacher stepped out and started talking about education and not let the administrators do it for him.

The next step is to have better teachers. For us to have enough teachers to do the job properly, we would have to use almost all the people at our top intelligence level. Since we do not have enough of them, and since we know that many of our children are being deprived of an adequate education, would it not be smart for us to identify those children who can benefit by better education and to see that they get it, instead of chaining all of them to a common-core curriculum, as we do all over under the false name of "democracy," and saying that this is "the democratic way" to teach? We say this in the schoolroom and then, lo and behold, at recess time the kids get out on the playground, where it is immediately evident that some of them do some things better than others. We deny that some people are better mentally than others, and this is blasphemy because God created human beings as unique individuals, and to say that any two of us are identical is blasphemous. The great genius of the human race is that we are all different, that we cannot all be measured by standard tests. It is impossible to teach all children the same way. This "philosophy" arose at a time when education was being broadened in this country and "progressive" methods seemed to make it easier to teach large numbers of people. It also meant that inferior teaching personnel could take care of the job.

So I say that we must have better teachers. We must get the best people in this country into the profession. In order to do that, since we are essentially a commercial society, we will have to increase the salaries of teachers. I, for one, think that any teacher worth his salt should get more than a senator—or even an admiral. And if there is not enough money to pay for education, I would take it out of the military funds because education is more important than the military.

The next necessity is standards. Nothing can be changed or even improved unless standards have been set. We have standards for medicine, we place an inspector's stamp on a side of beef, our coffee is standardized, our clothes are standardized. But we have no standard in education. Consequently, we have some 40,000 school boards in the United States, each trying to set its own standard of education. The argument is that the Constitution did not give any right for education to the federal government. And yet the federal government, ever since the Northwest Ordinance of 1787, has been granting funds and other property to education. It now amounts to $2 billion a year.

Every other modern country in the world that has been able to improve its educational system in a short period of time has necessarily had to adopt standards. There is no other way. There are not enough people with a good knowledge of education to man 40,000 school boards. Certainly the PTA's, who concern themselves with the Christmas play and matters of that kind, are not going to solve the problem. I think they are an infernal nuisance and ought to be abolished. The women ought to stay home and take care of their husbands rather than bother the school teachers.

I do not advocate a *mandatory* national standard. I advocate a *permissive* standard, which every community could adapt as it wished. Educational standards abroad are set by the central government, but the local communities decide how much of it they want to carry out and what teachers they want to hire in order to carry it out.

These are my three points: Turn teaching back to the teachers; set up a standard; and have our teachers the best educated and, preferably, the best paid people in the country.

ROSEMARY PARK

President, Barnard College

THE problem at issue here is not in any sense a technological problem. We have the tools. The problem is a human problem. Man finds himself today in a world with tremendous power at his disposal, and he also finds himself in a world that has begun to narrow. Spengler makes the point that the sense of infinitude has been the primary stamp of the quality of Western civilization. But today I suggest that all of us sense a kind of narrowing. We do not think that we can go on forever as we are. There is limitless space outside of us, but in spite of our powerful tools, we feel impotent to come to grips with it. Rather than facing a great infinitude with a perpetual gushing forth of novelty, as Bergson said, we face a limited universe, and we are uncertain of the direction in which our powerful tools should be used.

This produces frustration, and so we look at the educator and say: What should we do with these tools? Our technological skills have given us this remarkable civilization, affluent and luxurious beyond anything we have ever attained before. But they have also encouraged the rapid growth of population, so that one of our fundamental problems is how to care for the mass of people desiring education when we know that in its uttermost reality education is a changing of the *individual* human being. How can we reach to the core of this individual when the tools of education, the institutions, are so overwhelmed that scarcely any man-to-man relationship remains through which the conversion that education should provide can take place?

The question becomes: Can the machine accomplish the same kind of conversion that the human being used to—not every time at all, but perhaps more often than not. My answer is that the machine, properly used in certain parts of the educational process, can probably accomplish quite a bit, but it can never do the job of the human being. Our problem, therefore, is to save the human being for those parts of the educational process which no machine can properly touch. The production of specialists is, I think, pretty well under control; we can produce the specialists we need. But the further question is whether we are producing the human individuals to direct this specialization.

I am inclined to think that we are not, simply because we have lost sight of our sense of "citizenship," which, at least for the Greeks, meant a kind of ethical discipline. This kind of citizenship has slipped through our fingers. We no longer, any of us, I think, honestly believe that because we are members of a democracy we have submitted to certain ethical disciplines in order to carry out the mandates of that society. This is the innermost part of the human being, the area in which he decides not to do certain things even though he would be able to do them. This is the area with which education has to be most vitally concerned, and it is the area in which up to date, I am afraid, we have been totally remiss.

Education, and those of us who are engaged in it, can only reflect the standards and the hopes of the society that supports it. Our society today is one that has very largely lost hope. It has lost hope in the sense that it does not adhere to any accepted, basic thought about reality into which hope is built. It does not accept the Marxist hope, for instance, that the lapse of time and history will produce the classless society after we get over the dictatorship of the proletariat. It does not adhere—except with undue sentimentality—to the Christian insight that the Kingdom of God may and will come. It has failed to hold on to the basic insight of science, or at least of nineteenth century science, that reason will produce progress and that continued control over nature will also produce progress.

The only way that we may come to a definition of a hope that would give direction to our society and cohesion to the discipline expected of our citizens is to face clearly the things we most desperately fear—the disappearance of this stage of human life by complete destruction of the world, and, second, a horrible, nagging suspicion that we are continually surrendering our freedom in order to achieve a more luxurious life. If we fear these things sufficiently, and if we maintain that "hope" is a matter of willpower, not a matter of knowing history or a matter of indoctrination, then we may be able to say, as many philosophers have always held, that "hope is hope in spite of . . ."—in spite of fear, in spite of the horror that is around us, in spite of the vulgarity of much of our society.

Our deep sense of uncertainty and concern is reflected in the ideals of our younger generation. They wish that there was something to hope. They wish that they could fight with us, the older generation, because they disapprove of what little we do hope. But it *is* so little that there is small opportunity to fight with us. We have, then, an educational system that can produce specialists but that is rather short on producing the kind of disciplined citizen the Greek state aimed to produce. If we have good fortune, and if we hope, we may make, possibly in our lifetime, some step toward achieving true citizenship.

7.

The Prospects
for Democracy

ADLAI E. STEVENSON

U. S. Representative to the United Nations

I SAID some ten years ago: "Self-criticism is the secret weapon of democracy. . . . We dare not just look back on great yesterdays. We must look forward to great tomorrows. What counts now is not just what we are *against*, but what we are *for*. *Who* leads us is less important than *what* leads us—what convictions, what courage, what faith."

I should like to think that these words apply to the Center for the Study of Democratic Institutions and the work that goes on there. Bernard Shaw said that democracy was a device that insures that we shall be governed no better than we deserve. The Center for the Study of Democratic Institutions, as I understand it, can be thought of, then, as a kind of national insurance plan, a way of making certain that we will deserve better and better. I am proud to lend my endorsement to what the Center has already done and what it promises to do in the years ahead.

We have all learned that modern technology can strengthen the despot's hand and the dictator's grasp—and for that reason, if no other, we know that democracy is more necessary now than it ever was. Of course, democracy is not self-executing. We have to make it work, and to make it work we have to understand it. Sober thought and fearless criticism are impossible without critical thinkers and thinking critics. Such persons must be given the opportunity to come together, to see new facts in the light of old principles, to evaluate old principles in the light of new facts, and by deliberation, debate, and dialogue to hammer out the consensus that makes democracy possible. And this, as we all know well, though some of us forget from time to time, requires intellectual independence, impenitent speculation, and freedom from political pressure. In a word, it requires centers of the kind found on Eucalyptus Hill in Santa Barbara.

I hope the day may come when such centers are multiplied the world over. For democracy's need for wisdom will remain as perennial as its need for liberty. Not only external vigilance but unending self-examination must be the perennial price of liberty, because the work of self-government never ceases. The work of an institution like this Center in Santa Barbara is similar to the work of the church in this regard— it will be required as long as final salvation eludes us, which will be until the end of time.

The study of democratic institutions—how to create them, how to sustain them, how to preserve them—will be necessary as long as men continue to seek faith in themselves, continue to harbor hope in their own capacity to progess, and cherish the charity that unites them in a common cause. And with the world undergoing such rapid change in geography, politics, and economics, the need to adapt our old and venerated institutions to the changes is urgent.

I suppose whether democracy can prevail in the great upheaval of our time is a valid question. Certainly, after 150 years of uninterrupted expansion of the idea of government by consent of the governed, it has recently met with mounting and formidable challenges all over the world from Fascist, Nazi, Communist authoritarians, and a variety of dictatorships. And we have good reason to know how clumsy, slow, inefficient, and costly it is compared to the celerity, certainty, and secrecy of absolutism. But the important thing is that it *has* survived. The important thing is that even the absolutists masquerade as democrats; even the military and quasi-military dictatorships strive in the name of democracy to manage the public business. And all of them say that authoritarianism is only a necessary transition to democracy.

Why? Because it is the most popular form of government yet devised; because it is, as it always has been, not only the prize of the steadfast and the courageous but the privilege of those who are better off; because, in short, as Jefferson said, it is "the only form of government which is not eternally at open or secret war with the rights of the people."

I have, therefore, no doubt that, distant as it may be for many people, it will ultimately prevail, that it will rewin lost ground, that it will expand its dominion—that it can withstand the winds that are blowing through the world—if, and I repeat if, we who are its custodians continually re-examine and adapt its principles to the changing needs of our changing times.

Years ago, Reinhold Niebuhr observed that "man's capacity for justice makes democracy possible; but man's inclination to injustice makes democracy necessary." And I suppose most of us, if we were asked to name the most profound issues at stake in the world today, would say the issues of freedom and democracy. We would say that the Western world, for all its errors and shortcomings, has for centuries tried to evolve a society in which the individual has enough legal, social, and political elbowroom to be not the puppet of the community but his own autonomous self.

And we would say, too, that the enemies of freedom, whatever the magnificent ends they propose—the brotherhood of man, the kingdom of saints, "from each according to his ability, to each according to his needs"—miss just this essential point: that man is greater than the social purposes to which he can be put. He must not be kicked about even with the most high-minded objectives. He is not a means or an instrument. He is an end in himself.

This, I take it, is the essence of what we mean by democracy—not so much voting systems or parliamentary systems or economic or legal systems—though they all enter in—as an irrevocable and final dedication to the dignity of man.

In this sense, democracy is perhaps mankind's most audacious experiment. This dignity, this equality of the human person, could hardly be further removed from the existential facts of human existence. There is precious little dignity, precious little equality, in our natural state. Most human beings have to spend their lives in utter vulnerability, all are murderable, all are torturable, and survive only through the restraint shown by more powerful neighbors. All are born unequal in terms of capacity or of strength. All are born to the inherent frailty of the human condition, naked and helpless, vulnerable all through life to the will of others, limited by ignorance, limited by physical weakness, limited by fear, limited by the phobias that fear engenders. It is not surprising that, given this basic defenselessness, the natural condition of man has not been far removed from Hobbes's definition of it as "nasty, brutish, and short."

For nearly 3,000 years, the political and social genius of what we can permissibly call "Western man" has struggled with these brute facts of our unsatisfactory existence. Ever since the Hebrews discovered personal moral responsibility, and the Greeks discovered the autonomy of the citizen, the effort has been made, with setbacks and defeats, with dark ages and interregnums, to create a social order in which weak, fallible, obstinate, silly, magnificent man can maintain his dignity and exercise his free and responsible choice.

The task has never been easy. Each step has been a groping in the dark, the dark of violence, of brute power, and of overweening arrogance. What we seek to defend today against new critics and new adversaries is essentially a great body of *experience,* not theories or untried ideals, but a solid mass of lived-through facts.

Equality before the law has been expanded and safeguarded by consultation and by representation—in other words, by the vote, which is not simply a device for peacefully changing government, although it is that too. It is not only a means of allowing the wearer to say where the shoe pinches. It is, in addition, a means of offsetting the natural inequalities that grow up in any society, however organized, as a result of the unequal endowment of people. The head of, say, General Electric has more means of influencing society than a small-town electrician. Against the advantage of brains and money, the vote is the only advantage the small man has. His voice, or vote, added to millions of other voices, offsets the accumulated power of society's entrenched positions. But equality before the law and the ballot box are only strands in the seamless robe in which all of our liberties are woven together; carelessly unravel one and the robe itself may come apart.

Another strand is enough social and economic opportunity for each man, even the poorest, to hold his dignity intact. The widest access to education and to training, equal opportunity for talent to find its niche, security of income and of work, the chance of health—all these belong to a social order of responsible and respected citizens. We no longer define democracy solely in political terms. The great effort in this century has been to work out its economic and social implications.

We are profoundly concerned with the extension of the concept of democracy—extension in depth, for we now believe that no human being, however lowly his occupation or poor his resources, can be excluded from the dignity of man; and extension in space, for the whole world is now a community, and we have to find ways in which the idea of a truly human society can be realized on a planetary scale. The two processes going forward simultaneously in every part of the globe make up the vast revolutionary ferment of our time. What we have to attempt today is the building of intercontinental forms of free community—certainly the most testing experiment of all those made so far by free men. Yet our past achievements give us the right to hope for future success.

One form of association already exists between virtually all the nations of the globe; and, whatever work we may accomplish on a regional basis, the progress at the United Nations in the direction of a free society of equals must be part of our effort to extend the principle of liberty as the essential working principle of mankind.

How are we to set about this formidable task? There is one method that I most profoundly hope we shall avoid, and that is the method of self-righteous exhortation. We have, I fear, displayed an unattractive tendency to lecture new governments on their constitutional shortcomings and to point sometimes openly, sometimes implicitly, to the superior performance of the West. We can proudly admit that free government is a Western invention—by all odds its finest political achievement. But there are several things we must remember as well. We must remember that it took about eight centuries to develop these patterns of life in our own culture. We must remember that our form of democracy is the most subtle, the most sophisticated form of government in the world. Other more primitive, still developing peoples cannot be expected to master it overnight, but move toward it they will; and such institutions as the United Nations help to train their leadership in our ways. Moreover, new states always face appalling problems of readjustment, and we must be smart enough to recognize when and how these alien leaderships move our way.

If now we see in Africa single-party rule, dominated by one leader, with changing policies and political choice severely restricted, we should not hold up our hands in horror, but rather remember that this is not far from our politics of two centuries ago. We might even have the modesty to admit that in Northern Ireland and in the American South, for example, we, too, practice single-party government.

Where we have every right to express our alarm, however, is in the breakdown of constitutional protection by the law. The danger lies not so much in parliamentary failure as in judicial failure. Yet, even here, our alarm should be expressed in modest terms. In eighteenth century England a man could be hanged for stealing a sheep, and horrible ships took convicts to Australia for no more than petty larceny. Nor was Europe's recent Fascist experiment precisely a law-abiding mode of government.

No, the way ahead does not lie through sermonizing carried on by people whose own eyes are too full of beams to judge clearly the others' motes. It lies, rather, in a sustained effort to work out within the United Nations and in international partnerships the chief lines of advance toward a more coherent, a more viable world community with freedom as its working principle and constitutionalism as its political habit. No one is likely to underestimate the appalling complexities of this task, but the outlook must have seemed as daunting to the lawyers struggling against Stuart despotism or to the Founding Fathers attempting to turn federalism into a workable system. The task is indeed "piled high with difficulty." We should attempt it, therefore, with all the more vigor and clarity, and I would suggest that the three criteria that I have stressed in domestic democracy are relevant too to the global democracy we painfully must try to build.

Today, the first of all tasks is to restrain the nation-states from taking the law into their own hands; in other words, from using force to assert its will, or, in the final word, from making war. From domestic society we know that the only way to banish lawless violence and fratricidal strife is by accepting rules of peaceful change and adjustment and building an impartial peace force to enforce the peaceful solutions that are agreed. This, I take it, to be a task of the United Nations. However, some of our vast modern states are still like the medieval barons, too powerful to be controlled in their feudal fastnesses. But perhaps we have reached a first stage of restraint on arbitrary power. Troubled areas—Palestine, the Congo, Laos—are policed not by rivals whose rivalry would lead to war, but by an external and impartial third force.

Could we not extend the principle? Could we not aim at the policing by the United Nations of more and more areas in which the rival interests of powerful states threaten to clash? Global systems of restraint may still evade us, but history suggests that we can start from the particular instance and then extend the principle, and every area withdrawn from the naked arbitrament of force is an area saved for the constitutional working of a sane human society.

Does the second principle I have picked out, the procedure of equal voting, apply to the building of a free world society? The critics say that the new states, holding the balance of power by means of their combined vote, drive the United Nations on toward ferocious extremes of anticolonialism and attempt to impose other imprudent policies on the great powers that must disrupt the whole organization. Meanwhile, the great foot the bill.

There is much to be said on this score. For the moment, let me say only that in world society the small nation—like the small man in domestic society—is most likely to be vulnerable. His equal voice, his capacity to unite it with other small voices, is a measure of protection against his inequality. We see the need for this countervailing power inside our states, so let us not be too quick to denounce it in the world at large.

There is a further reason for being cautious and patient about the workings inside the United Nations of the potential ex-colonial majority. If we turn to the third principle of democracy—equality of esteem, equal dignity, equal access to the social and economic possibilities of society—we find that the disproportions that distort true community inside our nations are present in world society, too. This Afro-Asian bloc—a misnomer, for, save on the colonial issue, there is no bloc—represents most of the world's most truly underprivileged peoples. If they cling to their United Nations status, the reason is that, as citizens of our planet, they have not yet much else to cling to. Pushed to the first outskirts of modernity by Western investment and trade, emancipated before they have received either the training or the powers of creating wealth that are needed for a modern society, they are caught between two worlds, the powerful, affluent expanding world of the developed "North" and the traditional, pretechnological, largely poor world of the underdeveloped "South."

This division in world society is a great obstacle to the expansion of the confidence and the community the world needs for a truly human society And it threatens to become worse if such experiments as the European Common Market or the Atlantic Community prove to be, vis-à-vis the less fortunate parts of the world, a rich man's club, exclusive in its commerce, its investments, its arrangements, and its interests. The gap exists. We must not make it worse.

What can we do? I would like to suggest two lines to follow if we in this generation are to make our full contribution to the advance of world democracy.

I know there is much dissatisfaction about economic assistance, about foreign aid, much feeling that it is wasted, that it never achieves a breakthrough, that it dribbles down thousands of unspecified drains and ratholes. Yet, just so did the Victorians talk about tax money devoted to lifting the standard of the very poor in early industrial society. There were the "good poor," who said "please" and "thank you" and touched their forelocks. Then there were the "bad poor," who kept coal in the bath tub. But over a couple of generations, it was the raising of all this unfortunate mass of humanity that turned Western society into the first social order in history in which everyone could expect something of an equal chance.

After ten years, we are only at the beginning of this experiment in international aid. We are learning greatly. We see the relevance of some policies, the supreme obstacles offered by others. We discriminate more. We are learning to be better givers.

Our second task is harder. It is harder for us than for any other member of the world's wealthy elite. It is to see that the last vestiges of discrimination inside our own society are speedily abolished. It is no use talking of ourselves as the "vanguard of freedom and of democracy" while any of our fellow Americans can be treated like a James Meredith at the University of Mississippi. Must we not, as lovers of freedom, and as, too often, self-styled prophets of the free way of life, sometimes lapse into a shamed silence when we even have to talk about social injustice let alone deal with it—one hundred years after the Emancipation Proclamation?

I must end as I began. The essence of democracy is the dignity of man. We shall create a free world order on no other basis. If we attack Communism—as we must—for its contempt for political dignity, we must as unrelentingly attack lapses in social dignity.

It sometimes seems to me as though running through all of the great issues of the day—the anticolonial revolution, the political contest with Communism, the unification of Europe, the clamor of poorer lands for advance—there runs the underlying desire for some lasting realization of the dignity of man, man with a measure of political autonomy, man with the economic elbowroom to live above the torturing doubts of food and of work, man with the dignity to look his neighbor in the face and to see a friend. Isolate the problems, measure their magnitude, measure our progress in dealing with them —and you have my answer to the question of what the prospects for democracy are around the world.

And this, I take it, is what the Center for the Study of Democratic Institutions is all about: The steady effort to discover the common good in democratic fashion, by assembling together persons from varied backgrounds, with diverse specialties and diverse competences for discussion and debate. The Center may be a pioneering effort, but its roots are sunk deep in the Academy of ancient Greece, the medieval university, the New England Town Meeting, and a long list of later devices to make democracy work: getting good men to think together, though not to think alike; bringing the cumulative wisdom of such persons to bear on present and emerging problems; and, through publications, broadcasts, and meetings, widening the circles of discussion and debate.

In these remarks I have quoted some moderns. I should like to close with a few words from an ancient. Plutarch wrote: "Only those persons who live in obedience to reason are worthy to be accounted free. Only they live as they will who have learned what they ought to will."

If there is no engraving over the door of the Center for the Study of Democratic Institutions, that quotation is worth considering.

NOTES ON THE CONTRIBUTORS

WILLIAM BENTON is Chairman of the Board and Publisher of Encyclopaedia Britannica, Inc. and U.S. Ambassador to UNESCO. Co-founder of Benton & Bowles, he has also been Vice-President of the University of Chicago and has held several government posts, including Assistant Secretary of State for Public Affairs, member of the Constitutional Conference for UNESCO, and Chairman of the U.S. UNESCO delegation at the Conferences in Paris and Mexico City. From 1949–52, he was Senator from Connecticut.

ADOLF A. BERLE, JR., practices law in New York. He has been Professor of Law at Columbia University, Assistant Secretary of State, and Ambassador to Brazil. He has written *Studies in Corporation Finance, The Modern Corporation and Private Property,* and *The 20th Century Capitalist Revolution.*

BARRY BINGHAM has been associated with the Louisville *Courier-Journal* and *Times* since 1930, as reporter, secretary, associate publisher, publisher, president, and editor-in-chief. He is a member of the Pulitzer Prize advisory board.

HARRISON BROWN is Professor of Geochemistry at the California Institute of Technology, where he has been associated since 1946. Formerly he served as Assistant Director of Chemistry at Clinton Labs at Oak Ridge and participated in the plutonium project at the University of Chicago. He has written *The Challenge of Man's Future* and *The Next Hundred Years.* He is an editor-at-large for the *Saturday Review* and a Consultant to the Center for the Study of Democratic Institutions.

ARTHUR F. BURNS is now President of the National Bureau of Economic Research, where he has been associated since 1930. During this period, he has also been on the staffs of Rutgers and Columbia universities and served on various government assignments, including the President's Council of Economic Advisers, the Advisory Board on Economic Growth and Stability, and the President's Advisory Committee on Labor and Management Policy. He has written *Economic Resources and the Keynesian Thinking of Our Times, The Frontier of Economic Knowledge,* and *Prosperity Without Inflation* (with W. C. Mitchell).

JOSEPH S. CLARK has been a U.S. Senator since 1957. Mayor of Philadelphia from 1952–56 and City Controller from 1949–51, he had previously practiced law in Philadelphia.

LORD FRANCIS-WILLIAMS is an author, broadcaster, and journalist who has been on the staff of various newspapers and held various government posts connected with communications. His books include *Plan for Peace, No Man Is an Island, Transmitting News: A Study of Telecommunication and the Press,* and *Dangerous Estate: The Anatomy of Newspapers.*

CHARLES FRANKEL is Professor of Philosophy at Columbia University. His books include *The Faith of Reason.*

J. WILLIAM FULBRIGHT has been in Congress since 1943. Before that time he had been President and Lecturer in Law at the University of Arkansas and Instructor in Law at George Washington University.

VISCOUNT HAILSHAM is Minister for Science of the United Kingdom. He has held many posts in the British Government, including Under-Secretary to the Air Ministry, First Lord of the Admiralty, Privy Counsellor, Minister of Education, Lord President of the Council, Chairman of the Conservative Party, Lord Privy Seal, and Leader of the House of Lords. His writings include *The Law of Arbitration, Making Peace,* and *The Purpose of Parliament.*

ROBERT L. HEILBRONER's first book, *The Worldly Philosophers,* has become a standard introduction to economic history for college courses. His articles about economics and social affairs have appeared in many magazines, and he has lectured widely, including courses at the New School for Social Research. Other books are *The Future as History, The Great Economist,* and *The Making of Economic Society.*

ROBERT M. HUTCHINS, President of The Fund for the Republic, Inc., was formerly Associate Director of the Ford Foundation. He is also Chairman of the Board of Editors of Encyclopaedia Britannica, Inc. Mr. Hutchins was President and Chancellor of the University of Chicago for twenty-two years after a period as Dean of the Yale Law School. He has written *No Friendly Voice, The Conflict in Education,* and *Some Observations on American Education.*

LORD JAMES OF RUSHOLME is Vice-Chancellor of the University of York. He was High Master of the Manchester Grammar School from 1945 to 1962, and has been a member of the University Grants Committee and Central Advisory Council on Education. His writings include *Science and Education* (in part), *An Essay on the Content of Education, Education and Leadership,* and numerous papers in scientific and educational fields.

SOL M. LINOWITZ has been associated with the law firm of Harris, Beach, Keating, Wilcox, Dale & Linowitz in Rochester, New York, since 1958. He is Chairman of the Board of the Xerox Corporation.

PIERRE MENDÈS-FRANCE has been active in the government of France since 1932. He was tried by the Vichy Administration in 1940 and escaped to serve with the Fighting French Air Force. Subsequently, he was Finance Minister with the French Provisional Government, Head of the French Finance Missions at Washington and Bretton Woods, and Minister of National Economics before becoming Prime Minister in 1954–55.

NEWTON N. MINOW resigned as Chairman of the Federal Communications Commission in May, 1963, to join Encyclopaedia Britannica, Inc. Before 1961, he had been a partner in the Chicago law firm of Stevenson, Rifkind & Wirtz and Administrative Assistant to Governor Adlai E. Stevenson.

LEWIS MUMFORD is President of the American Academy of Arts and Letters. He has been Professor of City and Regional Planning at the University of Pennsylvania and Visiting Professor at MIT. His books include *Sticks and Stones, The Brown Decades, Technics and Civilization, The Culture of Cities,* and *The City in History.*

JOHN COURTNEY MURRAY, S.J., is Professor of Philosophy at Woodstock College, where he has been associated since 1937. He has been Visiting

Professor at Yale on medieval philosophy and culture and Lecturer and member of the advisory board for the Committee on International Relations at Notre Dame. He is editor of *Theological Studies* and has written many articles in theological and secular periodicals, as well as the book *We Hold These Truths*. He is a Consultant to the Center for the Study of Democratic Institutions.

GUNNAR MYRDAL has been associated with Stockholm University since 1927. He has served as a government adviser on financial, social, and economic questions, as well as Minister of Trade and Commerce and Executive Secretary of the UN Economic Commission for Europe. His books include *The Cost of Living in Sweden, 1830–1930; Population: A Problem for Democracy; An American Dilemma: The Negro Problem and Modern Democracy;* and *Value in Social Theory*.

ROSEMARY PARK became President of Barnard College in 1962. Until assuming that post, she had been associated with Wheaton College since 1935 in the capacities of Professor of German, Dean, and President. She has served on many state and national advisory committees.

GERARD PIEL is publisher of *Scientific American*. He has been with the magazine since 1947. Previously, he was science editor for *Life* magazine.

EDWARD REED, editor of this book, is Director of Publications of the Center for the Study of Democratic Institutions. He has been associated with the Fund for the Republic since 1954. A graduate of Princeton, he has been an editor of several magazines.

WALTER REUTHER is President of the United Auto Workers and Vice-President of the AFL-CIO. He organized the auto workers in 1935, having started his career as an apprentice tool and die maker at General Motors and Ford in Detroit.

HYMAN G. RICKOVER is Chief of the Naval Reactors Branch of the Atomic Energy Commission. He has been associated with the atomic submarine project since its inception. His writings include *Education and Freedom*.

ADOLPH W. SCHMIDT is Vice-President and Governor of T. Mellon & Sons. Until he joined that organization in 1946, he was associated with various banks in Pittsburgh. He has frequently served on advisory boards for Pennsylvania affairs.

ADLAI E. STEVENSON is U.S. Representative to the United Nations. Governor of Illinois from 1949–53, he has also held posts in the Department of the Navy, the Department of State, and served as chief U.S. delegate to the Preparatory Commission of the United Nations in London in 1945.

ROBERT C. WEAVER, Administrator of the Housing and Home Finance Agency, has held posts in the Department of the Interior, U.S. Housing Authority, and New York housing agencies since 1933. He has also taught at Teachers College, Columbia University, and New York University and been associated with the John Hay Whitney Foundation.

SYLVESTER L. WEAVER, JR., is President of McCann-Erickson Productions. He has long served in the fields of television, radio, and advertising. In recent years, he has been Chairman of the Board of the National Broadcasting Company and marketing and advertising consultant to Kaiser Industries.

W. WILLARD WIRTZ, Secretary of Labor, has practiced law and been active in government agencies, including the War Labor Board and the National Wage Stabilization Board. He was a member of the Advisory Committee to the Trade Union Study of the Center for the Study of Democratic Institutions.

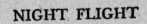

NIGHT FLIGHT

NIGHT
FLIGHT

by
Antoine de Saint-Exupéry

Preface by André Gide

Translated by Stuart Gilbert

TRIANGLE BOOKS

NEW YORK

TRIANGLE BOOKS, 14 West Forty-ninth Street,
New York, N. Y.

PRINTED AND BOUND IN THE UNITED STATES OF AMERICA
BY THE AMERICAN BOOK—STRATFORD PRESS, INC., N. Y. C.

PREFACE

The *sine qua non* for the air-line companies was to compete in speed with all other systems of transport. In the course of this book Rivière, that leader to the manner born, sums up the issues. "It is a matter of life and death for us; for the lead we gain by day on ships and railways is lost each night." This night service—much criticized at the start but subsequently, once the experimental stage was over, accepted as a practical proposition—still involved at the time of this narrative considerable risks. For to the impalpable perils of all air-routes and their manifold surprises accrued the night's dark treachery. I hasten to add that, great though these risks still are, they are growing daily less, for each successive trip facilitates and improves the prospects of the next one. Aviation, like the exploration of uncharted lands, has its early heroic age and "Night Flight," which describes the tragic adventure of one of these pioneers of the air, sounds, naturally enough, the authentic epic note.

Much as I liked Saint Exupéry's first book, I prefer this one by far. In his "Courrier Sud" there runs, through the experiences of an aviator described with vivid exactitude, a vein of sentiment which brings the hero nearer to ourselves. How human we feel him to be, how tenderhearted, and how vulnerable! But the hero of "Night Flight," though human through and through, rises to superhuman heights of valor. The quality which I think delights one most of all in this stirring narrative is its nobility. Too well we know man's failings, his cowardice and lapses, and our writers of to-day are only too proficient in exposing these; but we stood in need of one to tell us how a man may be lifted far above himself by his sheer force of will.

More striking even than the aviator himself is, in my opinion, Rivière, his chief. The latter does not act, himself; he impels to action, breathes into his pilots his own virtue and exacts the utmost from them, constraining them to dare greatly. His iron will admits no flinching, and the least lapse is punished by him. At first sight his severity may seem inhuman and excessive. But its target is not the man himself, whom Rivière aspires to mold, but the man's blemishes. In his portrayal of this character we feel the author's profound admiration. I am especially grateful to him for bringing out a paradoxical truth which seems to me of great psychological import; that man's happiness lies not in freedom but in his acceptance of a duty. Each of the characters in this book is whole-heartedly, passionately devoted to that which duty bids him do, and it is in fulfilling this perilous task, and only thus, that he attains contentedness and peace. Reading between the lines we discover that Rivière is anything but insensitive (the narrative of his interview with the wife of the lost pilot is infinitely touching) and he needs quite as much courage to give his orders as the pilots need to carry them out.

"To make oneself beloved," he says, "one need only show pity. I show little pity, or I hide it. . . . My power sometimes amazes me." And, again: "Love the men under your orders, but do not let them know it."

A sense of duty commands Rivière in all things, "the dark sense of duty, greater than that of love." Man is not to seek an end within himself but to submit and sacrifice his all to some strange thing that commands him and lives through him. It pleases me here to find that selfsame "dark sense" which inspired my Prometheus to his paradox: "Man I love not; I love that which devours him." This is the mainspring of every act of heroism. " 'We behave,' thought Rivière, 'as if there were something of higher value than human life. . . . But what thing?' " And again: "There is perhaps something else, something more lasting, to be saved; and perhaps it was to save this part of man that Rivière was working." A true saying.

In an age when the idea of heroism seems likely to quit the army, since manly virtues may play no part in those future wars whose horrors are foreshadowed by our scientists, does not aviation provide the most admirable and worthy field for the display of prowess? What would otherwise be rashness ceases to be such when it is part and parcel of an allotted task. The pilot who is forever risking his life may well smile at the current meaning we give to "courage." I trust that Saint Exupéry will permit me to quote an old letter of his dating from the time when he was flying on the Casablanca-Dakar air-route.

"I don't know when I shall be back, I have had so much to do for several months, searches for lost airmen, salvage of planes that have come down in hostile territory, and some flights with the Dakar mail.

"I have just pulled off a little exploit; spent two days and nights with eleven Moors and a mechanic, salving a plane. Alarums and excursions, varied and impressive. I heard bullets whizzing over my head for the first time. So now I know how I behave under such conditions; much more calmly than the Moors. But I also came to understand something which had always puzzled me—why Plato (Aristotle?) places courage in the last degree of virtues. It's a concoction of feelings that are not so very admirable. A touch of anger, a spice of vanity, a lot of obstinacy and a tawdry 'sporting' thrill. Above all, a stimulation of one's physical energies, which, however, is oddly out of place. One just folds one's arms, taking deep breaths, across one's opened shirt. Rather a pleasant feeling. When it happens at night another feeling creeps into it—of having done something immensely silly. I shall never again admire a merely brave man."

By way of epigraph I might append to

this quotation an aphorism from Quinton's book (which, however, I cannot commend without reserve). "A man keeps, like his love, his courage dark." Or, better still: "Brave men hide their deeds as decent folk their alms. They disguise them or make excuses for them."

Saint Exupéry in all he tells us speaks as one who has "been through it." His personal contact with ever-recurrent danger seasons his book with an authentic and inimitable tang. We have had many stories of the War or of imaginary adventures which, if they showed the author as a man of nimble wit, brought smiles to the faces of such old soldiers or genuine adventurers as read them. I admire this work not only on its literary merits but for its value as a record of realities, and it is the unlikely combination of these two qualities which gives "Night Flight" its quite exceptional importance.

ANDRÉ GIDE

CONTENTS

xiii

CONTENTS

xiv

CONTENTS

XV

I

ALREADY, BENEATH HIM, THROUGH THE GOLDEN EVENING—

NIGHT FLIGHT

I

ALREADY, beneath him, through the golden
evening, the shadowed hills had dug their
furrows and the plains grew luminous with
long-enduring light. For in these lands the
ground gives off this golden glow persist-
ently, just as, even when winter goes, the
whiteness of the snow persists.

Fabien, the pilot bringing the Patagonia
air-mail from the far south to Buenos Aires,
could mark night coming on by certain
signs that called to mind the waters of a
harbor—a calm expanse beneath, faintly
rippled by the lazy clouds—and he seemed
to be entering a vast anchorage, an immen-
sity of blessedness.

Or else he might have fancied he was taking a quiet walk in the calm of evening, almost like a shepherd. The Patagonian shepherds move, unhurried, from one flock to another; and he, too, moved from one town to another, the shepherd of those little towns. Every two hours he met another of them, drinking at its riverside or browsing on its plain.

Sometimes, after a hundred miles of steppes as desolate as the sea, he encountered a lonely farm-house that seemed to be sailing backwards from him in a great prairie sea, with its freight of human lives; and he saluted with his wings this passing ship.

"San Julian in sight. In ten minutes we shall land."

The wireless operator gave their position to all the stations on the line. From Magellan Strait to Buenos Aires the airports were strung out across fifteen hundred miles and more, but this one led toward the frontiers

4

of night, just as in Africa the last conquered hamlet opens on to the unknown.

The wireless operator handed the pilot a slip of paper: "There are so many storms about that the discharges are fouling my ear-phones. Shall we stop the night at San Julian?"

Fabien smiled; the sky was calm as an aquarium and all the stations ahead were signaling, *Clear sky: no wind.*

"No, we'll go on."

But the wireless operator was thinking: these storms had lodged themselves somewhere or other, as worms do in a fruit; a fine night, but they would ruin it, and he loathed entering this shadow that was ripe to rottenness.

As he slowed down his engine for the San Julian landing, Fabien knew that he was tired. All that endeared his life to man was looming up to meet him; men's houses, friendly little cafés, trees under which they walk. He was like some conqueror who, in the aftermath of victory, bends down upon his territories and now perceives the humble happiness of men. A need came over Fabien to lay his weapons down and feel the aching burden of his limbs—for even our misfortunes are a part of our belongings—and to stay, a simple dweller here, watching from his window a scene that would never change. This tiny village, he could gladly have made friends with it; the choice once made, a man accepts the issue of his venture and can love the life. Like love, it hems him in. Fabien would have wished to live a long while here—here to possess his morsel of eternity. These little towns, where he lived an hour, their gardens girdled by old walls over which he passed, seemed something apart and everlasting. Now the village was rising to meet the plane, opening out toward him. And there, he mused, were friendliness and gentle girls, white napery spread in quiet homes; all that is slowly shaped toward eternity. The village streamed past beneath his

6

wings, yielding the secrets of closed gardens that their walls no longer guarded. He landed; and now he knew that he had seen nothing at all, only a few men slowly moving amongst their stones. The village kept, by its mere immobility, the secret of its passions and withheld its kindly charm; for, to master that, he would have needed to give up an active life.

The ten minutes' halt was ended and Fabien resumed his flight. He glanced back toward San Julian; all he now could see was a cluster of lights, then stars, then twinkling star-dust that vanished, tempting him for the last time.

"I can't see the dials; I'll light up."

He touched the switches, but the red light falling from the cockpit lamps upon the dial-hands was so diluted with the blue evening glow that they did not catch its color. When he passed his fingers close before a bulb, they were hardly tinged at all.

"Too soon."

But night was rising like a tawny smoke

and already the valleys were brimming over with it. No longer were they distinguishable from the plains. The villages were lighting up, constellations that greeted each other across the dusk. And, at a touch of his finger, his flying-lights flashed back a greeting to them. The earth grew spangled with light-signals as each house lit its star, searching the vastness of the night as a lighthouse sweeps the sea. Now every place that sheltered human life was sparkling. And it rejoiced him to enter into this one night with a measured slowness, as into an anchorage.

He bent down into the cockpit; the luminous dial-hands were beginning to show up. The pilot read their figures one by one; all was going well. He felt at ease up here, snugly ensconced. He passed his fingers along a steel rib and felt the stream of life that flowed in it; the metal did not vibrate, yet it was alive. The engine's five-hundred horse-power bred in its texture a very gentle current, fraying its ice-cold rind into a velvety bloom. Once again the pilot in full flight experienced neither giddiness nor any thrill; only the mystery of metal turned to living flesh.

So he had found his world again. . . . A few digs of his elbow, and he was quite at home. He tapped the dashboard, touched the contacts one by one, shifting his limbs a little, and, settling himself more solidly, felt for the best position whence to gage the faintest lurch of his five tons of metal, jostled by the heaving darkness. Groping with his fingers, he plugged in his emergency-lamp, let go of it, felt for it again, made sure it held; then lightly touched each switch, to be certain of finding it later, training his hands to function in a blind man's world. Now that his hands had learnt their rôle by heart, he ventured to turn on a lamp, making the cockpit bright with polished fittings and then, as on a submarine about to dive, watched his passage into night upon the dials only. Nothing shook or rattled, neither gyroscope nor altimeter flickered in the least, the engine was running smoothly; so now he relaxed his limbs a little, let his neck sink back into the leather padding and fell into the deeply meditative mood of flight, mellow with inexplicable hopes.

Now, a watchman from the heart of night, he learnt how night betrays man's presence, his voices, lights, and his unrest. That star down there in the shadows, alone; a lonely house. Yonder a fading star; that house is closing in upon its love. . . . Or on its lassitude. A house that has ceased to flash its signal to the world. Gathered round their lamp-lit table, those peasants do not know the measure of their hopes; they do not guess that their desire carries so far, out into the vastness of the night that hems them in. But Fabien has met it on his path, when, coming from a thousand miles away, he feels the heavy ground-swell raise his panting plane and let it sink, when he has crossed a dozen storms like lands at war, between them neutral tracts of moonlight, to reach at last those lights, one following the other—and knows himself a conqueror. They think, these peasants, that their lamp shines only for that little table; but, from fifty miles away, some one has felt the summons of their light, as though it were a desperate signal from some lonely island, flashed by shipwrecked men toward the sea.

II

THUS THE THREE PLANES OF THE AIR-MAIL SERVICE—

II

THUS the three planes of the air-mail service, from Patagonia, Chile, and Paraguay, were converging from south, west, and north on Buenos Aires. Their arrival with the mails would give the signal for the departure, about midnight, of the Europe postal plane.

Three pilots, each behind a cowling heavy as a river-barge, intent upon his flight, were hastening through the distant darkness, soon to come slowly down, from a sky of storm or calm, like wild, outlandish peasants descending from their highlands.

Rivière, who was responsible for the entire service, was pacing to and fro on the Buenos Aires landing-ground. He was in silent mood, for, till the three planes had come in, he could not shake off a feeling of apprehension which had been haunting him all day. Minute by minute, as the telegrams were passed to him, Rivière felt that he had scored another point against fate, reduced the quantum of the unknown, and was drawing his charges in, out of the clutches of the night, toward their haven.

One of the hands came up to Rivière with a radio message.

"Chile mail reports: Buenos Aires in sight."

"Good."

Presently, then, Rivière would hear its drone; already the night was yielding up one of them, as a sea, heavy with its secrets and the cadence of the tides, surrenders to the shore a treasure long the plaything of the waves. And soon the night would give him back the other two.

Then to-day's work would be over. Worn out, the crews would go to sleep, fresh crews replace them. Rivière alone would have no respite; then, in its turn, the Europe mail would weigh upon his mind. And so it would always be. Always. For the

16

first time in his life this veteran fighter caught himself feeling tired. Never could an arrival of the planes mean for him the victory that ends a war and preludes a spell of smiling peace. For him it meant just one more step, with a thousand more to follow, along a straight, unending road. Rivière felt as though for an eternity he had been carrying a crushing load on his uplifted arms; an endless, hopeless effort.

"I'm aging." If he no longer found a solace in work and work alone, surely he was growing old. He caught himself puzzling over problems which hitherto he had ignored. There surged within his mind, like a lost ocean, murmuring regrets, all the gentler joys of life that he had thrust aside. "Can it be coming on me—so soon?" He realized that he had always been postponing for his declining years, "when I have time for it," everything that makes life kind to men. As if it were ever possible to "have time for it" one day and realize at life's end that dream of peace and happiness! No, peace there could be none; nor any victory, perhaps. Never could all the air-mails land in one swoop once for all.

Rivière paused before Leroux; the old foreman was hard at work. Leroux, too, had forty years of work behind him. All his energies were for his work. When at ten o'clock or midnight Leroux went home it certainly was not to find a change of scene, escape into another world. When Rivière smiled toward him, he raised his heavy head and pointed at a burnt-out axle. "Jammed it was, but I've fixed it up." Rivière bent down to look; duty had regained its hold upon him. "You should tell the shop to set them a bit looser." He passed his finger over the trace of seizing, then glanced again at Leroux. As his eyes lingered on the stern old wrinkled face, an odd question hovered on his lips and made him smile.

"Ever had much to do with love, Leroux, in your time?"

"Love, sir? Well, you see—"

"Hadn't the time for it, I suppose—like me."

"Not a great deal, sir."

Rivière strained his ears to hear if there were any bitterness in the reply; no, not a trace of it. This man, looking back on life, felt the quiet satisfaction of a carpenter who has made a good job of planing down a board: "There you are! *That's* done."

"There you are," thought Rivière. "My life's done."

Then, brushing aside the swarm of somber thoughts his weariness had brought, he walked toward the hangar; for the Chile plane was droning down toward it.

III

THE SOUND OF THE DISTANT ENGINE SWELLED AND THICKENED—

III

THE sound of the distant engine swelled
and thickened; a sound of ripening. Lights
flashed out. The red lamps on the light-
tower silhouetted a hangar, radio standards,
a square landing-ground. The setting of a
gala night.

"There she comes!"

A sheaf of beams had caught the ground-
ing plane, making it shine as if brand-new.
No sooner had it come to rest before the
hangar than mechanics and airdrome hands
hurried up to unload the mail. Only Pellerin, the pilot, did not move.

"Well, aren't you going to get down?"

The pilot, intent on some mysterious
task, did not deign to reply. Listening, perhaps, to sounds that he alone could hear,
long echoes of the flight. Nodding reflec-
tively, he bent down and tinkered with

some unseen object. At last he turned toward the officials and his comrades, gravely taking stock of them as though of his possessions. He seemed to pass them in review, to weigh them, take their measure, saying to himself that he had earned his right to them, as to this hangar with its gala lights and solid concrete and, in the offing, the city, full of movement, warmth, and women. In the hollow of his large hands he seemed to hold this folk; they were his subjects, to touch or hear or curse, as the fancy took him. His impulse now was to curse them for a lazy crowd, so sure of life they seemed, gaping at the moon; but he decided to be genial instead.

". . . Drinks are on you!"

Then he climbed down.

He wanted to tell them about the trip.

"If only you knew . . . !"

Evidently, to his thinking, that summed it up, for now he walked off to change his flying gear.

As the car was taking him to Buenos Aires in the company of a morose inspector and Rivière in silent mood, Pellerin suddenly felt sad; of course, he thought, it's a fine thing for a fellow to have gone through it and, when he's got his footing again, let off a healthy volley of curses. Nothing finer in the world! But afterwards . . . when you look back on it all; you wonder, you aren't half so sure!

A struggle with a cyclone, that at least is a straight fight, it's *real*. But not that curious look things wear, the face they have when they think they are alone. His thoughts took form. "Like a revolution it is; men's faces turning only the least shade paler, yet utterly unlike themselves."

He bent his mind toward the memory.

He had been crossing peacefully the Cordillera of the Andes. A snow-bound stillness brooded on the ranges; the winter snow had brought its peace to all this vastness, as in dead castles the passing centuries

25

spread peace. Two hundred miles without a man, a breath of life, a movement; only sheer peaks that, flying at twenty thousand feet, you almost graze, straight-falling cloaks of stone, an ominous tranquillity.

It had happened somewhere near the Tupungato Peak. . . .

He reflected. . . . Yes, it was there he saw a miracle take place.

For at first he had noticed nothing much, felt no more than a vague uneasiness—as when a man believes himself alone, but is not; some one is watching him. Too late, and how he could not comprehend, he realized that he was hemmed in by anger. Where was it coming from, this anger? What told him it was oozing from the stones, sweating from the snow? For nothing seemed on its way to him, no storm was lowering. And still—another world, like it and yet unlike, was issuing from the world around him. Now all those quiet-looking peaks, snow-caps, and ridges, growing faintly grayer, seemed to spring to life, a people of the snows. And an inexplicable anguish gripped his heart.

Instinctively he tightened his grasp on the controls. Something he did not understand was on its way and he tautened his muscles, like a beast about to spring. Yet, as far as eye could see, all was at peace. Peaceful, yes, but tense with some dark potency.

Suddenly all grew sharp; peaks and ridges seemed keen-edged prows cutting athwart a heavy head wind. Veering around him, they deployed like dreadnoughts taking their positions in a battle-line. Dust began to mingle with the air, rising and hovering, a veil above the snow. Looking back to see if retreat might still be feasible, he shuddered; all the Cordillera behind him was in seething ferment.

"I'm lost!"

On a peak ahead of him the snow swirled up into the air—a snow volcano. Upon his right flared up another peak and, one by one, all the summits grew lambent with gray fire, as if some unseen messenger had touched them into flame. Then the first squall broke and all the mountains round the pilot quivered.

Violent action leaves little trace behind it and he had no recollection of the gusts that buffeted him then from side to side. Only one clear memory remained; the battle in a welter of gray flames.

He pondered.

"A cyclone, that's nothing. A man just saves his skin! It's what comes before it— the thing one meets upon the way!"

But already, even as he thought he had recalled it, that one face in a thousand, he had forgotten what it was like.

IV

RIVIÈRE GLANCED AT THE PILOT.

IV

RIVIÈRE glanced at the pilot. In twenty minutes Pellerin would step from the car, mingle with the crowd, and know the burden of his lassitude. Perhaps he would murmur: "Tired out as usual. It's a dog's life!" To his wife he would, perhaps, let fall a word or two: "A fellow's better off here than flying above the Andes!" And yet that world to which men hold so strongly had almost slipped from him; he had come to know its wretchedness. He had returned from a few hours' life on the other side of the picture, ignoring if it would be possible for him ever to retrieve this city with its lights, ever to know again his little human frailties, irksome yet cherished childhood friends.

"In every crowd," Rivière mused, "are certain persons who seem just like the rest, yet they bear amazing messages. Unwittingly, no doubt, unless—" Rivière was chary of a certain type of admirers, blind to the higher side of this adventure, whose vain applause perverted its meaning, debased its human dignity. But Pellerin's inalienable greatness lay in this—his simple yet sure awareness of what the world, seen from a special angle, signified, his massive scorn of vulgar flattery. So Rivière congratulated him: "Well, how did you bring it off?" And loved him for his knack of only "talking shop," referring to his flight as a blacksmith to his anvil.

Pellerin began by telling how his retreat had been cut off. It was almost as if he were apologizing about it. "There was nothing else for it!" Then he had lost sight of everything, blinded by the snow. He owed his escape to the violent air-currents which had driven him up to twenty-five thousand feet. "I guess they held me all the way just above the level of the peaks." He mentioned his trouble with the gyroscope and how he had had to shift the air-inlet, as the snow was clogging it; "forming a frost-glaze, you see." After that another set of air-currents had driven Pellerin down and, when he was only at ten thousand feet or so, he was puzzled why he had not run into anything. As a matter of fact he was already above the plains. "I spotted it all of a sudden when I came out into a clear patch." And he explained how it had felt at that moment; just as if he had escaped from a cave.

"Storm at Mendoza, too?"

"No. The sky was clear when I made my landing, not a breath of wind. But the storm was at my heels all right!"

It was such a damned queer business, he said; that was why he mentioned it. The summits were lost in snow at a great height while the lower slopes seemed to be streaming out across the plain, like a flood of black lava which swallowed up the villages one by one. "Never saw anything like it before. . . ." Then he relapsed into silence, gripped by some secret memory.

Rivière turned to the inspector.

"That's a Pacific cyclone; it's too late to take any action now. Anyhow these cyclones never cross the Andes."

No one could have foreseen that this particular cyclone would continue its advance toward the east.

The inspector, who had no ideas on the subject, assented.

The inspector seemed about to speak. Then he hesitated, turned toward Pellerin, and his Adam's apple stirred. But he held his peace and, after a moment's thought, resumed his air of melancholy dignity, looking straight before him.

That melancholy of his, he carried it about with him everywhere, like a hand-bag. No sooner had he landed in Argentina than Rivière had appointed him to certain vague functions, and now his large hands and inspectorial dignity got always in his way. He had no right to admire imagination or ready wit; it was his business to

34

commend punctuality and punctuality alone. He had no right to take a glass of wine in company, to call a comrade by his Christian name or risk a joke; unless, of course, by some rare chance, he came across another inspector on the same run.

"It's hard luck," he thought, "always having to be a judge."

As a matter of fact he never judged; he merely wagged his head. To mask his utter ignorance he would slowly, thoughtfully, wag his head at everything that came his way, a movement that struck fear into uneasy consciences and ensured the proper upkeep of the plant.

He was not beloved—but then inspectors are not made for love and such delights, only for drawing up reports. He had desisted from proposing changes of system or technical improvements since Rivière had written: *Inspector Robineau is requested to supply reports, not poems. He will be putting his talents to better use by speeding up the personnel.* From that day forth

Inspector Robineau had battened on human frailties, as on his daily bread; on the mechanic who had a glass too much, the airport overseer who stayed up of nights, the pilot who bumped a landing.

Rivière said of him: "He is far from intelligent, but very useful to us, such as he is." One of the rules which Rivière rigorously imposed—upon himself—was a knowledge of his men. For Robineau the only knowledge that counted was knowledge of the *orders*.

"Robineau," Rivière had said one day, "you must cut the punctuality bonus whenever a plane starts late."

"Even when it's nobody's fault? In case of fog, for instance?"

"Even in case of fog."

Robineau felt a thrill of pride in knowing that his chief was strong enough not to shrink from being unjust. Surely Robineau himself would win reflected majesty from such overweening power!

"You postponed the start till six fifteen,"

36

he would say to the airport superintendents. "We cannot allow your bonus."

"But, Monsieur Robineau, at five thirty one couldn't see ten yards ahead!"

"Those are the *orders*."

"But, Monsieur Robineau, we couldn't sweep the fog away with a broom!"

He alone amongst all these nonentities knew the secret; if you only punish men enough, the weather will improve!

"He never thinks at all," said Rivière of him, "and that prevents him from thinking wrong."

The pilot who damaged a plane lost his no-accident bonus.

"But supposing his engine gives out when he is over a wood?" Robineau inquired of his chief.

"Even when it occurs above a wood."

Robineau took to heart the *ipse dixit*.

"I regret," he would inform the pilots with cheerful zest, "I regret it very much indeed, but you should have had your breakdown somewhere else."

"But, Monsieur Robineau, one doesn't choose the place to have it."

"Those are the orders."

The orders, thought Rivière, are like the rites of a religion; they may look absurd but they shape men in their mold. It was no concern to Rivière whether he seemed just or unjust. Perhaps the words were meaningless to him. The little townsfolk of the little towns promenade each evening round a bandstand and Rivière thought: It's nonsense to talk of being just or unjust toward them; they don't exist.

For him, a man was a mere lump of wax to be kneaded into shape. It was his task to furnish this dead matter with a soul, to inject will-power into it. Not that he wished to make slaves of his men; his aim was to raise them above themselves. In punishing them for each delay he acted, no doubt, unjustly, but he bent the will of every crew to punctual departure; or, rather, he bred in them the will to keep to time. Denying his men the right to welcome foggy weather as the pretext for a leisure hour, he kept them so breathlessly eager for the fog to lift that even the humblest mechanic felt a twinge of shame for the delay. Thus they were quick to profit by the least rift in the armor of the skies.

"An opening on the north; let's be off!"

Thanks to Rivière the service of the mails was paramount over twenty thousand miles of land and sea.

"The men are happy," he would say, "because they like their work, and they like it because I am hard."

And hard he may have been—still he gave his men keen pleasure for all that. "They need," he would say to himself, "to be urged on toward a hardy life, with its sufferings and its joys; only that matters."

As the car approached the city, Rivière instructed the driver to take him to the Head Office. Presently Robineau found himself alone with Pellerin and a question shaped itself upon his lips.

V

ROBINEAU WAS FEELING TIRED TO-NIGHT.

V

ROBINEAU was feeling tired to-night. Looking at Pellerin—Pellerin the Conqueror—he had just discovered that his own life was a gray one. Worst of all, he was coming to realize that, for all his rank of inspector and authority, he, Robineau, cut a poor figure beside this travel-stained and weary pilot, crouching in a corner of the car, his eyes closed and hands all grimed with oil. For the first time, Robineau was learning to admire. A need to speak of this came over him and, above all, to make a friend.

He was tired of his journey and the day's rebuffs and felt perhaps a little ridiculous. That very evening, when verifying the gasoline reserve, he had botched his figures and the agent, whom he had wanted to catch out, had taken compassion and totted them up for him. What was worse, he had commented on the fitting of a Model B.6 oil-pump, mistaking it for the B.4 type, and the mechanics with ironic smiles had let him maunder on for twenty minutes about this "inexcusable stupidity"—his own stupidity.

He dreaded his room at the hotel. From Toulouse to Buenos Aires, straight to his room he always went once the day's work was over. Safely ensconced and darkly conscious of the secrets he carried in his breast, he would draw from his bag a sheet of paper and slowly inscribe *Report* on it, write a line or two at random, then tear it up. He would have liked to save the company from some tremendous peril; but it was not in any danger. All he had saved so far was a slightly rusted propeller-boss. He had slowly passed his finger over the rust with a mournful air, eyed by an airport overseer, whose only comment was: "Better call up the last halt; this plane's only just

44

in." Robineau was losing confidence in himself.

At a venture he essayed a friendly move. "Would you care to dine with me?" he asked Pellerin. "I'd enjoy a quiet chat; my job's pretty exhausting at times."

Then, reluctant to quit his pedestal too soon, he added: "The responsibility, you know."

His subordinates did not much relish the idea of intimacy with Robineau; it had its dangers. "If he's not dug up something for his report, with an appetite like his, I guess he'll just eat me up!"

But Robineau's mind this evening was full of his personal afflictions. He suffered from an annoying eczema, his only real secret; he would have liked to talk about his trouble, to be pitied and, now that pride had played him false, find solace in humility. Then again there was his mistress over there in France, who had to hear the nightly tale of his inspections whenever he

45

returned. He hoped to impress her thus and earn her love but—his usual luck!—he only seemed to aggravate her. He wanted to talk about her, too.

"So you'll come to dinner?"

Good-naturedly Pellerin assented.

VI

THE CLERKS WERE DROWSING IN THE BUENOS AIRES OFFICE—

VI

THE clerks were drowsing in the Buenos Aires office when Rivière entered. He had kept his overcoat and hat on, like the incessant traveler he always seemed to be. His spare person took up so little room, his clothes and graying hair so aptly fitted into any scene, that when he went by hardly any one noticed it. Yet, at his entry, a wave of energy traversed the office. The staff bustled, the head clerk hurriedly compiled the papers remaining on his desk, typewriters began to click.

The telephonist was busily slipping his plugs into the standard and noting the telegrams in a bulky register. Rivière sat down and read them.

All that he read, the Chile episode excepted, told of one of those favored days when things go right of themselves and each

49

successive message from the airports is another bulletin of victory. The Patagonia mail, too, was making headway; all the planes were ahead of time, for fair winds were bearing them northward on a favoring tide.

"Give me the weather reports."

Each airport vaunted its fine weather, clear sky, and clement breeze. The mantle of a golden evening had fallen on South America. And Rivière welcomed this friendliness of things. True, one of the planes was battling somewhere with the perils of the night, but the odds were in its favor.

Rivière pushed the book aside.

"That will do."

Then, a night-warden whose charge was half the world, he went out to inspect the men on night duty, and came back.

Later, standing at an open window, he took the measure of the darkness. It con-

tained Buenos Aires yonder, but also, like
the hull of some huge ship, America. He
did not wonder at this feeling of immen-
sity; the sky of Santiago de Chile might be
a foreign sky, but once the air-mail was in
flight toward Santiago you lived, from end
to journey's end, under the same dark
vault of heaven. Even now the Patagonian
fishermen were gazing at the navigation
lights of the plane whose messages were being awaited here. The vague unrest of an
aëroplane in flight brooded not only on
Rivière's heart but, with the droning of the
engine, upon the capitals and little towns.

Glad of this night that promised so well,
he recalled those other nights of chaos,
when a plane had seemed hemmed in with
dangers, its rescue well-nigh a forlorn hope,
and how to the Buenos Aires Radio Post its
desperate calls came faltering through,
fused with the atmospherics of the storm.
Under the leaden weight of sky the golden
music of the waves was tarnished. Lament

51

in the minor of a plane sped arrowwise against the blinding barriers of darkness, no sadder sound than this!

Rivière remembered that the place of an inspector, when the staff is on night duty, is in the office.

"Send for Monsieur Robineau."

Robineau had all but made a friend of his guest, the pilot. Under his eyes he had unpacked his suitcase and revealed those trivial objects which link inspectors with the rest of men; some shirts in execrable taste, a dressing-set, the photograph of a lean woman, which the inspector pinned to the wall. Humbly thus he imparted to Pellerin his needs, affections, and regrets. Laying before the pilot's eyes his sorry treasures, he laid bare all his wretchedness. A moral eczema. His prison.

But a speck of light remained for Robineau, as for every man, and it was in a mood of quiet ecstasy that he drew, from the bottom of his valise, a little bag care-

fully wrapped up in paper. He fumbled
with it some moments without speaking.
Then he unclasped his hands.

"I brought this from the Sahara."

The inspector blushed to think that he
had thus betrayed himself. For all his cha-
grins, domestic misadventures, for all the
gray reality of life he had a solace, these
little blackish pebbles—talismans to open
doors of mystery.

His blush grew a little deeper. "You find
exactly the same kind in Brazil."

Then Pellerin had slapped the shoulder
of an inspector poring upon Atlantis and,
as in duty bound, had asked a question.

"Keen on geology, eh?"

"Keen? I'm mad about it!"

All his life long only the stones had not
been hard on him.

Hearing that he was wanted, Robineau
felt sad but forthwith resumed his air of
dignity.

"I must leave you. Monsieur Rivière

needs my assistance for certain important problems."

When Robineau entered the office, Rivière had forgotten all about him. He was musing before a wall-map on which the company's air-lines were traced in red. The inspector awaited his chief's orders. Long minutes passed before Rivière addressed him, without turning his head.

"What is your idea of this map, Robineau?"

He had a way of springing conundrums of this sort when he came out of a brown study.

"The map, Monsieur Rivière? Well—"

As a matter of fact he had no ideas on the subject; nevertheless, frowning at the map, he roved all Europe and America with an inspectorial eye. Meanwhile Rivière, in silence, pursued his train of thought. "On the face of it, a pretty scheme enough—but it's ruthless. When one thinks of all the lives, young fellows' lives, it has cost us! It's a fine, solid thing and we must bow to its authority, of course; but what a host of problems it presents!" With Rivière, however, nothing mattered save the end in view.

Robineau, standing beside him with his eyes fixed on the map, was gradually pulling himself together. Pity from Rivière was not to be expected; that he knew. Once he had chanced it, explaining how that grotesque infirmity of his had spoilt his life. All he had got from Rivière was a jeer, "Stops you sleeping, eh? So much the better for your work!"

Rivière spoke only half in jest. One of his sayings was: "If a composer suffers from loss of sleep and his sleeplessness induces him to turn out masterpieces, what a profitable loss it is!" One day, too, he had said of Leroux: "Just look at him! I call it a fine thing, ugliness like that—so perfect that it would warn off any sweetheart!" And perhaps, indeed, Leroux owed what was finest in him to his misfortune, which obliged him to live only for his work.

"Pellerin's a great friend of yours, isn't he, Robineau?"

"Well—"

"I'm not reproaching you."

Rivière made a half-turn and with bowed head, taking short steps, paced to and fro with Robineau. A bitter smile, incomprehensible to Robineau, came to his lips.

"Only . . . only you are his chief, you see."

"Yes," said Robineau.

Rivière was thinking how to-night, as every night, a battle was in progress in the southern sky. A moment's weakening of the will might spell defeat; there was, perhaps, much fighting to be done before the dawn.

"You should keep your place, Robineau." Rivière weighed his words. "You may have to order this pilot to-morrow night to start on a dangerous flight. He will have to obey you."

"Yes."

"The lives of men worth more than you are in your hands." He seemed to hesitate. "It's a serious matter."

For a while Rivière paced the room in silence, taking his little steps.

"If they obey you because they like you, Robineau, you're fooling them. You have no right to ask any sacrifice of them."

"No, of course not."

"And if they think that your friendship will get them off disagreeable duties, you're fooling them again. They have to obey in any case. Sit down."

With a touch of his hand Rivière gently propelled Inspector Robineau toward the desk.

"I am going to teach you a lesson, Robineau. If you feel run down it's not these men's business to give you energy. You are their chief. Your weakness is absurd. Now write!"

"I—"

"Write. *Inspector Robineau imposes the penalty stated hereunder on Pellerin, Pilot, on the following grounds. . . .* You will discover something to fill in the blanks."

"Sir!"

"Act as though you understood, Robineau. Love the men under your orders—but do not let them know it."

So, once more, Robineau would supervise the cleaning of each propeller-boss, with zest.

An emergency landing-ground sent in a radio message. *Plane in sight. Plane signals: Engine Trouble; about to land.*

That meant half an hour lost. Rivière felt that mood of irritation the traveler knows when his express is held up by a signal and the minutes no longer yield their toll of passing hedgerows. The large clock-hand was turning now an empty hemicycle, within whose compass so many things might have fitted in. To while away the interval Rivière went out and now the night seemed hollow as a stage without an actor. Wasted—a night like this! He nursed a grudge against that cloudless sky with its wealth of stars, the moon's celestial beacon, the squandered gold of such a night. . . .

But, once the plane had taken off, the night once more grew full of beauty and enthralment; for now the womb of night was carrying life, and over it Rivière kept his watch.

"What weather have you?"

He had the query transmitted to the crew. Ten seconds later the reply came in: "Very fine."

There followed a string of names, towns over which the plane had passed and, for Rivière's ears, these were so many names of cities falling one by one before a conqueror.

VII

AN HOUR LATER THE WIRELESS OPERATOR ON THE PATAGONIA MAIL—

VII

An hour later the wireless operator on the Patagonia mail felt himself gently lifted as though some one were tugging at his shoulder. He looked around; heavy clouds were putting out the stars. He leaned toward the earth, trying to see the village lights, shining like glowworms in the grass, but in those fields of darkness no light sparkled.

He felt depressed; a hard night lay before him, marches and countermarches, advances won and lost. He did not understand the pilot's tactics; a little further on and they would hit against that blackness, like a wall.

On the rim of the horizon in front he now could see a ghostly flicker, like the glow above a smithy. He tapped Fabien's shoulder, but the pilot did not stir.

Now the first eddies of the distant storm assailed them. The mass of metal heaved gently up, pressing itself against the operator's limbs; and then it seemed to melt away, leaving him for some seconds floating in the darkness, levitated. He clung to the steel bulwarks with both hands. The red lamp in the cockpit was all that remained to him of the world of men and he shuddered to know himself descending helpless into the dark heart of night, with only a little thing, a miner's safety-lamp, to see him through. He dared not disturb the pilot to ask his plans; he tightened his grip on the steel ribs and, bending forward, fixed his eyes upon the pilot's shadowed back.

In that obscurity the pilot's head and shoulders were all that showed themselves. His torso was a block of darkness, inclined a little to the left; his face was set toward the storm, bathed intermittently, no doubt, by flickering gleams. He could not see that face; all the feelings thronging there to meet the onset of the storm were hidden from his eyes; lips set with anger and resolve, a white face holding elemental colloquy with the leaping flashes ahead.

Yet he divined the concentrated force that brooded in that mass of shadow, and he loved it. True, it was carrying him toward the tempest, yet it shielded him. True, those hands, gripping the controls, pressed heavy on the storm, as on some huge beast's neck, but the strong shoulders never budged, attesting vast reserves of force. And after all, he said to himself, the pilot's responsible. So, carried like a pillion-rider on this breakneck gallop into the flames, he could relish to its full the solid permanence, the weight and substance implicit in that dark form before him.

On the left, faint as a far revolving light, a new storm-center kindled.

The wireless operator made as if to touch Fabien's shoulder and warn him, but then he saw him slowly turn his head, fix his eyes a while on this new enemy and then as slowly return to his previous position, his neck pressed back against the leather pad, shoulders unmoving as before.

VIII

RIVIÈRE WENT OUT FOR A SHORT WALK—

VIII

RIVIÈRE went out for a short walk, hoping
to shake off his malaise, which had returned. He who had only lived for action,
dramatic action, now felt a curious shifting
of the crisis of the drama, toward his own
personality. It came to him that the little people of these little towns, strolling
around their bandstands, might seem to
lead a placid life and yet it had its tragedies; illness, love, bereavements, and that
perhaps— His own trouble was teaching
him many things, "opening windows," as
he put it to himself.

Toward eleven he was breathing more
easily and turned back toward the offices,
slowly shouldering his way through the
stagnant crowds around the cinemas. He
glanced up at the stars which glinted on the
narrow street, well-nigh submerged by glar-

ing sky-signs, and said to himself: "To-night, with my two air-mails on their way, I am responsible for all the sky. That star up there is a sign that is looking for me amongst this crowd—and finds me. That's why I'm feeling out of things, a man apart."

A phrase of music came back to him, some notes from a sonata which he had heard the day before in the company of friends. They had not understood. "That stuff bores us and bores you too, only you won't admit it!"

"Perhaps," he had replied.

Then, as to-night, he had felt lonely, but soon had learnt the bounty of such loneli-ness. The music had breathed to him its message, to him alone amongst these ordi-nary folk, whispered its gentle secret. And now the star. Across the shoulders of these people a voice was speaking to him in a tongue that he alone could understand.

On the pavement they were hustling him about, "No," he said to himself, "I won't get annoyed. I am like the father of a sick child walking in the crowd, taking short steps, who carries in his breast the hushed silence of his house."

He looked upon the people, seeking to discover which of them, moving with little steps, bore in his heart discovery or love—and he remembered the lighthouse-keeper's isolation.

Back in the office, the silence pleased him. As he slowly walked from one room to another, his footsteps echoed emptiness. The typewriters slept beneath their covers. The big cupboard doors were closed upon the serried files. Ten years of work and effort. He felt as if he were visiting the cellars of a bank where wealth lies heavy on the earth. But these registers contained a finer stuff than gold—a stock of living energy, living but, like the hoarded gold of banks, asleep.

Somewhere he would find the solitary clerk on night duty. Somewhere here a man was working that life and energy should persevere and thus the work goes on from post to post that, from Toulouse to Buenos Aires, the chain of flights should stay unbroken.

"That fellow," thought Rivière, "doesn't know his greatness."

Somewhere, too, the planes were fighting forward; the night flights went on and on like a persistent malady, and on them watch must be kept. Help must be given to these men who with hands and knees and breast to breast were wrestling with the darkness, who knew and only knew an unseen world of shifting things, whence they must struggle out, as from an ocean. And the things they said about it afterward were—terrible! "I turned the light on to my hands so as to see them." Velvet of hands bathed in a dim red dark-room glow; last fragment, that must be saved, of a lost world.

Rivière opened the door of the Traffic Office. A solitary lamp shone in one corner, making a little pool of light. The clicking of a single typewriter gave meaning to the silence, but did not fill it. Sometimes the telephone buzzed faintly and the clerk on duty rose obedient to its sad, reiterated call. As he took down the receiver that invisible distress was soothed and a gentle, very gentle murmur of voices filled the coign of shadow.

Impassive the man returned to his desk, for drowsiness and solitude had sealed his features on a secret unconfessed. And yet—what menace it may hold, a call from the outer darkness when two postal planes are on their way! Rivière thought of telegrams that invaded the peace of families sitting round their lamp at night and that grief which, for seconds that seem unending, keeps its secret on the father's face. Waves, so weak at first, so distant from the call they carry, and so calm; and yet each quiet purring of the bell held, for Rivière, a faint echo of that cry. Each time the man came back from the shadow toward his lamp, like a diver returning to the surface, the solitude made his movements heavy with their secret, slow as a swimmer's in the undertow.

"Wait! I'll answer."

Rivière unhooked the receiver and a world of murmurs hummed in his ears.

"Rivière speaking."

Confused sounds, then a voice: "I'll put you on the radio station."

A rattle of plugs into the standard, then another voice: "Radio Station speaking. I'll pass you the messages."

Rivière noted them, nodding. "Good. . . . Good . . ."

Nothing important, the usual routine news. Rio de Janeiro asking for information, Montevideo reporting on the weather, Mendoza on the plant. Familiar sounds.

"And the planes?" he asked.

"The weather's stormy. We don't hear them to-night."

"Right!"

The night is fine here and starry, Rivière

74

thought, yet those fellows can detect in it the breath of the distant storm.

"That's all for the present," he said.

As Rivière rose the clerk accosted him: "Papers to sign, sir."

Rivière discovered that he greatly liked this subordinate of his who was bearing, too, the brunt of night. "A comrade in arms," he thought. "But he will never guess, I fancy, how to-night's vigil brings us near each other."

IX

AS HE WAS RETURNING TO HIS PRIVATE OFFICE—

As HE was returning to his private office,
a sheaf of papers in his hand, Rivière felt
the stab of pain in his right side which had
been worrying him for some weeks past.

"That's bad. . . ."

He leaned against the wall a moment.

"It's absurd!"

Then he made his way to his chair.

Once again he felt like some old lion
fallen in a trap and a great sadness came
upon him.

"To think I've come to this after all
those years of work! I'm fifty; all that time
I've filled my life with work, trained myself, fought my way, altered the course of
events and here's this damned thing getting
a hold of me, obsessing me till it seems the
only thing that matters in the world. It's
absurd!"

He wiped away a drop or two of sweat, waited till the pain had ebbed and settled down to work, examining the memoranda on his table.

"In taking down Motor 301 at Buenos Aires we discovered that . . . The employee responsible will be severely punished."

He signed his name.

"The Florianopolis staff, having failed to comply with orders . . ."

He signed.

"As a disciplinary measure Airport Supervisor Richard, is transferred on the following grounds. . . ."

He signed.

Then, as the pain in his side, slumbering but persistent, new as a new meaning in life, drove his thoughts inward toward himself, an almost bitter mood came over him.

"Am I just or unjust? I've no idea. All I know is that when I hit hard there are fewer accidents. It isn't the individual that's responsible but a sort of hidden force

80

and I can't get at it without—getting at every one! If I were merely just, every night flight would mean a risk of death."

A sort of disgust came over him, that he had given himself so hard a road to follow. Pity is a fine thing, he thought. Lost in his musings, he turned the pages over.

"Roblet, as from this day, is struck off the strength. . . ."

He remembered the old fellow and their talk the evening before.

"There's no way out of it, an example must be made."

"But, sir. . . . It was the only time, just once in a way, sir . . . and I've been hard at it all my life!"

"An example must be made."

"But . . . but, sir. Please see here, sir."

A tattered pocket-book, a newspaper picture showing young Roblet standing beside an aëroplane. Rivière saw how the old hands were trembling upon this little scrap of fame.

"It was in nineteen ten, sir. That was the

first plane in Argentina and I assembled it.
I've been in aviation since nineteen ten,
think of it, sir! Twenty years! So how can
you say . . . ? And the young 'uns, sir,
won't they just laugh about it in the shop!
Won't they just chuckle!"

"I can't help that."

"And my kids, sir. I've a family."

"I told you you could have a job as a
fitter."

"But there's my good name, sir, my
name . . . after twenty years' experience.
An old employee like me!"

"As a fitter."

"No, sir, I can't see my way to that. I
somehow can't, sir!"

The old hands trembled and Rivière
averted his eyes from their plump, creased
flesh which had a beauty of its own.

"No, sir, no. . . . And there's something more I'd like to say."

"That will do."

Not he, thought Rivière, it wasn't he
whom I dismissed so brutally, but the mis-

chief for which, perhaps, he was not responsible, though it came to pass through him.
For, he mused, we can command events and
they obey us; and thus we are creators.
These humble men, too, are things and we
create them. Or cast them aside when mischief comes about through them.

"There's something more I'd like to
say." What did the poor old fellow want to
say? That I was robbing him of all that
made life dear? That he loved the clang of
tools upon the steel of airplanes, that all
the ardent poetry of life would now be lost
to him . . . and then, a man must live?

"I am very tired," Rivière murmured
and his fever rose, insidiously caressing
him. "I liked that old chap's face." He
tapped the sheet of paper with his finger. It
came back to him, the look of the old man's
hands and he now seemed to see them shape
a faltering gesture of thankfulness. "That's
all right," was all he had to say. "That's
right. Stay!" And then— He pictured the
torrent of joy that would flow through

those old hands. Nothing in all the world, it seemed to him, could be more beautiful than that joy revealed not on a face, but in those toil-worn hands. Shall I tear up this paper? He imagined the old man's home-coming to his family, his modest pride.

"So they're keeping you on?"

"What do you think? It was I who assembled the first plane in Argentina!"

The old fellow would get back his prestige, the youngsters cease to laugh.

As he was asking himself if he would tear it up, the telephone rang.

There was a long pause, full of the resonance and depth that wind and distance give to voices.

"Landing-ground speaking. Who is there?"

"Rivière."

"No. 650 is on the tarmac, sir."

"Good."

"We've managed to fix it up, but the electric circuit needed overhauling at the last minute, the connections had been bungled."

"Yes. Who did the wiring?"

"We will inquire and, if you agree, we'll make an example. It's a serious matter when the lights give out on board."

"You're right."

If, Rivière was thinking, one doesn't uproot the mischief whenever and wherever it crops up, the lights may fail and it would be criminal to let it pass when, by some chance, it happens to unmask its instrument; Roblet shall go.

The clerk, who had noticed nothing, was busy with his typewriter.

"What's that?"

"The fortnightly accounts."

"Why not ready?"

"I . . . I . . ."

"We'll see about that."

Curious, mused Rivière, how things take the upper hand, how a vast dark force, the force that thrusts up virgin forests, shows itself whenever a great work is in the making! And he thought of temples dragged asunder by frail liana tendrils.

A great work. . . .

And, heartening himself, he let his thought flow on. These men of mine, I love them; it's not they whom I'm against, but what comes about through them. . . . His heart was throbbing rapidly and it hurt him. . . . No, I cannot say if I am doing right or what precise value should be set on a human life, or suffering, or justice. How should I know the value of a man's joys? Or of a trembling hand? Of kindness, or pity?

Life is so full of contradictions; a man muddles through it as best he can. But to endure, to create, to barter this vile body. . . .

As if to conclude his musings he pressed the bell-push.

"Ring up the pilot of the Europe mail and tell him to come and see me before he leaves."

For he was thinking: I must make sure he doesn't turn back needlessly. If I don't stir my men up the night is sure to make them nervous.

X

ROUSED BY THE CALL, THE PILOT'S WIFE—

X

ROUSED by the call, the pilot's wife looked musingly at her husband. I'll let him sleep a bit longer, she thought.

She admired that spanned bared chest of his and the thought came to her of a well-built ship. In the quiet bed, as in a harbor, he was sleeping and, lest anything should spoil his rest, she smoothed out a fold of the sheet, a little wave of shadow, with her hand, bringing calm upon the bed, as a divine hand calms the sea.

Rising, she opened the window and felt the wind on her face. Their room overlooked Buenos Aires. A dance was going on in a house near by and the music came to her upon the wind, for this was the hour of leisure and amusement. In a hundred thousand barracks this city billeted its men and all was peaceful and secure; but, the woman thought, soon there'll be a cry "To arms!" and only one man—mine—will answer it. True, he rested still, yet his was the ominous rest of reserves soon to be summoned to the front. This town at rest did not protect him; its light would seem as nothing when, like a young god, he rose above its golden dust. She looked at the strong arms which, in an hour, would decide the fortune of the Europe mail, bearing a high responsibility, like a city's fate. The thought troubled her. That this man alone, amongst those millions, was destined for the sacrifice made her sad. It estranged him from her love. She had cherished him, watched over him, caressed him, not for herself but for this night which was to take him. For struggles, fears, and victories which she would never know. Wild things they were, those hands of his, and only tamed to tenderness; their real task was dark to her. She knew this man's smile, his gentle ways of love, but not his godlike fury in the storm. She might snare him in a fragile net of music, love and flowers, but, at each departure, he would break forth without, it seemed to her, the least regret.

He opened his eyes. "What time is it?"

"Midnight."

"How's the weather?"

"I don't know."

He rose and, stretching himself, walked to the window. "Won't be too cold. What's the wind?"

"How should I know?"

He leaned out. "Southerly. That's top-hole. It'll hold as far as Brazil anyhow."

He looked at the moon and reckoned up his riches and then his gaze fell upon the town below. Not warm or kind or bright it seemed to him; already in his mind's eye its worthless, shining sands were running out.

"What are you thinking about?"

He was thinking of the fog he might encounter toward Porto Allegre.

"I've made my plans. I know exactly where to turn."

He still was bending down, inhaling deeply like a man about to plunge, naked, into the sea.

"You don't even seem to mind it! How long will you be away?" she asked.

A week or ten days, he couldn't say. "Mind it?" Why should he? All those cities, plains, and mountains. . . . In freedom he was going out to conquer them. In under an hour, he thought, he would have annexed Buenos Aires and tossed it aside!

He smiled at his thoughts. This town . . . it will soon be left behind. It's fine starting out at night. One opens out the gas, facing south, and ten seconds later swings the landscape roundabout, heading up north. The town looks like the bottom of the sea.

She thought of all a man must lay aside to conquer. "So you don't like your home?"

"I do like my home."

94

But his wife knew that he was already on his way and even now his sturdy shoulders were pressing up against the sky.

She pointed to the sky. "A fine night. See, your road is paved with stars!"

He laughed. "Yes."

She rested her hand on his shoulder and its moist warmth disquieted her; did some danger threaten this young flesh of his?

"I know how strong you are, but—do take care!"

"Of course I'll take care."

Then he began dressing. For the occasion he chose the coarsest, roughest fabrics, the heaviest of leather—a peasant's kit. The heavier he grew, the more she admired him. Herself she buckled his belt, helped to pull his boots on.

"These boots pinch me!"

"Here are the others."

"Bring a cord for my emergency-lamp."

She looked at him, set to rights the last flaw in his armor; all fell into place.

95

"You look splendid."

Then she noticed that he was carefully brushing his hair.

"For the benefit of the stars?" she questioned.

"I don't want to feel old."

"I'm jealous."

He laughed again and kissed her, pressing her to his heavy garments. Then he lifted her from the ground between his outstretched arms, like a little girl, and, laughing still, deposited her on the bed.

"Go to sleep!"

He shut the door behind him and, passing amongst the indistinguishable folk of night, took the first step toward his conquests.

She remained, sadly looking at these flowers and books, little friendly things which meant for him no more than the bottom of the sea.

XI

RIVIÈRE GREETED HIM.

RIVIÈRE greeted him.

"That's a nice trick you played on me, your last trip! You turned back though the weather reports were good. You could have pushed through all right. Got the wind up?"

Surprised, the pilot found no answer. He slowly rubbed his hands one on the other. Then, raising his head, he looked Rivière in the eyes.

"Yes," he answered.

Deep in himself Rivière felt sorry for this brave fellow who had been afraid. The pilot tried to explain.

"I couldn't see a thing. No doubt, further on . . . perhaps . . . the radio said. . . . But my lamp was getting weak and I couldn't see my hands. I tried turning on my flying-light so as to spot a wing anyhow, but I saw nothing. It was like being at the bottom of a huge pit, and no getting out of it. Then my engine started a rattle."

"No."

"No?"

"No, we had a look at it. In perfect order. But a man always thinks the engine's rattling when he gets the wind up."

"And who wouldn't? The mountains were above me. When I tried to climb I got caught in heavy squalls. When one can't see a damned thing, squalls, you know. . . . Instead of climbing I lost three hundred feet or more. I couldn't even see the gyroscope or the manometers. It struck me that the engine was running badly and heating up, and the oil-pressure was going down. And it was dark as a plague of Egypt. Damned glad I was to see the lights of a town again."

"You've too much imagination. That's what it is."

The pilot left him.

Rivière sank back into the arm-chair and ran his fingers through his grizzled hair.

The pluckiest of my men, he thought. It was a fine thing he did that night, but I've stopped him from being afraid.

He felt a mood of weakness coming over him again.

To make oneself beloved one need only show pity. I show little pity, or I hide it. Sure enough it would be fine to create friendships and human kindness around me. A doctor can enjoy that in the course of his profession. But I'm the servant of events and, to make others serve them too, I've got to temper my men like steel. That dark necessity is with me every night when I read over the flight reports. If I am slack and let events take charge, trusting to routine, always mysteriously something seems to happen. It is as if my will alone forbade the plane in flight from breaking or the storm to hold the mail up. My power sometimes amazes me.

His thoughts flowed on.

Simple enough, perhaps. Like a gardener's endless labor on his lawn; the mere pressure of his hand drives back into the soil the virgin forest which the earth will engender time and time again.

His thoughts turned to the pilot.

I am saving him from fear. I was not attacking *him* but, across him, that stubborn inertia which paralyzes men who face the unknown. If I listen and sympathize, if I take his adventure seriously, he will fancy he is returning from a land of mystery, and mystery alone is at the root of fear. We must do away with mystery. Men who have gone down into the pit of darkness must come up and say—there's nothing in it! This man must enter the inmost heart of night, that clotted darkness, without even his little miner's davy, whose light, falling only on a hand or wing, suffices to push the unknown a shoulder's breath away.

Yet a silent communion, deep within

them, united Rivière and his pilots in the battle. All were like shipmates, sharing a common will to victory.

Rivière remembered other battles he had joined to conquer night. In official circles darkness was dreaded as a desert unexplored. The idea of launching a craft at a hundred and fifty miles an hour against the storm and mists and all the solid obstacles night veils in darkness might suit the military arm; you leave on a fine night, drop bombs and return to your starting-point. But regular night-services were doomed to fail. "It's a matter of life and death," said Rivière, "for the lead we gain by day on ships and railways is lost each night."

Disgusted, he had heard them prate of balance-sheets, insurance and, above all, public opinion. "Public opinion!" he exclaimed. "The public does as it's told!" But it was all waste of time, he was saying to himself. There's something far above all that. A living thing forces its way through, makes its own laws to live and nothing can resist it. Rivière had no notion when or how commercial aviation would tackle the problem of night-flying but its inevitable solution must be prepared for.

Those green table-cloths over which he had leaned, his chin propped on his arm, well he remembered them! And his feeling of power as he heard the others' quibbles! Futile these had seemed, doomed from the outset by the force of life. He felt the weight of energy that gathered in him. And I shall win, thought Rivière, for the weight of argument is on my side. That is the natural trend of things. They urged him to propose a utopian scheme, devoid of every risk. "Experience will guide us to the rules," he said. "You cannot make rules precede practical experience."

After a hard year's struggles, Rivière got his way. "His faith saw him through," said some, but others: "No, his tenacity. Why, the fellow's as obstinate as a bear!" But Rivière put his success down to the fact that he had lent his weight to the better cause.

Safety first was the obsession of those early days. Planes were to leave only an hour before dawn, to land only an hour after sunset. When Rivière felt surer of his ground, then and only then did he venture to send his planes into the depth of night. And now, with few to back him, disowned by nearly all, he plowed a lonely furrow.

Rivière rang up to learn the latest messages from the planes in flight.

XII

NOW THE PATAGONIA MAIL WAS
ENTERING THE STORM—

XII

Now the Patagonia mail was entering the storm and Fabien abandoned all idea of circumventing it; it was too widespread for that, he reckoned, for the vista of lightning-flashes led far inland, exposing battlement on battlement of clouds. He decided to try passing below it, ready to beat a retreat if things took a bad turn.

He read his altitude, five thousand five hundred feet, and pressed the controls with his palms to bring it down. The engine started thudding violently, setting all the plane aquiver. Fabien corrected the gliding angle approximately, verifying on the map the height of the hills, some sixteen hundred feet. To keep a safety margin he determined to fly at a trifle above two thousand, staking his altitude as a gambler risks his fortune.

An eddy dragged him down, making the plane tremble still more harshly and he felt the threat of unseen avalanches that toppled all about him. He dreamt an instant of retreat and its guerdon of a hundred thousand stars, but did not shift his course by one degree.

Fabien weighed his chances; probably this was just a local storm, as Trelew, the next halt, was signaling a sky only three-quarters overcast. A bare twenty minutes more of solid murk and he would be through with it. Nevertheless the pilot felt uneasy. Leaning to his left, to windward, he sought to catch those vague gleams which, even in darkest nights, flit here and there. But even those vagrant gleams were gone; at most there lingered patches in the mass of shadow where the night seemed less opaque, or was it only that his eyes were growing strained?

The wireless operator handed him a slip of paper.

"Where are we?"

Fabien would have given much to know. "Can't say exactly," he answered. "We are flying by compass across a storm."

He leaned down again. The flame from the exhaust was getting on his nerves. There it was, clinging to the motor like a spray of fire-flowers, so pale it seemed that moonlight would have quelled it, but, in this nothingness, engulfing all the visible world. He watched it streaming stiffly out into the wind, like a torch-flame.

Every thirty seconds Fabien bent down into the cockpit to check the gyroscope and compass. He dared not light the dim red lamps which would have dazzled his eyes for some moments, but the luminous dial-hands were ceaselessly emitting their pale and starry radiance. And in all those needles and printed figures the pilot found an illusive reassurance, as in the cabin of a ship swept by the waves. For, like a very sea of strange fatality, the night was rolling

111

up against him with all its rocks and reefs and wreckage.

"Where are we?" the operator asked again.

Fabien drew himself up and, leaning to the left, resumed his tremendous vigil. He had no notion left how many hours more and what efforts would be needed to deliver him from fettering darkness. Would he ever come clear, he wondered, for he was staking his life on this little slip of dirty, crumpled paper, which he unfolded and re-read a thousand times to nurse his hopes: *Trelew. Sky three-quarters overcast. Westerly breeze.* If there still remained a clear patch over Trelew, he would presently glimpse its lights across a cloud-rift. Unless. . . .

That promise of a faint gleam far ahead beckoned him on; but, to make sure, he scribbled a message to the radio operator. "Don't know if I can get through. Ask if the weather's holding out behind."

The answer appalled him.

"Commodoro reports: Impossible return here. Storm."

He was beginning to measure this unforeseen offensive, launched from the Cordillera toward the sea. Before he could make them the storm would have burst upon the cities.

"Get the San Antonio weather report."

"San Antonio reports: West wind rising. Storm in the west. Sky three-quarters overcast. San Antonio picking up badly on account of interferences. I'm having trouble too. I shall have to pull up the aërial on account of the lightning. Will you turn back? What are your plans?"

"Stow your damned questions! Get Bahia Blanca!"

"Bahia Blanca reports: Violent westerly gale over Bahia Blanca expected in less than twenty minutes."

"Ask Trelew."

"Trelew reports: Westerly gale; a hundred feet per second; rain squalls."

"Inform Buenos Aires: We are cut off

on all sides; storm developing over a depth of eight hundred miles; no visibility. What shall we do?"

A shoreless night, the pilot thought, leading to no anchorage (for every port was unattainable, it seemed), nor toward dawn. In an hour and twenty minutes the fuel would run out. Sooner or later he must blindly founder in the sea of darkness. Ah, if only he could have won through to daylight!

Fabien pictured the dawn as a beach of golden sand where a man might get a foothold after this hard night. Beneath him the plains, like friendly shores, would spread their safety. The quiet land would bear its sleeping farms and flocks and hills. And all the flotsam swirling in the shadows would lose its menace. If it were possible, how gladly he would swim toward the strand of daylight! But, well he knew, he was surrounded; for better or for worse the end would come within this murk of darkness. . . . Sometimes, indeed, when day-break came, it seemed like convalescence after illness.

What use to turn his eyes towards the east, home of the sun? Between them lay a gulf of night so deep that he could never clamber up again.

XIII

THE ASUNCION MAIL IS MAKING GOOD HEADWAY—

XIII

"THE Asuncion mail is making good headway; it should be in at about two. The Patagonia mail, however, seems to be in difficulties and we expect it to be much overdue."

"Very good, Monsieur Rivière."

"Quite possibly we won't make the Europe mail wait for it; as soon as Asuncion's in, come for instructions, please. Hold yourself in readiness."

Rivière read again the weather reports from the northern sectors. "Clear sky; full moon; no wind." The mountains of Brazil were standing stark and clear against the moonlit sky, the tangled tresses of their jet-black forests falling sheer into a silver tracery of sea. Upon those forests the moonbeams played and played in vain, tingeing their blackness with no light. Black, too, as drifting wreckage, the islands flecked the sea. But all the outward air-route was flooded by that exhaustless fountain of moonlight.

If Rivière now gave orders for the start, the crew of the Europe mail would enter a stable world, softly illuminated all night long. A land which held no threat for the just balance of light and shade, unruffled by the least caress of those cool winds which, when they freshen, can ruin a whole sky in an hour or two.

Facing this wide radiance, like a prospector eyeing a forbidden gold-field, Rivière hesitated. What was happening in the south put Rivière, sole protagonist of night flights, in the wrong. His opponents would make such moral capital out of a disaster in Patagonia that all Rivière's faith would henceforth be unavailing. Not that his faith wavered; if, through a fissure in his work, a tragedy had entered in, well, the tragedy might prove the fissure—but it proved nothing else. Perhaps, he thought, it would be well to have look-out posts in the west. That must be seen to. "After all," he said to himself, "my previous arguments hold good as ever and the possibilities of accident are reduced by one, the one to-night has illustrated." The strong are strengthened by reverses; the trouble is that the true meaning of events scores next to nothing in the match we play with men. Appearances decide our gains or losses and the points are trumpery. And a mere semblance of defeat may hopelessly checkmate us.

He summoned an employee. "Still no radio from Bahia Blanca?"

"No."

"Ring up the station on the phone."

Five minutes later he made further inquiries. "Why don't you pass on the messages?"

"We can't hear the mail."

"He's not sending anything?"

"Can't say. Too many storms. Even if

he was sending we shouldn't pick it up."

"Can you get Trelew?"

"We can't hear Trelew."

"Telephone."

"We've tried. The line's broken."

"How's the weather your end?"

"Threatening. Very sultry. Lightning in the west and south."

"Wind?"

"Moderate so far. But in ten minutes the storm will break; the lightning's coming up fast."

Silence.

"Hullo, Bahia Blanca! You hear me? Good. Call me again in ten minutes."

Rivière looked through the telegrams from the southern stations. All alike reported: No message from the plane. Some had ceased by now to answer Buenos Aires and the patch of silent areas was spreading on the map as the cyclone swept upon the little towns and one by one, behind closed doors, each house along the lightless streets grew isolated from the outer world, lonely as a ship on a dark sea. And only dawn would rescue them.

Rivière, poring on the map, still hoped against hope to discover a haven of clear sky, for he had telegraphed to the police at more than thirty up-country police-stations and their replies were coming in. And the radio-posts over twelve hundred miles of country had orders to advise Buenos Aires within thirty seconds if any message from the plane was picked up, so that Fabien might learn at once whither to fly for refuge.

The employees had been warned to attend at 1 A. M. and were now at their posts. Somehow, mysteriously, a rumor was gaining ground that perhaps the night flights would be suspended in future and the Europe mail would leave by day. They spoke in whispers of Fabien, the cyclone and, above all, of Rivière whom they pictured near at hand and point by point capitulating to this rebuff the elements had dealt.

Their chatter ceased abruptly; Rivière was standing at his door, his overcoat tight-buttoned across his chest, his hat well down upon his eyes, like the incessant traveler he always seemed. Calmly he approached the head clerk.

"It's one ten. Are the papers for the Europe mail in order?"

"I—I thought—"

"Your business is to carry out orders, not to think."

Slowly turning away, he moved toward an open window, his hands clasped behind his back. A clerk came up to him.

"We have very few replies, sir. We hear that a great many telegraph lines in the interior have been destroyed."

"Right!"

Unmoving, Rivière stared out into the night.

Thus each new message boded new peril for the mail. Each town, when a reply could be sent through before the lines were broken, announced the cyclone on its way, like an invading horde. "It's coming up from the Cordillera, sweeping everything before it, toward the sea."

To Rivière the stars seemed over-bright, the air too moist. Strange night indeed! It was rotting away in patches, like the substance of a shining fruit. The stars, in all their host, still looked down on Buenos Aires—an oasis, and not to last. A haven out of Fabien's range, in any case. A night of menace, touched and tainted by an evil wind. A difficult night to conquer.

Somewhere in its depths an airplane was in peril; here, on the margin, they were fighting to rescue it, in vain.

XIV

FABIEN'S WIFE TELEPHONED.

XIV

FABIEN's wife telephoned.

Each night she calculated the progress of the homing Patagonia mail. "He's leaving Trelew now," she murmured. Then went to sleep again. Presently: "He's getting near San Antonio, he has its lights in view." Then she got out of bed, drew back the curtains and summed up the sky. "All those clouds will worry him." Sometimes the moon was wandering like a shepherd and the young wife was heartened by the faithful moon and stars, the thousand presences that watched her husband. Toward one o'clock she felt him near her. "Not far to go, Buenos Aires is in sight." Then she got up again, prepared a meal for him, a nice steaming cup of coffee. "It's so cold up there!" She always welcomed him as if he had just descended

from a snow-peak. "You *must* be cold!"
"Not a bit." "Well, warm yourself anyhow!" She had everything ready at a
quarter past one. Then she telephoned. To-
night she asked the usual question.

"Has Fabien landed?"

The clerk at the other end grew flus-
tered. "Who's speaking?"

"Simone Fabien."

"Ah! A moment, please. . . ."

Afraid to answer, he passed the receiver
to the head clerk.

"Who's that?"

"Simone Fabien."

"Yes. What can I do for you?"

"Has my husband arrived?"

After a silence which must have baffled
her, there came a monosyllable. "No."

"Is he delayed?"

"Yes."

Another silence. "Yes, he is delayed."

"Ah!"

The cry of a wounded creature. A little

delay, that's nothing much, but when it lasts, when it lasts. . . .

"Yes. And when—when is he expected in?"

"When is he expected? We . . . we don't know exactly . . ."

A solid wall in front of her, a wall of silence, which only gave her back the echo of her questions.

"Do please tell me, where is he now?"

"Where is he? Wait. . . ."

This suspense was like a torture. Something was happening there, behind that wall.

At last, a voice! "He left Commodoro at seven thirty this evening."

"Yes? And then?"

"Then—delayed, seriously delayed by stormy weather."

"Ah! A storm!"

The injustice of it, the sly cruelty of that moon up there, that lazing moon of Buenos Aires! Suddenly she remembered that it took barely two hours to fly from Commodoro to Trelew.

"He's been six hours on the way to Trelew! But surely you've had messages from him. What does he say?"

"What does he say? Well, you see, with weather like that . . . it's only natural . . . we can't hear him."

"Weather like—?"

"You may rest assured, madame, the moment we get news of him, we will ring you up."

"Ah! You've no news."

"Good-night, madame."

"No! No! I want to talk to the director."

"I'm sorry, he's very busy just now; he has a meeting on—"

"I can't help that. That doesn't matter. I insist on speaking to him."

The head clerk mopped his forehead. "A moment, please."

He opened Rivière's door.

"Madame Fabien wants to speak to you, sir."

"Here," thought Rivière, "is what I was dreading." The emotional elements of the drama were coming into action. His first impulse was to thrust them aside; mothers and women are not allowed in an operating theater. And all emotion is bidden to hold its peace on a ship in peril; it does not help to save the crew. Nevertheless he yielded.

"Switch on to my phone."

No sooner did he hear that far off, quavering voice, than he knew his inability to answer it. It would be futile for both alike, worse than futile, to meet each other.

"Do not be alarmed, madame, I beg you. In our calling it so often happens that a long while passes without news."

He had reached a point where not the problem of a small personal grief but the very will to act was in itself at issue. Not so much Fabien's wife as another theory of life confronted Rivière now. Hearing that timid voice, he could but pity its infinite distress—and know it for an enemy! For action and individual happiness have no truck with each other; they are eternally at war. This woman, too, was championing a self-coherent world with its own rights and duties, that world where a lamp shines at nightfall on the table, flesh calls to mated flesh, a homely world of love and hopes and memories. She stood up for her happiness and she was right. And Rivière, too, was right, yet he found no words to set against this woman's truth. He was discovering the truth within him, his own inhuman and unutterable truth, by an humble light, the lamplight of a little home!

"Madame . . . !"

She did not hear him. Her hands were bruised with beating on the wall and she lay fallen, or so it seemed to him, almost at his feet.

One day an engineer had remarked to Rivière, as they were bending above a wounded man, beside a bridge that was being erected: "Is the bridge worth a man's crushed face?" Not one of the peasants using the road would ever have wished to mutilate this face so hideously just to save the extra walk to the next bridge. "The welfare of the community," the engineer had continued, "is just the sum of individual welfares and has no right to look beyond them." "And yet," Rivière observed on a subsequent occasion, "even though human life may be the most precious thing on earth, we always behave as if there were something of higher value than human life. . . . But what thing?"

Thinking of the lost airmen, Rivière felt his heart sink. All man's activity, even the building of a bridge, involves a toll of suffering and he could no longer evade the issue— "Under what authority?"

These men, he mused, who perhaps are lost, might have led happy lives. He seemed to see as in a golden sanctuary the evening lamplight shine on faces bending side by side. "Under what authority have I taken them from all this?" he wondered. What was his right to rob them of their personal happiness? Did not the highest of all laws ordain that these human joys should be safeguarded? But he destroyed them. And yet one day, inevitably, those golden sanctuaries vanish like mirage. Old age and death, more pitiless than even he, destroy them. There is, perhaps, some other thing, something more lasting, to be saved; and, perhaps, it was to save this part of man that Rivière was working. Otherwise there could be no defense for action.

To love, only to love, leads nowhere. Rivière knew a dark sense of duty, greater than that of love. And deep within it there might lie another emotion and a tender one, but worlds away from ordinary feelings. He recalled a phrase that he once had read: "The one thing is to make them everlasting. . . . That which you seek within yourself will die." He remembered a temple of the sun-god, built by the ancient Incas of Peru. Tall menhirs on a mountain. But for these what would be left of all that mighty civilization which with its massive stones weighs heavy, like a dark regret, on modern man? Under the mandate of what strange love, what ruthlessness, did that primeval leader of men compel his hordes to drag this temple up the mountainside, bidding them raise up their eternity? And now another picture rose in Rivière's mind; the people of the little towns, strolling by nights around their bandstands. That form of happiness, those shackles . . . he thought. The leader of those ancient races may have had scant compassion for man's sufferings, but he had a boundless pity for his death. Not for his personal death, but pity for his race, doomed to be blotted out beneath a sea of sand. And so he bade his folk set up these stones at least, something the desert never would engulf.

XV

THAT SCRAP OF FOLDED PAPER
MIGHT PERHAPS SAVE
HIM YET—

XV

THAT scrap of folded paper might perhaps save him yet; gritting his teeth, Fabien unfolded it.

"Impossible communicate Buenos Aires. Can't even touch the key, the shocks are numbing my hands."

In his vexation Fabien wanted to reply, but the moment his hands left the controls to write, a vast groundswell seemed to surge up across his body; the eddies lifted him in his five tons of metal and rocked him to and fro. He abandoned the attempt.

Again he clenched his hands upon the tempest and brought it down. Fabien was breathing heavily. If that fellow pulled up the aërial for fear of the storm, Fabien would smash his face in when they landed. At all costs they must get in touch with

Buenos Aires—as though across the thousand miles and more a safety-line might be flung to rescue them from this abyss! If he could not have one vagrant ray of light, not even the flicker of an inn-lamp—of little help indeed, yet shining like a beacon, earnest of the earth—at least let him be given a voice, a single word from that lost world of his. The pilot raised his fist and shook it in the red glow, hoping to make the man behind him understand the tragic truth, but the other was bending down to watch a world in ruins, with its buried cities and dead lights, and did not see him.

Let them shout any order whatever to him and Fabien would obey. If they tell me to go round and round, he thought, I'll turn in circles and if they say I must head due south. . . . For somewhere, even now, there still were lands of calm, at peace beneath the wide moon-shadows. His comrades down there, omniscient folk like clever scientists, knew all about them, poring upon the maps beneath their hanging lamps, pretty as flower-bells. But he, what could he know save squalls and night, this night that buffeted him with its swirling spate of darkness? Surely they could not leave two men to their fate in these whirlwinds and flaming clouds! No, that was unthinkable! They might order Fabien to set his course at two hundred and forty degrees, and he would do it. . . . But he was alone.

It was as if dead matter were infected by his exasperation; at every plunge the engine set up such furious vibrations that all the fuselage seemed convulsed with rage. Fabien strained all his efforts to control it; crouching in the cockpit, he kept his eyes fixed on the artificial horizon only, for the masses of sky and land outside were not to be distinguished, lost both alike in a welter as of worlds in the making. But the hands of the flying instruments oscillated more and more abruptly, grew almost impossible to follow. Already the pilot, misled by their vagaries, was losing altitude, fighting against odds, while deadly quicksands sucked him down into the darkness. He read his height, sixteen hundred—just the level of the hills. He guessed their towering billows hard upon him, for now it seemed that all these earthen monsters, the least of which could crush him into nothingness, were breaking loose from their foundations and careering about in a drunken frenzy. A dark tellurian carnival was thronging close and closer round him.

He made up his mind. He would land no matter where, even if it meant cracking up! To avoid the hills anyhow, he launched his only landing flare. It sputtered and spun, illumining a vast plain, then died away; beneath him lay the sea!

His thoughts came quickly. Lost—forty degrees' drift—yes, I've drifted, sure enough—it's a cyclone—where's land? He turned due west. Without another flare, he thought, I'm a goner. Well, it was bound to happen one day. And that fellow behind there! Sure thing he's pulled up the aërial.

. . . But now the pilot's anger had ebbed away. He had only to unclasp his hands and their lives would slither through his fingers like a trivial mote of dust. He held the beating heart of each—his own, his comrade's—in his hands. And suddenly his hands appalled him.

In these squalls that battered on the plane, to counteract the jerks of the wheel, which else would have snapped the control cables, he clung to it with might and main, never relaxing his hold for an instant. But now he could no longer feel his hands, numbed by the strain. He tried to shift his fingers and get some signal they were there, but he could not tell if they obeyed his will. His arms seemed to end in two queer foreign bodies, insentient like flabby rubber pads. "Better try hard to think I'm gripping," he said to himself. But whether his thought carried as far as his hands he could not guess. The tugs upon the wheel were only felt by him as sudden twinges in his shoulders. "I'll let go for sure. My fin-

gers will open." His rashness scared him—
that he had dared to even think such words!
—for now he fancied that his hands, yielding to the dark suggestion of his thought,
were opening slowly, slowly opening in the
shadow, to betray him.

He might keep up the struggle, chance
his luck; no destiny attacks us from outside. But, within him, man bears his fate
and there comes a moment when he knows
himself vulnerable; and then, as in a
vertigo, blunder upon blunder lures him.

And, at this very moment, there gleamed
above his head, across a storm-rift, like a
fatal lure within a deep abyss, a star or two.

Only too well he knew them for a trap.
A man sees a few stars at the issue of a pit
and climbs toward them, and then—never
can he get down again but stays up there
eternally, chewing the stars. . . .

But such was his lust for light that he
began to climb.

XVI

HE CLIMBED AND IT GREW EASIER TO CORRECT THE PLUNGES—

XVI

HE CLIMBED and it grew easier to correct the plunges for the stars gave him his bearings. Their pale magnet drew him up; after that long and bitter quest for light, for nothing in the world would he forgo the frailest gleam. If the glimmer of a little inn were all his riches, he would turn around this token of his heart's desire until his death! So now he soared toward the fields of light.

Little by little he spiraled up, out of the dark pit which closed again beneath him. As he rose the clouds began to shed their slime of shadow, flowing past him in cleaner, whiter billows. Fabien rose clear.

And now a wonder seized him; dazzled by that brightness, he had to keep his eyes closed for some seconds. He had never dreamt the night-clouds could dazzle thus.

But the full moon and all the constellations were changing them to waves of light.

In a flash, the very instant he had risen clear, the pilot found a peace that passed his understanding. Not a ripple tilted the plane but, like a ship that has crossed the bar, it moved across a tranquil anchorage. In an unknown and secret corner of the sky it floated, as in a harbor of the Happy Isles. Below him still the storm was fashioning another world, thridded with squalls and cloudbursts and lightnings, but turning to the stars a face of crystal snow.

Now all grew luminous, his hands, his clothes, the wings, and Fabien thought that he was in a limbo of strange magic; for the light did not come down from the stars but welled up from below, from all that snowy whiteness.

The clouds beneath threw up the flakes the moon was pouring on them; on every hand they loomed like towers of snow. A milky stream of light flowed everywhere, laving the plane and crew. When Fabien turned he saw the wireless operator smile.

"That's better!" he cried.

But his words were drowned by the rumor of the flight; they conversed in smiles. I'm daft, thought Fabien, to be smiling, we're lost.

And yet—at last a myriad dark arms had let him go; those bonds of his were loosed, as of a prisoner whom they let walk a while in liberty amongst the flowers.

"Too beautiful," he thought. Amid the far-flung treasure of the stars he roved, in a world where no life was, no faintest breath of life, save his and his companion's. Like plunderers of fabled cities they seemed, immured in treasure-vaults whence there is no escape. Amongst these frozen jewels they were wandering, rich beyond all dreams, but doomed.

XVII

ONE OF THE WIRELESS OPERATORS AT THE COMMODORO RIVADAVIA STATION—

XVII

ONE of the wireless operators at the Commodoro Rivadavia station in Patagonia made a startled gesture and all the others keeping helpless vigil there crowded round to read the message.

A harsh light fell upon the blank sheet of paper over which they bent. The operator's hand seemed loath to do its task and his pencil shook. The words to write were prisoned in his hand, but already his fingers twitched.

"Storms?"

He nodded assent; he could hardly hear for interferences. Then he scrawled some illegible signs, then words; then, at last, the text came out.

"Cut off at 12,000 feet, above the storm. Proceeding due west toward interior; found we had been carried above sea. No visibility

155

below. Impossible know if still flying over sea. Report if storm extends interior."

By reason of the storms the telegram had to be relayed from post to post to Buenos Aires, bearing its message through the night like bale-fires lit from tower to tower.

Buenos Aires transmitted a reply. "Storm covers all interior area. How much gasoline left?"

"For thirty minutes." These words sped back from post to post to Buenos Aires.

In under half an hour the plane was doomed to plunge into a cyclone which would crash it to the earth.

XVIII

RIVIÈRE WAS MUSING, ALL HOPE LOST—

XVIII

RIVIÈRE was musing, all hope lost; somewhere this plane would founder in the darkness. A picture rose in his mind of a scene which had impressed him in his boyhood; a pond that was being emptied to find a body. Thus, till this flood of darkness had been drained off the earth and daylight turned toward the plains and cornfields, nothing would be found. Then some humble peasants perhaps would come on two young bodies, their elbows folded on their faces, like children asleep amid the grass and gold of some calm scene. Drowned by the night.

Rivière thought of all the treasure buried in the depths of night, as in deep, legendary seas. Night's apple-trees that wait upon the dawn with all their flowers that serve as yet no purpose. Night, perfume-laden, that hides the lambs asleep and flowers that have no color yet.

Little by little the lush tilth, wet woods, and dew-cool meadows would swing toward the light. But somewhere in the hills, no longer dark with menace, amid the fields and flocks, a world at peace again, two children would seem to sleep. And something would have flowed out of the seen world into that other.

Rivière knew all the tenderness of Fabien's wife, the fears that haunted her; this love seemed only lent her for a while, like a toy to some poor child. He thought of Fabien's hand which, firm on the controls, would hold the balance of his fate some minutes yet; that hand had given caresses and lingered on a breast, wakening a tumult there; a hand of godlike virtue, it had touched a face, transfiguring it. A hand that brought miracles to pass.

Fabien was drifting now in the vast splendor of a sea of clouds, but under him there lay eternity. Among the constellations

still he had his being, their only denizen.
For yet a while he held the universe in his
hand, weighed it at his breast. That wheel
he clutched upbore a load of human treasure and desperately, from one star to the
other, he trafficked this useless wealth, soon
to be his no more.

A single radio post still heard him. The
only link between him and the world was
a wave of music, a minor modulation. Not
a lament, no cry, yet purest of sounds that
ever spoke despair.

XIX

ROBINEAU BROKE IN UPON HIS THOUGHTS.

XIX

Robineau broke in upon his thoughts.

"I've been thinking, sir. . . . Perhaps we might try—"

He had nothing really to suggest but thus proclaimed his good intentions. A solution, how he would have rejoiced to find it! He went about it as if it were a puzzle to be solved. Solutions were his *forte,* but Rivière would not hear of them. "I tell you, Robineau, in life there are no solutions. There are only motive forces, and our task is to set them acting—then the solutions follow." The only force that Robineau had to activate was one which functioned in the mechanics' shop; a humble force which saved propeller-bosses from rusting.

But this night's happenings found Robineau at fault. His inspectorial mandate could not control the elements, nor yet a phantom ship that, as things were, struggled no longer to win a punctuality-bonus but only to evade a penalty which canceled all that Robineau imposed, the penalty of death.

There was no use for Robineau now and he roamed the offices, forlorn.

Rivière was informed that Fabien's wife wished to see him. Tormented by anxiety, she was waiting in the clerks' office till Rivière could receive her. The employees were stealing glances at her face. She felt shy, almost shamefast, and gazed nervously around her; she had no right of presence here. They went about their tasks as usual and to her it was as if they were trampling on a corpse; in their ledgers no human sorrow but dwindled to dross of brittle figures. She looked for something that might speak to her of Fabien; at home all things confessed his absence—the sheets turned back upon the bed, the coffee on the table, a vase of flowers. Here there was nothing of him;

all was at war with pity, friendship, memories. The only word she caught (for in her presence they instinctively lowered their voices) was the oath of an employee clamoring for an invoice. "The dynamo account, God blast you! The one we send to Santos." Raising her eyes she gazed toward this man with a look of infinite wonder. Then to the wall where a map hung. Her lips trembled a little, almost imperceptibly.

The realization irked her that in this room she was the envoy of a hostile creed and almost she regretted having come; she would have liked to hide somewhere and, fearful of being remarked, dared neither cough nor weep. She felt her presence here misplaced, indecent, as though she were standing naked before them. But so potent was *her* truth, the truth within her, that furtively their eyes strayed ever and again in her direction, trying to read it on her face. Beauty was hers and she stood for a holy thing, the world of human happiness. She vouched for the sanctity of that material something with which man tampers when he acts. She closed her eyes before their crowded scrutiny, revealing all the peace which in his blindness man is apt to shatter.

Rivière admitted her.

So now she was come to make a timid plea for her flowers, the coffee waiting on the table, her own young body. Again, in this room, colder even than the others, her lips began to quiver. Thus, too, she bore witness to her truth, unutterable in this alien world. All the wild yearning of her love, her heart's devotion, seemed here invested with a selfish, pestering aspect. And again she would have liked to leave this place.

"I am disturbing you—"

"No," said Rivière, "you are not disturbing me. But unfortunately neither you nor I can do anything except—wait."

There was a faint movement of her shoulders and Rivière guessed its meaning. "What is the use of that lamp, the dinner waiting, and the flowers there when I return?" Once a young mother had confided in Rivière. "I've hardly realized my baby's death as yet. It's the little things that are so cruel—when I see the baby-clothes I had ready, when I wake up at night and there rises in my heart a tide of love, useless now, like my milk . . . all useless!" And for this woman here, Fabien's death would only just begin to-morrow—in every action, useless now, in trivial objects . . . useless. Little by little Fabien would leave his home. A deep, unuttered pity stirred in Rivière's heart.

"Madame—"

The young wife turned and left him with a weak smile, an almost humble smile, ignoring her own power.

Rivière sat down again rather heavily. "Still she is helping me to discover the thing I'm looking for."

He fingered absent-mindedly the messages from the northern airports. "We do not pray for immortality," he thought, "but only not to see our acts and all things stripped suddenly of all their meaning; for then it is the utter emptiness of everything reveals itself."

His gaze fell on the telegrams.

"These are the paths death takes to enter here—messages that have lost their meaning."

He looked at Robineau. Meaningless, too, this fellow who served no purpose now. Rivière addressed him almost gruffly.

"Have I got to tell you what your duties are?"

Then he pushed open the door that led into the Business Office and saw how Fabien's disappearance was recorded there in signs his wife could not have noticed. The slip marked *R.B.903,* Fabien's machine, was already inserted in the wall-index of Unavailable Plant. The clerks preparing the papers for the Europe mail were working slackly, knowing it would be delayed. The airport was ringing up for orders respecting

170

the staff on night duty whose presence was no longer necessary. The functions of life were slowing down. That is death! thought Rivière. His work was like a sailing-ship becalmed upon the sea.

He heard Robineau speaking. "Sir, they had only been married six weeks."

"Get on with your work!"

Rivière, watching the clerks, seemed to see beyond them the workmen, mechanics, pilots, all who had helped him in his task, with the faith of men who build. He thought of those little cities of old time where men had murmured of the "Indies," built a ship and freighted it with hopes. That men might see their hope outspread its wings across the sea. All of them magnified, lifted above themselves and saved—by a ship! He thought: The goal, perhaps, means nothing, it is the thing done that delivers man from death. By their ship those men will live.

Rivière, too, would be fighting against death when he restored to those telegrams

171

their full meaning, to these men on night duty their unrest and to his pilots their tragic purpose; when life itself would make his work alive again, as winds restore to life a sailing-ship upon the sea.

XX

COMMODORO RIVADAVIA COULD
HEAR NOTHING NOW—

XX

Commodoro Rivadavia could hear nothing now, but twenty seconds later, six hundred miles away, Bahia Blanca picked up a second message.

"Coming down. Entering the clouds. . . ."

Then two words of a blurred message were caught at Trelew.

". . . see nothing . . ."

Short waves are like that; here they can be caught, elsewhere is silence. Then, for no reason, all is changed. This crew, whose position was unknown, made itself heard by living ears, from somewhere out of space and out of time, and at the radio station phantom hands were tracing a word or two on this white paper.

Had the fuel run out already or was the pilot, before catastrophe, playing his last card: to reach the earth again without a crash?

Buenos Aires transmitted an order to Trelew.

"Ask him."

The radio station looked like a laboratory with its nickel and its copper, manometers and sheaves of wires. The operators on duty in their white overalls seemed to be bending silently above some simple experiment. Delicately they touched their instruments, exploring the magnetic sky, dowsers in quest of hidden gold.

"No answer?"

"No answer."

Perhaps they yet might seize upon its way a sound that told of life. If the plane and its lights were soaring up to join the stars, it might be they would hear a sound— a singing star!

The seconds flowed away, like ebbing blood. Were they still in flight? Each second killed a hope. The stream of time was wearing life away. As for twenty centuries it beats against a temple, seeping through the granite, and spreads the fane in ruin, so centuries of wear and tear were thronging in each second, menacing the airmen.

Every second swept something away; Fabien's voice, his laugh, his smile. Silence was gaining ground. Heavy and heavier silence drowned their voices, like a heavy sea.

"One forty," some one murmured. "They're out of fuel. They can't be flying any more."

Then silence.

A dry and bitter taste rose on their lips, like the dry savor of a journey's end. Something mysterious, a sickening thing, had come to pass. And all the shining nickel and trellised copper seemed tarnished with the gloom that broods on ruined factories. All this apparatus had grown clumsy, futile, out of use; a tangle of dead twigs.

One thing remained; to wait for day-break. In a few hours all Argentina would swing toward the sun, and here these men were standing, as on a beach, facing the net that was being slowly, slowly drawn in toward them, none knowing what its take would be.

To Rivière in his office came that quiet aftermath which follows only on great disasters, when destiny has spent its force. He had set the police of the entire country on the alert. He could do no more; only wait.

But even in the house of death order must have its due. Rivière signed to Robineau.

"Circular telegram to the northern airports. *Considerable delay anticipated Patagonia mail. To avoid undue delay Europe mail, will ship Patagonia traffic on following Europe mail.*"

He stooped a little forward. Then, with an effort, he called something to mind, something important. Yes, that was it. Better make sure.

"Robineau!"

"Sir."

"Issue an order, please. Pilots forbidden

178

to exceed 1900 revs. They're ruining my engines."

"Very good, sir."

Rivière bowed his head a little more. To be alone—that was his supreme desire.

"That's all, Robineau. Trot off, old chap!"

And this, their strange equality before the shades, filled Robineau with awe.

XXI

ROBINEAU was drifting aimlessly about the office. He felt despondent. The company's life had come to a standstill, since the Europe mail, due to start at two, would be countermanded and only leave at daybreak. Morosely the employees kept their posts, but their presence now was purposeless. In steady rhythm the weather reports from the north poured in, but their "no wind," "clear sky," "full moon" evoked the vision of a barren kingdom. A wilderness of stones and moonlight. As Robineau, hardly aware what he was up to, was turning over the pages of a file on which the office super-intendent was at work, he suddenly grew conscious that the official in question was at his side, waiting with an air of mocking deference to get his papers back. As if he were saying: "That's my show. Suppose you leave me to it, eh?"

Shocked though he was by his subordinate's demeanor, the inspector found himself tongue-tied and, with a movement of annoyance, handed back the documents. The superintendent resumed his seat with an air of grand punctilio. "I should have told him to go to the devil," thought Robineau. Then, to save his face, he moved away and his thoughts returned to the night's tragedy. For with this tragedy all his chief's campaign went under and Robineau lamented a twofold loss.

The picture of Rivière alone there in his private office rose in Robineau's mind; "old chap," Rivière had said. Never had there been a man so utterly unfriended as he, and Robineau felt an infinite compassion for him. He turned over in his mind vague sentences that hinted sympathy and consolation, and the impulse prompting him struck Robineau as eminently laudable. He knocked gently at the door. There was no answer. Not daring in such a silence to knock louder, he turned the handle. Rivière was there. For the first time Robineau entered Rivière's room almost on an equal footing, almost as a friend; he likened himself to the N.C.O. who joins his wounded general under fire, follows him in defeat and, in exile, plays a brother's part. "Whatever happens I am with you"—that was Robineau's unspoken message.

Rivière said nothing; his head was bowed and he was staring at his hands. Robineau's courage ebbed and he dared not speak; the old lion daunted him, even in defeat. Phrases of loyalty, of ever-growing fervor, rose to his lips; but every time he raised his eyes they encountered that bent head, gray hair and lips tight-set upon their bitter secret. At last he summoned up his courage.

"Sir!"

Rivière raised his head and looked at him. So deep, so far away had been his dream that till now he might well have been unconscious of Robineau's presence there.

And what he felt, what was that dream and what his heart's bereavement, none would ever know. . . . For a long while Rivière looked at Robineau as at the living witness of some dark event. Robineau felt ill at ease. An enigmatic irony seemed to shape itself on his chief's lips as he watched Robineau. And the longer his chief watched him, the more deeply Robineau blushed and the more it grew on Rivière that this fellow had come, for all his touching and unhappily sincere good-will, to act as spokesman for the folly of the herd.

Robineau by now had quite lost his bearings. The N.C.O., the general, the bullets—all faded into mist. Something inexplicable was in the air. Rivière's eyes were still intent on him. Reluctantly he shifted his position, withdrew his hand from his pocket. Rivière's eyes were on him still. At last, hardly knowing what he said, he stammered a few words.

"I've come for orders, sir."

Composedly Rivière pulled out his watch.

"It is two. The Asuncion mail will land at two ten. See that the Europe mail takes off at two fifteen."

Robineau bruited abroad the astounding news; the night flights would continue. He accosted the office superintendent.

"Bring me that file of yours to check."

The superintendent brought the papers.

"Wait!"

And the superintendent waited.

XXII

THE ASUNCION MAIL SIGNALED THAT IT WAS ABOUT TO LAND.

XXII

THE Asuncion mail signaled that it was
about to land. Even at the darkest hour,
Rivière had followed, telegram by telegram,
its well-ordered progress. In the turmoil of
this night he hailed it as the avenger of his
faith, an all-conclusive witness. Each message telling of this auspicious flight augured
a thousand more such flights to come. "And,
after all," thought Rivière, "we don't get a
cyclone every night! Once the trail is blazed,
it must be followed up."

Coming down, flight by flight, from Paraguay, as from an enchanted garden set with
flowers, low houses and slow waters, the
pilot had just skirted the edge of a cyclone
which never masked from him a single star.
Nine passengers, huddled in their traveling-
rugs, had pressed their foreheads on the

window, as if it were a shop-front glittering with gems. For now the little towns of Argentina were stringing through the night their golden beads, beneath the paler gold of the star-cities. And at his prow the pilot held within his hands his freight of lives, eyes wide open, full of moonlight, like a shepherd. Already Buenos Aires was dyeing the horizon with pink fires, soon to flaunt its diadem of jewels, like some fairy hoard. The wireless operator strummed with nimble fingers the final telegrams, last notes of a sonata he had played *allegro* in the sky— a melody familiar to Rivière's ears. Then he pulled up the aërial and stretched his limbs, yawning and smiling; another journey done.

The pilot who had just made land greeted the pilot of the Europe mail, who was lolling, his hands in his pockets, against the plane.

"Your turn to carry on?"

"Yes."

"Has the Patagonia come in?"

"We don't expect it; lost. How's the weather? Fine?"

"Very fine. Is Fabien lost then?"

They spoke few words of him, for that deep fraternity of theirs dispensed with phrases.

The transit mail-bags from Asuncion were loaded into the Europe mail while the pilot, his head bent back and shoulders pressed against the cockpit, stood motionless, watching the stars. He felt a vast power stirring in him and a potent joy.

"Loaded?" some one asked. "Then, contact!"

The pilot did not move. His engine was started. Now he would feel in his shoulders that pressed upon it the airplane come to life. At last, after all those false alarms—to start or not to start—his mind was easy. His lips were parted and in the moon his keen white teeth glittered like a jungle cub's.

"Watch out! The night, you know . . . !"

He did not hear his comrade's warning. His hands thrust in his pockets and head bent back, he stared toward the clouds, mountains and seas and rivers, and laughed silently. Soft laughter that rustled through him like a breeze across a tree, and all his body thrilled with it. Soft laughter, yet stronger, stronger far, than all those clouds and mountains, seas and rivers.

"What's the joke?"

"It's that damned fool Rivière, who said . . . who thinks I've got the wind up!"

XXIII

IN A MINUTE HE WOULD BE
LEAVING BUENOS AIRES—

XXIII

IN A minute he would be leaving Buenos Aires and Rivière, on active service once again, wanted to hear him go. To hear his thunder rise and swell and die into the distance like the tramp of armies marching in the stars.

With folded arms Rivière passed among the clerks and halted at a window to muse and listen. If he had held up even one departure, that would be an end of night flights. But, by launching this other mail into the darkness, Rivière had forestalled the weaklings who to-morrow would disclaim him.

Victory, defeat—the words were meaningless. Life lies behind these symbols and life is ever bringing new symbols into being. One nation is weakened by a victory, another finds new forces in defeat. To-night's defeat conveyed perhaps a lesson which would speed the coming of final victory. The work in progress was all that mattered.

Within five minutes the radio stations would broadcast the news along the line and across a thousand miles the vibrant force of life give pause to every problem.

Already a deep organ-note was booming; the plane.

Rivière went back to his work and, as he passed, the clerks quailed under his stern eyes; Rivière the Great, Rivière the Conqueror, bearing his heavy load of victory.

(11)